PRAISE FOR DAN WAKEFIELD'S
How Do We Know When It's God?

"By taking an unsparingly honest look at his own life and faith, Dan Wakefield challenges us to look honestly at our own."
— Rabbi Harold S. Kushner, author of *When Bad Things Happen to Good People* and *How Good Do We Have to Be?*

"Wakefield may have been reborn as a spiritual seeker, but his sense of humor is still in good working order — and he does not spare himself from his own barbed wit. . . . He keeps us informed of what is going on in his heart and mind at every step along the spiritual path."
— Jonathan Kirsch, *Los Angeles Times Book Review*

"Wakefield's religious reawakening in the 1980s was just a beginning. *How Do We Know When It's God?* chronicles what came after, acknowledging doubts, questions, backsliding, and even a loss of faith in his ability to discern God's will in his life. It could be described as a 'how-not-to-do-it book.'"
— Connie Lauerman, *Chicago Tribune*

"An honest, humorous look at the role spirituality has played in helping Wakefield get past various life crises. . . . Unpretentious and well-written." — *San Francisco Examiner Magazine*

"I could no more stop reading than I could save half a chocolate bar for later. . . . *How Do We Know When It's God?* is both wickedly titillating and profoundly stirring."
— Peggy Payne, *Virginia-Pilot*

"What I like about this book is its honesty, its willingness to stay in the confusion and to show how failure points the way. . . . For anyone who can't get over having made mistakes, this book might give you hope. . . . This is the kind of 'spiritual' writing I treasure — grounded, undefined, generously human."
— Thomas Moore, author of *Care of the Soul* and *The Soul of Sex*

How Do We Know When It's God?

HOW
DO WE KNOW
WHEN IT'S
GOD?

A Spiritual Memoir

———◆———

Dan Wakefield

LITTLE, BROWN AND COMPANY

Boston   New York   London

For Theresa Mackin
Shaun O'Connell
April Smith

LOVED ONES ALL

Originally published in hardcover by
Little, Brown and Company, August 1999
First Back Bay paperback edition, August 2000

Library of Congress Cataloging-in-Publication Data

Wakefield, Dan.
How do we know when it's God? / by Dan Wakefield. — 1st ed.
p. cm.
ISBN 0-316-91778-8 (hc)/0-316-91719-2 (pb)
1. Wakefield, Dan — Religion. 2. Unitarian Universalists — United
States — Biography. 3. Authors, American — 20th century — Biography.
4. Christian biography — United States. I. Title.
BX9869.W18A3 1999
289.1'092 — dc21
[B] 99-19733

10 9 8 7 6 5 4 3 2 1

Q-FF

Book design by Steve Dyer

Printed in the United States of America

Spare me the theology; just give me the story.

— TIM WINTON,
Australian novelist, in an interview with
Image: A Journal of Religion and the Arts

Be kind, for everyone you meet is fighting a great battle.

— PHILO OF ALEXANDRIA

CONTENTS

ACKNOWLEDGMENTS

I am grateful to Bill Phillips for the kind of detailed as well as conceptual editorial direction that is becoming increasingly rare in the current publishing world. I cannot imagine a more careful, perceptive, and enlightening job. The book wouldn't be here without it.

Friends, as always, make it possible, and I am especially grateful for valuable early readings of the manuscript-in-progress from Barbara Graham, Brock Brower, April Smith, Sara Davidson, and Lydia Webster.

For general life support I want to thank (as well as the above readers) Les Standiford and my colleagues and students at Florida International University; Lynn Nesbit and Tina Bennett of Janklow and Nesbit; Gene and Fay Hale, Charles and Adelaide Ketchum Perry, Judith Hirsch, Mark Matousek, Joe Brenner, Dr. Howard Hartley, the Reverend Carl Scovel, Maureen Langer, Vicki Hendricks, Carolina Garcia-Alvarez, Pam Gordon, Mary Beth Coudal and Chris Jones, Frank and Marian del Vecchio, Lisa Almy, and my friends and neighbors at 301. And to K. M. P., a special gift of thanks.

How Do We Know When It's God?

Chapter 1

THE QUEST

◆

We and God have business with each other; and in opening ourselves to His influence our deepest destiny is fulfilled. The universe, as those parts of it which our personal being constitutes, takes a turn genuinely for the worse or for the better in proportion as each of us fulfills or evades God's demands.

—William James,
The Varieties of Religious Experience

YES! MY FELLOW PARISHIONERS AND I WHO HAVE COME on this retreat agree wholeheartedly with William James that our lives are better or worse to the extent that each of us "fulfills or evades" God's demands. But that still leaves us with the question that plagues us, the question we have come to explore and try to answer on a weekend of prayer and discussion at a Benedictine monastery outside of Boston.

How do we know when it's God?

That's the riddle that overrides our other concerns, the puzzle that each of us is trying to solve on our particular path of life as we come to the turning points, the big and small decisions that we know will shape our fate, that will lead us up or down, closer or farther away from that fulfillment of the heart and soul we all seek, that sense of being in tune, on track, in synch with ourselves and the universe. If only God would speak to us, boom out instructions from a voice on high, we would gladly go into battle or up the mountain or into the rushing path of charging horses or foaming seas. If only we knew.

For sure.

The way.

We are gathered here during Lent, season of penitence and contemplation, beginning with Ash Wednesday, when we remind ourselves we are dust, and to dust we shall return, yet on this retreat we are not so much considering the transitory nature of our time on earth but rather how to find the right path to take, how to fulfill our true destiny. Outside, the bare limbs of trees, still winter-stripped, reach for the sky like our own yearning. We are mostly middle-aged, middle-class, college-educated people, seeking a different knowledge than we find in books, the far more elusive wisdom of the heart. We sit on chairs or on the floor in the library of the guest house, wearing sweaters and jeans, corduroys or sweatpants, comfortably dressed to address the big questions, ready if need be to wrestle our angel, as Jacob did, and perhaps in the process to find our true name.

A woman in our group who's been going out with the same man for several years but doesn't know if she should marry him prays and meditates about it. Yes, she sees a therapist, but when she asks the therapist a question, the therapist asks her another question back. One day she thinks she sees a sign. She's sitting on the floor in her living room trying to pray about it, and the way the sunlight falls on the carpet seems to form a letter of the alphabet — the first letter of the man's name. Is this a "sign"? Is this the guidance she is praying for? Is it God's way of telling her to marry the man? Or is it just an accident, is it only the way she's sitting or looking or squinting that makes her think she sees this and wonder if it might be a "message"?

A man wonders if he ought to take a job that would pay more money but require him to move to another city and leave his friends and the neighborhood he loves. He makes a list of the pros and cons, totaling up each column, trying to figure if the greater number of reasons on one side means that's the right thing to do, the best course to take, or should each reason be weighted, given a number value according to its importance? And even so, does it all "add up" to an answer, *the* answer, the course that he should follow?

Like most of our contemporaries, our peers, we wrestle with deciding what's "the right thing to do" with the help of psychiatrists, tests, courses, the advice of friends and experts. Those of us who have a religious faith or try to follow a spiritual path also look to God or Spirit or Higher Power as we understand it for aid or affirmation in such decisions, feeling perhaps that this other dimension is a deeper one, more meaningful and true. We are looking for the kind of guidance and wisdom from God or Spirit that theology calls "discernment," which translated into lay people's language means "how do we know when it's God?" That's what we've titled this retreat and offered as its theme.

We're volunteer members of our church's adult religious education committee, and our job is to plan courses, classes, activities, and retreats that respond to the concerns of our fellow parishioners, the ones who come to church not only out of habit or social obligation or family tradition but as seekers; as men and women who, like so many in the world, want to know and learn how to live for more than the next paycheck or promotion, who want to find greater meaning and purpose in life by getting in tune with a spiritual dimension of experience and trying to live by such light.

My friends and I on this retreat in the spring of 1984 belong to King's Chapel, in Boston, a church described in the program for Sunday worship as "Unitarian in theology, Anglican in worship, and Congregational in governance," an amalgam resulting from the more than three centuries of history that make it a stop on the Freedom Trail, where it is identified as "the oldest continuing pulpit in America." We are one of a small percentage of Christian churches in the Unitarian-Universalist Association, most of whose members and churches are Humanist, making us an anomaly in our own denomination. Our liturgy features our own revised version of the Book of Common Prayer, and might be mistaken for a low Episcopal service, leading some denominational wags to refer to King's Chapel as "the St. Peter's of the Unitarians." Trying to explain all this to friends, I usually end up saying, "Just think of it as 'a Boston church.'"

That's how I think of it myself when I first walk into King's Chapel on Christmas Eve of 1980, little knowing it's going to change my life. It's a freezing Boston night and I'm shivering in church, too, maybe out of nervousness as well as the cold. What power do the carols and candles have, what stirs when I sing the Latin words of "Adeste Fidelis" that seem so much more haunting and true than the English? Was it only by chance that I heard a neighborhood man in a bar say he wanted to go to mass on Christmas Eve, and was prompted to look for a church service?

I'm trying to recover from a year of continuous midlife crisis that includes fleeing from Hollywood and network television in a state of financial and physical crisis, breaking up with the woman I've lived with for seven years whom I hoped and expected to be with the rest of my life, and attending the funerals of my father in May and my mother in November. The one saving grace in the midst of this tumult is finding Dr. Howard Hartley and nurse Jane Sherwood at the stress clinic of Massachusetts General Hospital and getting into an exercise and diet program that lowers my pulse from a runaway 120 (a condition called tachycardia) to a better than normal 60, and my weight from a blubbery 172 to a reasonable 155. Part of this program involves giving up drinking for a month — I've never gone longer than a week in my adult life and that experience left me scratching the walls — but in my healthy new condition I manage to make it. During this newfound state of clarity an impulse leads me to go to church on Christmas Eve for the first time (except for funerals and weddings) since I got out of college in 1955 with a B.A. in English and an informal degree in atheism.

I pick King's Chapel from an ad on the *Boston Globe* religion page because it's in walking distance and the promise of "candle-light service and carols" doesn't seem too threatening. Even after I start attending Sunday services, I don't pay much if any attention to what denomination it is, thinking of it as generic "church" as in one of those children's maps of Your Town identifying Church, School, Fire Station, Factory, and other institutions.

It later occurs to me I've stumbled into the most appropriate church imaginable for my own outlook. I'm a Christian from childhood, affirmed not only by baptism but a personal experience of Jesus, yet I'm not comfortable with the rules and regulations of particular dogmas, the requirements of belief. I'm somehow relieved and pleased when I learn that some of my fellow parishioners don't consider themselves Christians at all, but are Unitarians who believe only in "the interconnecting web of the universe." While I consider myself a Christian, I don't believe everyone else is wrong or damned or unenlightened. I want my spiritual life to be able to draw on the wisdom of other creeds and faiths, and to think of my friends who follow other beliefs as fellow pilgrims on a spiritual path rather than enemies or rivals whom I need to convert or compete with in some theological playoff.

Within a year I join the church and a year or so later I'm serving as co-chair of its adult religious education committee, finding my deepest fulfillment in planning and going on retreats such as this one at Glastonbury Abbey, in Hingham, a town on the South Shore forty-five minutes from Boston. The first time we go on retreat here, some of our more Humanist-oriented Unitarian members are concerned about the Roman Catholic aura of the setting, the crosses in every room, the monks in their robes going to chapel for prayers and Eucharist services, where we're welcome but not required to join them. The Benedictines' specialty is hospitality, and it usually happens that our skeptics are most charmed of all, sometimes making a special donation to Glastonbury in appreciation of its nonpressure, genuine service to us, and support of our program.

We don't find any answers to our theme of "how do we know when it's God?" but we learn that people throughout the ages have searched for such discernment. Religious leaders and even saints have spent most of their lives trying to learn not only how to do it themselves but also to teach other people how to try — and maybe the best we can do is try. I'm somehow cheered to know how difficult it is (I don't feel so dumb about the subject, knowing this) and that even the greatest authorities, actual certified saints, have trouble discerning the will of God.

St. Ignatius of Loyola, perhaps the greatest authority on discernment in the Christian tradition, who wrote the "Rules of Discernment of Spirits," had such difficulties himself. Although he was able to discern from daydreams that God was leading him into a new way of life, and the Madonna came to him in a vision, he still couldn't decide whether or not to kill a Moor who didn't believe in the virgin birth of Jesus. In an argument about the subject, the Moor saw how upset Ignatius was getting and wisely hurried on ahead, while Ignatius became more disturbed and wondered if he'd failed in his duty to defend the honor of the Madonna.

Ignatius wanted to pursue the Moor and stab him with his dagger, but he couldn't quite make up his mind to do it. He couldn't "discern" what to do, in other words. Luckily for the Moor, Ignatius let the mule he was riding make the decision, and the mule didn't follow the road the Moor took. After I read this account in *An Approach to the Spiritual Exercises of St. Ignatius of Loyola,* by the Jesuit spiritual director William Barry, I feel a sense of relief. If it's that hard for St. Ignatius to discern whether it's God's will for him to stab a Moor in a theological argument, perhaps those of us looking for signs in patterns of sunlight and lists of pros and cons are not so stupid or hopeless after all. Perhaps we too can learn to discern.

The year after our "how do we know when it's God?" retreat, I take a course in religious autobiography our minister gives. The Reverend Carl Scovel is a remarkable man, all the more so for trying to appear unremarkable — he is quiet, low-key, unassuming, with a sly perception and a wry sense of humor. In his seemingly everyday, commonplace way he gives us the most memorable sermons — never generalities, always specific insight and story — and teaches stimulating classes on Bible study, Christian and Unitarian history, everything pertinent to our spiritual growth.

A bony, pale New Englander whose favorite sport is hiking up New Hampshire's White Mountains, Carl jogs around Beacon Hill and over the bridges that span the Charles River, in old New Balance running shoes, wearing plain shorts and sloganless T-shirts, a man of little adornment and no pretension, clad for more formal occasions in frayed cuffs and collars and serviceable tweed sportcoat. Carl is my own age, our birthdays only a week apart, and he has lived a life almost opposite from mine — married once and for life, father of three children, minister of this church for almost all his career. For all our differences we communicate, and I resonate to his style — what in writing I would call "the plain style," the one I most admire. It's my special good fortune to have him as minister and friend, the guide of my return to church and faith.

His course in religious autobiography not only deepens my sense of belonging and being part of the church, it helps me see my own spiritual path from early childhood to the present. As part of the course I write an essay about my recent experience returning to faith. I've always written about what interests me most, and now I'm finding that the whole religious dimension from which I've closed myself for so long is the subject I find most fascinating. Later I hear this same feeling expressed by Michael Murphy, founder of the Esalen Institute, who says, "The great game, the game of games, the story of stories is the unfolding of the Divine."

The essay I write in my religious autobiography class, called "Returning to Church," is published in the *New York Times Magazine* in Christmas week of 1985 and draws a response of hundreds of letters, more mail than I've ever received about anything I've written. It leads to an offer from a publisher to write it more fully as a book, which becomes *Returning: A Spiritual Journey.*

, , ,

It's now — amazingly — eighteen years ago since I first walked into King's Chapel and began a whole new story of my life. The beginning of that story is told in *Returning,* a title, by the way, that means to me not just "going back" but more importantly "turning again," suggesting a new path. (I'm inspired and relieved when my minister explains that the word "conversion" in Hebrew and Greek does not mean "reborn" but "turning," which is much closer to my own experience.)

I want to tell now of the spiritual journey as it looks over the long haul, not just the first flush of rediscovery, and speak as honestly as I can of the pitfalls as well as the peaks of such experience. William James writes, in *The Varieties of Religious Experience,* "Nothing is more common in the pages of religious biography than the way in which seasons of lively and of difficult faith are described as alternating."

I have known the whole range now, from romance to disillusionment and anger, from honeymoon to separation. Whatever value my own story has is not because it's not unique, but common — the kind of thing others may expect beginning such a journey, or find reassuringly familiar if they've traveled it for long on their own.

Through all these highs and lows of the spirit over nearly two decades, I never in the deepest pit lost faith in God. What I did lose faith in was my own discernment, my own ability to answer the question *How do we know when it's God?* That question seems to me to carry the shape of my experience better than any other concept, the best lens to look through in tracing the map of my own journey. I could never have predicted its course, or anticipated how often I would fail in discernment, nor imagine I could still find forgiveness after all my mistakes. In a sense then, this is a "how not to do it" book, and as such I think may prove more useful and perhaps more encouraging to other stumbling pilgrims than the tomes that so confidently tell us the five or seven or ten easy steps to fulfillment, satori, salvation, and material (as well as spiritual) success.

My story does not relate the sort of tragedy that Rabbi Harold Kushner so eloquently addresses in his classic *When Bad Things Happen to Good People*. In fact, this memoir of mine could more aptly be titled *When Good People Do Bad Things* — or at least, stupid things, things that hurt themselves and others. And, of course, I'm presuming the grace of God and the reader's tolerance will allow me to call myself a good person. I think most sinners *do* think of themselves as good people, and their sins as aberrations, mistakes, false steps they indeed are responsible for, but seem alien from their intentions and out of kilter with their true identity. I am not the victim of a malevolent fate or a wrathful God, but rather the unintentional creator of the pain I've caused myself and others while at the same time trying to follow a spiritual path. Perhaps "following a spiritual path" simply means the effort to live in a decent, fruitful way with the talents and flaws you've been given and the circumstances you've been dealt (and dealt yourself), and attempting to do so by the light of some faith in God, a Higher Power, and/or religious tradition to guide you. That effort in my own experience has not made life "easier" or smoother, but in some ways more difficult and confusing, yet in spite of all the pitfalls and trials, more meaningful and ultimately fulfilling.

By laying bare my own mistakes and struggles, I hope to make fellow seekers aware of pitfalls they may face themselves, and that raising these flags of warning may provide on one level a kind of "guidebook-in-reverse" to their own journey. Perhaps I may alert them to contemporary kinds of delusion that lie in their path with all the shimmering hope of oases in the desert, only to prove illusory, leading one deeper into dry, barren places of the soul. In a happier way, I hope that others may profit from following the techniques and strategies I've found — or that found me — that helped me work my way out of the darkness, up from pits of despond that seemed bottomless, and back to a path of fulfillment, forgiveness, and contribution.

At the nadir of this journey I lost my most familiar and comfortable way of communication with my faith, when language itself, the ritual words and prayers and Psalms, the liturgy of belief, became meaningless to me. It was then I felt words fail me, as I put it in the title of a chapter describing that experience — the most discouraging and frightening prospect for one who has depended on words for his work, his living as a writer, and his inspiration as a person of faith. Yet out of that period of failure with words, I learned the power of silence and the spiritual healing to be found through the body, the wordless disciplines like hatha yoga that provide another, silent, way of prayer and enlarged my communication with Spirit.

I have learned from my own experience that the famous "dark night of the soul" on the path of illumination should not be spoken of in the singular, as it usually is described. I've learned there is not just one but many such tests and passages, and probably will continue to be, as long as one is on the path, as long as one is alive and seeking. Since emerging from that latest dark night of the soul when words failed me, my life has seemed more in the spirit of a prayer I learned from my friend Ann Brower, who has given up the practice of medicine to seek a theology degree and find a ministry. She carries a copy of this prayer, from *Guerrillas of Grace: Prayers for the Battle,* by Ted Loder, in her pocket:

> Help me to believe in beginnings,
>   to make a beginning,
>   to be a beginning
> So that I may not just grow old,
> But grow new each day
> To this wild, amazing life
> You call me to live
> With the passion of Jesus Christ.

Those who are not Christian may of course feel the same sentiment in being called to live with the passion of Mohammed or Krishna, Moses and Yahweh, or the Higher Power that some twelve-step followers imagine for themselves with idiosyncratic flair (my friend Ivan Gold posits his Higher Power as an image of a tap-dancing Sammy Davis, Jr., while a woman I know envisions hers as an owl.) Though my own image of my Higher Power is Jesus Christ, I respect all others, and ask only that mine be respected in return.

I am moved by Ann Brower's prayer because "beginning" is one of the continuing themes of my life, even before my return to church and faith. My first novel, *Going All the Way,* ends with the word: "Begin." My second novel is called *Starting Over.* One of my deep connections with Christianity is its emphasis on forgiveness and the offer of grace to be able to begin again. What is new for me in Ann's prayer is the admission of growing old, and the thrill and recognition that these years after sixty can more than ever be truly described as "this wild, amazing life you call me to live." I have never felt so alive, nor has my life ever seemed as amazing, as in "amazing grace" and in the sheer wonder of new, unexpected experience.

, , ,

When I finished *Returning,* I had the urge to "give back" the kind of experience I got from the religious autobiography course I took at King's Chapel, and I started leading workshops in "spiritual autobiography." I offer them to people of any faith, or even seekers without a faith, who simply want to look at their life in the context of "spirit" in its broadest sense (I use the *Oxford English Dictionary* definition of spirit as "the animating or vital principle in man [and animals] . . . in contrast to its purely material elements; the breath of life"). For the past decade I have given this workshop, as well as another in "Creating from the Spirit," throughout the U.S. and in Mexico and Northern Ireland, at adult education centers, churches, synagogues, retreats, health spas, and at Sing Sing prison. Whenever I offer this work, I confess my own faith and at the same time give assurance it is not my intent to proselytize, or to question — much less attack — the beliefs held sincerely by anyone else. I say the same now of these pages. I believe an assault on the spirit — an attack or undermining of anyone's sincerely held religious beliefs, whatever they may be — is a form of rape, and its perpetration is criminal.

My faith as a Christian is personal and intimate rather than intellectual or theological. It was deeply confirmed by a childhood experience that turns out to be perhaps the most defining moment of my life. One night when I am nine years old I go to bed, say the Lord's Prayer, and before going to sleep (I am clearly and vividly awake during this whole experience), I feel or sense — I *experience* — my whole body filling with light. The light is white and so bright that it seems almost silver. It is not accompanied by any voice or sound, but I know quite clearly the light is Christ, the presence of Jesus Christ. I am not transported anywhere, I am all the time in my room at the top of the stairs in our house at 6129 Winthrop, Indianapolis, Indiana, a place as familiar as my own hand. Everything is the same as always, my bed and the desk across from it, the pictures on the wall of my favorite football heroes, like Tommy Harmon of

Michigan. Everything is normal and solid and real, the only thing different is the Light, and after it has infused me, maybe I too am different, or in some way changed — not better or brighter or nicer but simply changed, the way a person is changed by deep experience, altered in how the world is perceived, more open to the unexplainable, the great mysteries, the gift of grace. The light is not frightening to me as a child, but reassuring, like a blessing. It is so real that in fact it seems today like the very bedrock of my existence.

In one of those hopeless arguments about religion with an atheist friend, when I cite this experience as part of my explanation of being a Christian, he asks in frustration, "You mean that has primacy?" I never heard that term before, but I get the gist and answer yes. Later in the year of that childhood experience I buy at the neighborhood dime store a framed picture of Jesus as a boy which is on the bureau in my bedroom today, the only possession I have from my childhood. In more than a half century of moves and travels all over the country and the world, I have lost or misplaced or given or thrown away everything else. Yes. It has primacy.

My parents have me baptized as a baby in the Presbyterian Church, and as a preschool child I enjoy and am moved by the Sunday school teaching of the minister's wife, round and apple-cheeked Amy Franz, who becomes a treasured friend and wise counselor of our family, and whose spirit still feels close to me. My religious feelings really catch fire, though, when a friend from my grade school and Cub Scout den invites me to go to a Bible class with him at a Baptist church, taught by a lively young minister and his wife who have come north from preaching in Kentucky, in the hills. They are both tall and bony and angular, and filled with a love of God and of Jesus that brightens and animates them. They convey their faith through stories they act out and illustrate, like Moses drawing water from a rock, which is represented by a brown paper bag tied over a drinking fountain that spouts a jet of water through the bag ("rock") at the crucial moment. We sing stirring hymns like "Throw out the lifeline, someone is drifting away" and gesture with our arms, tossing imaginary lifesavers to the spiritually drowning. At the end of the course I go forward with others who are so moved to proclaim my commitment to Jesus.

One can speculate that my experience of light is "caused" by the influence of the Bible school, yet I know of no others who had such an episode. It is not anything I invoke or try to create but is as totally surprising as it is awesome. I don't tell anyone about it at the time, and a few years later when I try to describe it to a friend in my grade school class, I can see he doesn't get it and finds it pretty weird, though he doesn't try to make fun of me about it (I pick him to tell because I know he isn't that kind of guy). I don't tell anyone else and later I worry it's a sign of being crazy, so I try to just forget about it.

I'm amazed and relieved when in college I read about this phenomenon in *The Varieties of Religious Experience* and learn there is even a psychological name for it: "photism." James writes that this kind of experience "possibly deserves special notice on account of its frequency. . . . Saint Paul's blinding heavenly vision seems to have been a phenomenon of this sort; so does Constantine's cross in the sky." Nor is this phenomenon limited to great historical figures; it comes up frequently in reports of nineteenth-century American religious experience, as in this account of one C. G. Finney:

"All at once the glory of God shone upon and roundabout me in a manner almost marvelous. . . . A light perfectly ineffable shone in my soul, that almost prostrated me on the ground. . . . I think I knew something then, by actual experience, of that light that prostrated Paul on the way to Damascus."

Nor is experience of "the light" limited to Christianity; it has come to people on all the great religious paths, and sometimes brought people with no religious faith to a spiritual transformation and a new life centered on God. One of the most famous examples is that of Bill Wilson, a drunkard who in 1936 fell to his knees in prayer, asking God to reveal himself if he really existed, and at that moment the room filled with a great white light. It brought with it "ecstasy" and "peace," as Wilson lost the urge to drink and with a doctor friend founded Alcoholics Anonymous, the model of all the life-saving twelve-step programs based on surrender to a Higher Power.

In his book on religious experience, James devotes a whole section to what he calls "the reality of the unseen," observing that "the things which we believe to exist, whether really or ideally . . . may be present to our senses, or they may be present only to our thought. In either case they elicit from us a reaction, and the reaction due to things of thought is notoriously in many cases as strong as that due to sensible presences. It may be even stronger." As James puts this concept another way, "God is real since He produces real effects."

What I learn again and again from my own experience and that of other seekers and believers is best summed up by the words of a man as humble and undogmatic as William James, the Benedictine Father Nicholas Morcone, abbot of Glastonbury Abbey. In a homily there one morning he speaks of his confusion after reading and rereading both the Old Testament lesson and the New Testament lesson in the lectionary that day, for the different view of God each presents is hard to reconcile. He admits he has been confused before by conflicting images of God he finds in the Bible and decides that "we must take God as he comes to each of us."

I accept however God comes to any sincere believer, whether Christian or Jew, Muslim or Buddhist, Quaker or Shaker or Sikh. I also accept whatever form God assumes in the mind and heart of believers, whether it is masculine or feminine or simply a "Cloud of Unknowing." It's easy for me to think of God as she, since I grew up with a mother who loved me and tried to provide me with everything I wanted. When I think of a stern God I think of a he, like my father, who also loved me but expressed it with rules and sometimes punishments (though more often threats of them) that I sometimes didn't understand but tried to accept as they were given, "for my own good."

Most often I think of God as Spirit, that Cloud of Unknowing, the ineffable divine mystery from which we come and to which we go. I also honor those seekers whose doubts may preclude a Deity, who look to what they conceive as a Higher Power; and those who are simply still looking, engaged in the quest, the great search for meaning that begins at the beginning and continues to the end, if end there be.

This is the story of my own continuing quest.

Chapter 2

CHASING
THE DEMONS

———◆———

WHAT AM I DOING IN A CHURCH BASEMENT ON A FRIDAY
night, eating a New England boiled dinner with a bunch of sub-
urbanite Bible students? Man, has my life changed in the last
four years! That's how long it's been since I went to that seemingly innocent "candlelight service with carols" on Christmas
Eve of 1980 and it led to a new way of life, including new
friends, habits, routines, and outlook, all tied in with my physical rebirth to new health, and a fresh, unexpected beginning as
I've entered my fifties. Four years before this I wondered if I'd
even make it to my fifties.

What happened to the cocky, carousing, hotshot novelist-
turned-television writer who guzzled his daily half-gallon of
wine and only entered churches for weddings and funerals? I
don't miss him, but still, as I stare at the nude-looking whiteness
of the boiled potato on my plate as prelude to a weekend Bible
study workshop in the suburbs, I wonder if maybe I'm pushing
my spiritual life too hard. Maybe it's the grim atmosphere of the

dank, dimly lit church basement suffused with the sad odor of boiled cabbage that makes me wonder if I shouldn't have gone to a movie instead. But it's too late now — they're bringing on the bread pudding.

I'm here at the suggestion of my minister, who thinks I'll pick up some good ideas for our adult religious education committee at King's Chapel, which I co-chair to help plan retreats and programs. He says that the roving theologian who's in town to teach this workshop has a "new approach" to Bible study, but I fear it's going to be as soggy as the meal I've been picking at. Much to my surprise, though, the man I've imagined as a dry-as-dust scholar bent over tomes of Biblical exegesis like a character out of Dickens turns out to be a "good old boy" from Texas named Walter Wink. Wearing a light-tan leather jacket and a Texas-size smile, rubbing his hands together in anticipation, Walter brings the dim basement and its overstuffed inhabitants to bright, energetic life.

Walter has us acting out Bible stories and relating their characters and situations to our own lives, rather than simply dissecting the text. I really get into it, especially the stories of healing — like Jesus giving blind Bartimaeus his sight, and stopping the flow of blood of the woman who touches the hem of his garment. I go home thinking how I too want to be healed; and that maybe through faith it's possible.

But wait, haven't I already been healed? I'm healthier than I've been since high school, I don't wake up with hangovers any more (though I still drink some carefully rationed glasses of wine), and my writing is going well. Besides all that I have a new girlfriend who is beautiful in spirit as well as in looks, and plenty of warm, loving friends in my neighborhood, my church, and my writing life. What more am I looking for? Isn't love and God supposed to fill the hole inside? What more do I want?

What's missing?

I think back to my year on the Nieman Fellowship in journalism at Harvard, when I met, laughed with, and drank Heaven

Hill bourbon with Robert Coles as we spoke of literature, psychoanalysis, and dreams (both the waking and sleeping kind). Crunching through the snow in Harvard Square or having sandwiches in a booth at the Wursthaus (a dark-wood Cambridge version of a German beer joint) or going in spring for ice cream cones with chocolate flakes called "jimmies" here, Coles sometimes in the midst of these good discussions might suddenly break out singing — with ironic gusto — the popular song that sums up in a single word our most human urge:

"*More* — da da da da dee dah, *More* . . ."

And my fellow Nieman fellow Wayne Kelley from Atlanta and I (and anyone else who was there) would burst out laughing, as if our deepest desire had been suddenly brought into the open, and we would join in singing, hitting it as hard as we could on "*More* . . ."

Of course I still would like "more" of all the good feelings and experiences (and a guarantee they continue!), but this time it doesn't describe the dissatisfaction, discomfort — fear, even — that's making me search for an answer I can't seem to find. It's not that anything's missing, but rather that some old hang-ups keep hanging on. I still get rattled when I have to make business decisions, and act on impulse (more like compulsion, it feels like), then realize when it's too late what I've done to sabotage myself. I buy an expensive condo on a whim that I realize is all wrong for me as soon as the deal is done. I make a deal for writing a television show — thinking I can handle it because it doesn't require moving to L.A. again — then back out of my commitment at the last minute, creating chaos for a dear professional and personal friend who trusted me. After these freakouts I go into horrible paroxysms of anguish and regret. I can't break out of these patterns, break free. It feels sometimes like I'm tied up, bound by ropes, or even chains — rusty now from being around me so long (since childhood, it feels like), but still strong. Yes! Chains is the right analogy.

There's a man like that in the Bible. And Jesus heals him.

I remember Walter Wink's method of "putting yourself in the story" and acting it out, trying to live it. Maybe I can "live" this story and be healed! I read this particular story over and over until I almost know it by heart. One afternoon I go to my bedroom with the Bible and close the door. I sit on the edge of my bed and pray, and then I stand up and try to act out the story, putting myself in it.

I'm the tormented man with an unclean spirit whom Jesus meets in the country of the Gadarenes, as told in the book of Mark, chapter 5, verses 1 to 20. As I read the story I feel not only an identification but a sense of relief, and hope that perhaps I too can be purged, set free, liberated. I read the story over and over, looking for clues, wanting to experience what the man experienced when Jesus rid him of the unclean spirit that was screwing him up. I read it like Sherlock Holmes, wanting to solve the mystery of the miracle, or like a literary critic who tries to understand every nuance of the text and get to the heart of the author's deepest meaning. I read it like a prayer, in hopes of being healed. This is the story as I read it in the King James version:

> And they came over unto the other side of the sea, into the country of the Gadarenes.
> And when he was come out of the ship, immediately there met him out of the tombs a man with an unclean spirit,
> Who had his dwelling among the tombs; and no man could bind him, no, not with chains:
> Because that he had been often bound with fetters and chains, and the chains had been plucked asunder by him, and the fetters broken in pieces: neither could any man tame him.
> And always, night and day, he was in the mountains, and in the tombs, crying, and cutting himself with stones.

But when he saw Jesus afar off, he ran and worshipped him,

And cried with a loud voice, and said, What have I to do with thee, Jesus, thou Son of the most high God? I adjure thee by God, that thou torment me not.

For he said unto him, Come out of the man, thou unclean spirit.

And he asked him, What is thy name? And he answered, saying, My name is Legion: for we are many.

And he besought him much that he would not send them away out of the country.

Now there was there nigh unto the mountains a great herd of swine feeding.

And all the devils besought him, saying, Send us into the swine, that we may enter into them.

And forthwith Jesus gave them leave. And the unclean spirits went out, and entered into the swine: and the herd ran violently down a steep place into the sea, (they were about two thousand;) and were choked in the sea.

And they that fed the swine fled, and told it in the city, and in the country. And they went out to see what it was that was done.

And they come to Jesus, and see him that was possessed with the devil, and had the legion, sitting, and clothed, and in his right mind: and they were afraid.

I not only pray with the story, I try to imagine myself into the story. I try to live the story. I want to be the man who is healed. I not only imagine myself in the story, I enact the story, in the role of the man with the unclean spirit. In the bedroom of my apartment at 140 Mt. Vernon Street on the flat of Beacon Hill, on a series of spring afternoons, I act it out.

Like this:

I'm pacing in my damned lair among the tombs, where I'm crying and cutting myself as the demons squawk inside me, taunting me with failure and reproof. This part of the role is easy for me to identify with — I actually cut my wrist long ago, and the inner voices recounting past mistakes and future fears are all too familiar. In the midst of my chaos among the tombs, I look out and see a boat reach the shore. A man in a white robe comes out of it: Jesus. I know who he is and that he heals. I run and worship him, falling at his feet. (I kneel on my bedroom floor.)

I read the story aloud, playing the different parts; I am the demon crying from within, and I speak the words of Jesus (the powerful words, the exorcising words) ordering the unclean spirit to come out, asking, "What is thy name?" and my demon answers, "My name is Legion." I hear the devils squawking to be let out so they can enter the herd of swine feeding nearby, and Jesus releases them. With relief I imagine the devils leaving me and entering the swine, and I picture them hurtling down to the sea and plunging in.

Gone at last! Disposed of!

I stand up, feeling lighter now, and sit on the edge of my bed. With a sense of calm, I picture myself as the man who is healed, clothed (in white), no longer tearing at myself but in my "right mind." Centered, at peace. Empty of the squabbling demons. Clean.

Sounds from the street and from other apartments intrude, breaking the spell — the baby cries in the next apartment, a car hums by outside. Such sounds were there before, I'm sure, but I put myself deeply enough in the story to shut them out. Emerging from it now, I'm aware again of the daily world, and I wonder — I hope and pray — that my amateur "exorcism" worked, that by trying to "be in" the story, and live it by acting it out in imagination, I have actually rid myself of my demons. To make sure, I repeat the story off and on in the coming weeks.

I don't tell anyone what I'm doing, not even my minister. It's between me and Jesus. That's how I think of it. It's not that hard for me to think of him as present — not a physical presence, but as Spirit, not like a "ghost" but an influence, a power, in and out of the world, in and out of me, beyond comprehension and yet knowable. I know the sure sense of this is based on my childhood experience of being filled with light — the light of Christ. Even in my long years of atheism I never denied or dismissed this experience — I simply didn't give it much thought or importance. After returning to church, I of course recall it with appreciation, and a confirmation of faith, as it is to me now.

, , ,

After going back to church my thirst for spiritual understanding leads me to seek out, with the recommendation of my minister, a "spiritual director" whom I meet with once or twice a month to receive counsel and guidance about prayer, sacred reading, and the still elusive "discernment." My spiritual director is a Roman Catholic nun who is part of an ongoing program at the Center for Religious Development in Cambridge, which trains people in the practice of spiritual direction and offers it to lay people as well as clergy.

Sister Madeline, a good and sincere woman with gray hair who could play a sympathetic nun in any movie, opens up many new ideas and avenues for me, urging me to establish a direct relationship to God. How? Why, just talk to him. Get quiet and ask what he wants to say to you. So I do. Back in my bedroom on lower Mt. Vernon Street, the same room where I act out the story of the exorcism of demons, I seriously, sincerely, ask God to speak to me, to give me some message.

He does. Not like a voice from outside, but an inner message that comes almost immediately, leaving me flabbergasted — and laughing. I cry, with delight and joy, and when I tell Sister Madeline about it, I cry again, and then when I come home from our session I write her, saying that another surprising aspect of the experience was how quickly it occurred:

> When I had settled down to pray, I expected I would be sitting there a long time, trying to maintain my concentration, but the words I told you about came almost at once, as if they were spontaneous, waiting to be said, a feeling like "Of course!" There was something wonderfully humorous about it, in the sense that I was known so totally — I was going to say "only in the way parents can know you." Sometimes my parents and I did make one another smile with such knowing . . .

So in recent adult experience as well as in childhood, I had felt the presence of God or Christ, which gave me hope that by acting out the demon story in Mark, I might in fact be able to get the same result. I think perhaps I can summon the healing power of Jesus to rid me of these inner forces I conceive as "demons" as he did for the man in the country of the Gadarenes.

But my demons don't go away. I still at crucial times feel gripped and whirled around, like someone being blindfolded and turned in circles and then cast off to try to walk a straight line and go reeling and careening off the sides of cliffs. I'm dizzy from it all — the compulsive decisions that seem to be made in the grip of panic and afterward look so obviously irrational and self-defeating. The most persistent and disturbing manifestation of it around this time is my firing literary agents.

The year after I get back from Hollywood I fire the good woman who has helped me professionally and been a friend for the past seven years. Then I go with the one who my publisher affirms is "the best agent in America," and when she makes a perfectly sane and reasonable suggestion to improve a book proposal I'm writing, I fire her too. Next I use a brilliant lawyer who is not familiar with the publishing world to negotiate my new book contract, and after that I feel I've made a big mistake and get rid of him too. Within a year I hire and fire still another agent for doing what I asked her to do, after I change my mind when it's too late. Of course I always believe I have good "reasons" at the time for splitting, yet even I begin to suspect there may be something wrong with me rather than all these successful professionals.

Yes, I'm seeing a therapist now, an extremely bright, sensitive, nondogmatic woman who sympathizes with my dilemmas. She is tall and graceful, her dark hair pulled back in a bun. Her brown eyes are sympathetic, actively engaged in trying to see me, trying to help me. Yet she can't seem to find any answer for me either — any more than my minister. Any more than Jesus. I rack my brain for answers, or rather for someone who can give me an answer, or point me the way to an answer. I think of an old Columbia friend who became a trusted confidant in my postcollegiate New York years and is now a successful lawyer, and I call and ask if he has any plans for coming to Boston soon. Could I take him to dinner and get some advice? He stops for a night on his way to vacation on Martha's Vineyard and I tell of my concerns. We go to my favorite restaurant, a homey Italian place on the border of Beacon Hill, and we talk by the light of a small electric candle as we fill ourselves with pasta and thick tomato sauce. There's comfort in the camaraderie, his caring and friendship renewed, but of course there's no magic answer in the mellow smoke that plumes up from his familiar pipe. Maybe I'm being too hard on myself, he tells me; we all make mistakes.

, , ,

How do people change? Hell, I've changed myself, through physical and spiritual disciplines, regaining my health and returning to a spiritual path. But the turn I began four years ago with diet and exercise and going back to church is not complete. I don't get drunk anymore, but I still cling to those one or two glasses of wine most nights, and to supplement them I smoke a little grass, rationalizing that it doesn't hurt my body and just brings a little surcease to the mind. Well, okay, but . . .

A line comes to mind I always loved, supposedly spoken after Carl Sandburg read a poem he had written about Sacco and Vanzetti to a group gathered to raise money for the two accused anarchists. When Sandburg finished reciting the poem, there was an uneasy silence from the audience. Then one of the sponsors of the event, the great Clarence Darrow, spoke up in response:

"It ain't enough," he said.

That's how I feel about my own transformation.

So how do people change? Or maybe the question is now — how do they keep changing?

One evening some six months after I came back to Boston from Hollywood in 1980, I see some old friends who have obviously undergone some sort of change — not only in their relationship, but their very attitude, their "outlook." The change is "for the good," yet it makes me uncomfortable, even suspicious. (How did they do it, and why, and was it for real?)

When they come to one of my homemade chili dinners on Beacon Hill (which is funkier than fancy in my own sublet apartment), Duncan and his wife, Bebe, appear to have taken some kind of happiness pill, perhaps the "soma" of the future forewarned by Aldous Huxley. (This is before the advent of Prozac and its derivatives, which would have made Huxley richer than Bill Gates if he'd patented a formula for it.) The eight of us at my apartment that night all know each other, but we don't seem to recognize good old Duncan and Bebe — at least by their behavior. They were perfectly pleasant people before, but now they are bursting with some kind of super-charged energy (are they on speed?) and mixed in with that happiness pill they seem to have swallowed is evidently some kind of love potion. They hold hands, gaze at one another like teenagers at the junior prom, and even smooch, right at the table — and this is a married couple, for God's sake! They have to leave just before midnight to go to some kind of "graduation" in the semi-seedy old Bradford Hotel in downtown Boston, which is part of this weird seminar thing they've done called "est." We all politely decline their invitation to come to this or future "guest events" of this program, and as soon as they're out the door we start dissecting them.

"What's happened to Duncan and Bebe . . . did you see them kissing?"

"They must be putting it on —"

"If you ask me, it's just an act."

"But why?"

"It's all part of this kooky self-improvement thing they're into — you go to these lectures or something, and supposedly improve your life."

Giggles. Groans.

"Why would anyone want to do that?" I ask.

We know it's impossible to alter "the human condition," which we've learned long ago as part of our college education, acquiring what F. Scott Fitzgerald called "the wise and tragic sense of life." What's all the more puzzling is that Bebe and Duncan are no dummies — he's a Ph.D. in English literature and an associate professor with tenure, she a Ph.D. in philosophy and a college instructor. How could people like that, whom we also think of as hip and "with it," fall for such nonsense, here at the dawn of what surely will be the Enlightened Eighties?

, , ,

But the memory stays, and now a few years later I wonder if this weird thing that changed Duncan and Bebe (Duncan says it kept their marriage from falling apart) could help change some things in my own life. By chance, I run into a bright woman I know walking up Mt. Vernon Street one afternoon, and she stops and asks me what I'm up to these days. For some reason, though I haven't said this to anyone yet, it pops into my mind to mention that I'm thinking of doing this seminar some friends of mine did called est.

Nancy looks stricken — as if I've just announced my plan to parachute off the Hancock Tower with a handkerchief.

"Don't do it!" she exclaims.

She grabs my shoulders.

"My last husband was a psychiatrist," she says. "And he told me never to do that thing — it's very damaging, it can screw you up. It's brainwashing stuff, they make you try to convert your friends. People get real aggressive when they do it, obnoxious. Listen, if you think you need to do something like that, take a course in assertiveness training. I'll find a course for you. I'll even pay for it — if you promise not to do est!"

I promise!

Maybe this chance meeting has saved me from a fate worse than death. I hear that some people think this est stuff is fascist. They won't let you go to the bathroom during the sessions — some former astronaut actually peed in his pants! The bathroom stuff has even been satirized in the Burt Reynolds movie *Semi-Tough*. This est thing got started in California (of course) by some former used-car salesman turned guru; in other words, an up-to-date snake-oil salesman.

I don't take Nancy up on her offer of assertiveness training courses, which really don't interest me. I go on with my church work, becoming co-chair of the adult religious education committee, planning retreats and programs at the parish house. Yet some of my old self-destructive habits are still hanging on, even though in modified form. I even smoke a joint one afternoon before going to a religious education committee meeting. My erratic patterns continue to repeat; I sell the condo I bought on a misguided whim a year earlier, creating atomic-level stress.

In early 1984 the thought returns that maybe in spite of all the bad stuff I've heard about it, this est thing could help me. Duncan continues to invite me to est guest seminars at the Bradford Hotel and I continue to decline, angry that he doesn't invite me to his new outdoor swimming pool instead. I've heard these "guest" events over at the Bradford are really a scam to get you to join — sign up for the program — and they lure you into little rooms and badger you until you say yes. I know that would turn me off, so when I decide to inquire about the seminar, I don't even mention it to Duncan and Bebe, but go to a new friend who someone else told me did est but has never tried to recruit me.

Sydney Rice is the manager of a restaurant on Charles Street where I go for lunch and take-out food, and I always enjoy stopping to talk with this bright, pleasant woman. She's short, with short dark hair and dark eyes, and has a fresh, crisp look about her. She speaks with a kind of clarity I admire, a no-nonsense straightforwardness that doesn't seem "assertive" so much as communicative. She also has a smile and a sense of humor that puts me at ease.

Over cappuccino at the neighborhood coffeehouse, Sydney answers my questions and concerns about doing est, and if she doesn't know the answer, she refers me to someone who does. When I tell her about my horrendous experience in Freudian analysis and say I'm afraid that doing est might bring on some of those hallucinatory nightmares, she sends me to talk with her friend Sarah Wolfe, a Boston therapist who's done a lot of "the work" of the est programs and believes it to be of value. Sarah is a hearty blond woman with the natural warmth of a favorite aunt, and I immediately trust her. When I pour out my fears, she tells me frankly, "Whatever is deepest in you will probably come up. It usually does." Well, at least she doesn't try to snow me. I'm so anxious to get at the root of my hang-ups — exorcise my demons — I'm willing to take that risk.

I can't stand any more anguishing over making decisions, fearing I'll make another wrong one — and then beating myself up because I think I've done it again! I say I'll go to New York to watch my good friend Ted perform as a star pitcher for his soft-ball team, reprising his athletic prowess from high school. Then at the last minute I fear if I don't stay home and work on a magazine article due the next week, I'll miss the deadline and get an important editor angry at me. As soon as it's too late to go, I fall into anxious depression, believing now that being a day or so late with the article isn't as important as supporting my friend. None of it's any big deal, except I torture myself as if it is, waking in a cold sweat, feeling like Benedict Arnold.

So now am I making the right decision doing something that seems so extreme as the est training? What if it interferes with my newfound spiritual life, my commitment to church and faith? Sydney assures me that many religious leaders, as well as believers of all faiths, have done this program. In fact, a whole group of Cistercian monks from St. Joseph's Monastery in Spencer, Massachusetts, took the est training right here in Boston.

A trusted writer friend in California who did one of the first est trainings with Werner Erhard himself (the guy who started it) tells me all the good things it did for her, and I ask "What's the worst thing about it?" She thinks a moment and says, "It doesn't last." I figure if that's the worst, I might as well take the plunge.

Before plunging, I decide to cover my tail with God, so I write to Sister Madeline to tell her of my decision. She's not too enthusiastic about it, but says it's up to me. Damn. I have to make another big decision by myself, without the aid of a divine intermediary. If it goes badly I'll only have me to blame — and oh, will I!

I tell Sydney to enroll me, but not to make me go to any guest events or introduction evenings first. I don't want to be turned off by any high-pressure selling tactics. Just tell me where and when to show up. I tell my girlfriend, Theresa, I'm going to do this, and she doesn't have to do it just because I am, but if she wants to join me, that's fine. She's heard about est herself, and thinks it might help her get a handle on some issues in her own life. Our relationship of a year or so is beginning to fray, and we both feel we have nothing to lose by doing this together. We need to tell people we won't be around the next weekend, but we don't want to admit what we're really doing. We don't want anyone to think we're kooks. So we tell everybody we're going to New Hampshire.

, , ,

There's a hundred or so people in the ballroom of the Bradford, some sitting on folding chairs facing the front, others still milling around or waiting in line to see one of the officials at the back tables who seem to be in charge of things, to make special requests. (We are all special, of course, and we want everyone to know it.) Theresa and I want to get special permission to sit in the back row so if we have to pee we can be excused and not be like that poor astronaut who had to do it in his pants. Sydney has assured me if I think I'll have to go and that's stopping me from doing the course, I can tell them I have a medical problem and get permission to sit in the back with others who have special needs. Theresa says she has a medical problem too. We both get to sit in the back row so we can sneak off and go to the bathroom anytime it's urgent, even before one of the regular breaks.

The first session lasts more than four hours, and neither of us even thinks about going to the bathroom. We are completely absorbed in what's going on. In fact, after the first break we turn in our special medical IDs so we can sit up front and not miss a damn thing. For the rest of the weekend and the following weekend, we sit for hours on end as close as possible to the front of the room without the least discomfort.

We "get it" that this part of the rules is not about deprivation or punishment or testing your bladder or willpower, but rather is about distraction. We are not used to paying attention to anyone or anything for more than a few minutes, and sitting still to listen for hours on end is almost unheard of in today's hyper world (a century and a half ago, debates like those between Lincoln and Douglas that lasted three or four hours were considered entertainment and drew big crowds). Now we smoke, drink coffee, turn on TV or radio, look at the paper, go to the bathroom, check the time, do anything to get out of simply concentrating, giving a subject our complete attention.

The man who's called the "trainer" (what the hell — are we animals or something?) is a tall, intense guy with dark hair who used to be a high school principal in a tough ghetto neighborhood in California. He acts and talks like it, barking out instructions, taking no shit, making sure we know he's boss. This is Ron. He strides across the front of the room, sipping from a tall silver mug something like a cocktail shaker with a top on it, and we wonder what the hell's in it — water, chicken soup, or maybe a version of Al Capp's "kickapoo joy juice" brewed in "Li'l Abner." There must be something powerful, because this guy never lets up, never gets tired, always looks neatly pressed, well combed, clear-eyed, sharp, on top of his game, whether it's four o'clock in the morning after going all day or three hours later when the whole thing starts up again. In fact, you can't help noticing that all the assistants and workers in the room, whether from the staff of est or volunteers, are neatly dressed and well groomed and stand or sit up straight, walk with purpose, speak clearly and directly. It's not natural. Damn. Have they all been brainwashed? Will such a dire fate befall me and Theresa?

I'm worried about another infamous part of the "training," where I've heard they call everybody assholes. The way I picture this, they take us off in small groups, maybe three or four or even six people, and "break us down" by yelling all kinds of names at us. But it turns out we don't ever split up into small groups; we're always sitting in the big ballroom, all hundred or so of us, so I don't feel personally threatened when Ron the trainer indeed calls the whole bunch of us assholes. And by the time he does it, I pretty much agree with him.

One of the rules that seems pretty simple is that no one is supposed to bring a watch into the room. That's so we can't keep glancing at our watches and losing our attention on what's going on, wondering how long it will be to the next break, checking how long or short a time we've been sitting here, and all the rest of the stuff people do when they're at lectures or seminars only paying attention with half their minds (or less) and letting their thoughts stray to important issues like what's for dinner and did I remember to turn off the toaster this morning. So leaving the watches outside the room doesn't seem too complicated, right?

Wrong.

It takes more than two hours to get every person in the room to give up their watch. Some people "forgot"; some people had a pocket watch instead of a wristwatch and figured that didn't count; some people took it off their wrist and put it in their purse or their pocket; others forgot they had taken it off their wrist and put it somewhere else on them; someone says his watch is very expensive and he's afraid it might be stolen; another person says tearfully her watch has deep sentimental value and she's afraid of losing it. You never could have guessed how many reasons there are for people to keep their watches. As this whole process drags on and on, and I see how people make up any excuse or trick of the mind or self-justification to get out of doing something they agreed to do, by the time Ron calls us a bunch of assholes, I agree.

Seeing how people behave in this way is like being in a laboratory in some experiment with guinea pigs, and we're the g.p.'s.

Of course this is still pretty impersonal for me so far. I haven't stood up to "share" or ask a question or make a comment yet. The way the whole thing works is, Ron puts forth different theories or ideas and then asks people to respond, and when he calls on them, one of these sharply dressed volunteers scurries down the aisle with a microphone and it's passed to the person who's standing up to speak.

A woman who speaks sincerely and well stands up to tell the story of why she and her husband got a divorce. She explains how his being from a different culture kept leading to conflicts that simply made the marriage impossible. She tells it in such an intelligent, low-key way that I believe her, and I'm shocked when Ron says, "That's not what happened — that's just your story of what happened."

The woman says, "No, it's what really happened — you could even have my sister-in-law come in here and she'd tell you the same thing."

"Well," says Ron with a smile, "what if we got your ex-husband in here. Would he say the same thing?"

"Oh, no!" the woman says. "He doesn't understand."

There is laughter — including mine.

"Oh, you mean he has a different story?"

In a flash I see myself, not the woman divorced from a foreign husband. I hear myself explaining, with all the low-key intelligence I heard and admired from that bright woman, just why I had to leave each of those literary agents, and I "get it" that these are just my stories, and God knows they have their own stories (versions) of what happened, just as convincing and damning as mine. And none of it's "true," it's just our stories, our self-justifying versions of our lives.

Ron teaches us to cut down our stories to the bare bones, to get to the real "what happened" rather than our opinions, judgments, and justifications, by constantly asking, "What happened?" Example: She called me a liar and I threw a vase at her, rather than "She went crazy and made me crazy too, and so I knew we didn't love each other and I was right to never make a commitment to her!" or: He didn't send my story to the *New Yorker* and I fired him, rather than "He never really had confidence in my work and I realized his literary taste was in the toilet, so I had to sever our relationship for the sake of my own larger vision of my career."

As the day progresses into the night (time becomes irrelevant), I begin to see myself in all the people who speak, argue, cry, and tell their stories. I "get it" that we are all the same, our secret fears and weird behaviors are not unique but are part of what it is to be human — and part of being human is try to hide the fact that we are human, to deny our "imperfections" and present to the world a facade that excludes all that — what Ron calls "our act."

This is more than intellectual learning, it is striking something deep in me, and I feel exhilarated. On one of our brief breaks when we hustle out to get juice or coffee, we pass a neighborhood bar and I look inside and am struck by what suddenly seems to me the wonder and strangeness of what they are doing in there. It's four in the afternoon, still light out, and these people are choosing to put themselves in a dim room to drink beverages that numb their senses. They seem as alien to me as the habitues in the bar scene in *Star Wars* — alien kinds of woogie creatures from other galaxies. My God. What makes it even stranger is that I realize how recently I'd have been in the bar looking out at people with name tags chugging tomato juice as if *they* were the aliens. I must really be "transforming."

All this is fascinating, but now we come to the nitty-gritty, the part I fear, the Pandora's box I'm afraid to open, the one that therapist told me would probably get pried open anyway. We are going deeper. We are going into our own unconscious — that house of horrors I unlocked in the last year of my Freudian analysis that nearly drove me crazy. Here I am risking messing with it again out of desperation to find the key I never found back then, the Open Sesame to life as it's supposed to be, without the demons, without the hang-ups that dog your steps and keep tormenting you, the life that's become so fulfilling now with church and Theresa and friends and work — if it weren't for the damn demons! Well, you have to take risks to get where you want to go.

Now Theresa and I are so intrigued by what's going on, we don't even mind the few hours' sleep we get (our Saturday session doesn't end until four in the morning, and we have to be back and in our seats by nine!). We can only have one big meal a day, but it becomes an adventure — we fortify ourselves with Paul Bunyan–style breakfasts at the Howard Johnson's on Stuart Street near the Bradford, and wolf down incredible stacks of pancakes, sausage, toast, muffins, fruit, orange juice, and coffee. We giggle as we grab for more food, like teenagers in an eating contest, and eagerly go off to our second day's session, eager to see what will happen next.

, , ,

Now comes the moment I fear the most. We move our chairs out of their ordered rows to sit with space between while we do something called a "process," which sounds like a kind of guided meditation. I feel like I'm about to go off the high diving board. I take a deep breath, try to relax, and say a prayer, bracing myself against what horrible images may come bursting out of the sewers and sinkholes of my unconscious, the terrors that arose in the last days of my Freudian psychoanalysis.

What appears in my mind is a pond in a pleasant place with trees and grass. Not so bad after all! Then I realize it's the pond in the Boston Public Garden. Uh-oh. That's a special place for me, the place I made a beeline for when I got back to Boston from Hollywood. It was there on a bench looking out onto the calm water that I thought again of the Psalm that I felt was my road map back: "He leadeth me beside the still waters. He restoreth my soul." The pond is a key place in my spiritual life, and I really don't want to get into that here. But I don't get to choose what my mind comes up with. I just try to be calm and watch.

Keeping my eyes shut, I see a line of men appear and begin to form a circle around the pond. They're dressed in armor like knights, or maybe Crusaders. Yes — on each of their chests there's a Crusader's cross. My worry about not wanting to get into religious issues begins to subside as I realize these must be "protectors" — Crusaders of the unconscious come to protect my pond, which I think of as the source of the sacred in me. So, just as I'm wanting to protect my religious beliefs from this "process," these guys appear, no doubt to protect those beliefs from attack. Now another figure joins the circle of Crusaders, but he wears no armor, only a robe. It is Jesus. He too must be protecting me, and I'm relieved that my faith is so staunchly guarded!

But now something awful happens — one by one, the Crusaders fall over, stiff as boards. It looks like they're being knocked down, like so many mannequins, yet I don't see anyone doing it. Last of all, Jesus falls over. I'm scared. They all were felled as simply as tipping over a doll. Now I feel vulnerable, unprotected. Does this little drama mean that my faith is not really solid, but only an illusion, a way to compensate for losing my home and mate in L.A. and my parents dying the same year? My deepest self is identified with my faith now, the faith that began in childhood, confirmed by "the light," as part of my very identity. Is it being taken away? Am I being stripped of this, too, in whatever this "process" is? Could this whole program be some kind of antireligious brainwashing? But nothing has been said about religion in any of our sessions. All this is coming up from my own depths. So maybe my fears were right, I shouldn't be digging into those depths.

We're given an opportunity to "share" the experience by asking for the microphone and addressing the trainer as the hundred or so other people in the room listen, but I wouldn't think of trying to explain this, it's too complicated. And too precarious. I keep quiet and listen to others "share" their experiences, positive and negative (each experience is precious and all-consuming to the person who has it), not really concentrating now on anything except my own disturbing riddle. Maybe my friend Nancy was right when she grabbed my shoulders and told me to stay away from this. Damn. What have I got myself into?

Can I get out?

This impulse is familiar. Since childhood, when I've been scared, I've quit. I've quit all kinds of things — summer camps, colleges, marriages, literary agents . . . Is this just another compulsive desire to cut and run when things get tough? Or do I need to run for my life? (How do we know when it's God?)

I hang in there until we finish about three o'clock Monday morning, go home, and flop into bed. I wake up at seven from a nightmare, groggy and frightened. I dreamed of the pond in the Public Garden, the very one that came up in the "process," and now from that source I consider sacred, a slimy black monster comes up! It's like a snake, but turns into something like a seal, and then a sea lion, which is much less frightening to me. But now, awake, I wonder what it might turn into next — in dreams or in waking images, like the ones that tormented me and drove me to the edge of madness or death at the end of the psychoanalysis. Maybe I've opened this Pandora's box again. Shit.

I call Joe Brenner, a shrink who helped me through my first divorce and later became a social friend. There's panic in my voice as I tell him what's going on, and he prescribes a Xanax to calm me down. But as part of the agreement of doing est, I promised not to drink or take any kind of drugs during the two weeks of training, and I want to do this thing right if I'm going to continue to do it at all. Joe says to ask someone if I can have permission to take a Xanax, so I call Sydney Rice, who says at once to go ahead: "You're responsible for your own health and well-being and you should take anything your doctor prescribes." As I hurry down Mt. Vernon Street to Gary Drug to get the pill, I wonder if all my senses are in working order, and I take off my glasses, only to have the brick sidewalk seem to move up toward me. Damn. I feel like I'm already on some drug, and I'd swear I'd been slipped something in the weekend sessions, except that we never ate or drank anything while we were in the room.

The Xanax calms me down a bit, but I'm still on edge and worrying whether I should risk going on with this thing — maybe I'm too screwed up to expose myself to such intense interior work — maybe I'll fall apart. I go to Joe Brenner's house in Cambridge that afternoon for advice.

Dr. Joseph Brenner is an Englishman who's head of psychiatry at M.I.T., and in the throes of my first divorce, in 1965, Robert Coles recommended him as a good man to help me through it. He did, and a year or so after I stopped going to him as a patient we ran into each other at a party in Cambridge. We enjoyed talking and began to invite one another to lunch and dinner or social events from time to time, talking of life, love, women, health, books, food, literature, and anything else that seemed of interest at the moment. Joe is a wry, thoughtful man who served as a doctor in the British Army in World War II, came to the U.S. to practice medicine, went into psychiatry, and ended up heading the department at M.I.T.

In the quiet of his kitchen on a leafy street in Cambridge, he gives me coffee, cake, and a saving insight. After hearing my worry about seeing the Crusaders and Jesus being knocked down at the pond, he says maybe those Crusaders weren't "spiritual" figures at all, but protectors whom I want to take care of me instead of being responsible myself. (Bull's-eye!) The real Crusaders, he says, were among the cruelest and bloodiest of warriors.

I laugh and say, "That's probably why I want them on my side!"

He also points out there seems something fake and doll-like about them, the way I describe them — even the Jesus figure — as if they were a child's toys that were being knocked down. Maybe this whole thing is about growing up — finally, at age fifty-two. That really hits home. And I realize the figure of Jesus was like the "cardboard Jesus" at the side of the baptismal well when I was dunked by full immersion at age eleven. I came up out of the water and the first thing I saw was that cardboard guy, and I felt cheated. Now all this is coming together like a puzzle being solved; but I still want more reassurance. I want to be reassured that this program isn't going to somehow suck my religion out of me, like a vampire drinking my blood.

Sydney — always at the ready — arranges for me to talk to one of the monks at St. Joseph's. I'm impressed that this is the monastery of the well-known religious author Father Basil Pennington, whose book *Centering Prayer* I know and admire. Father Pennington himself has done est but he is off on a speaking tour, so I talk to another monk at St. Joseph's. I express my fears to Father James, and tell him about the pond with the fallen Crusaders and Jesus, and about my return to church and its importance to me. He too says the figures at the pond sound like "toy soldiers"; perhaps I can now deal directly with the source of my own spirituality, as represented by the pond, without needing these other "protectors." He says that from his own experience doing est, I needn't worry about its having any adverse effect on my newly blooming spiritual life. His bottom-line message is: The only effect this program will have on your spiritual life will be to deepen it.

Once again I am reassured, though I remain edgy, worried about the next weekend and what it might bring up (from my "pond"). There's a Wednesday night "checking in" meeting for everyone in the training, just to make sure we're all okay and keeping our pledge not to drink or do drugs. Afterwards I go to one of the volunteers, the one with the brightest smile. I tell Lynn Hartness that "everything is coming up" for me — fears, nightmares, questions, health, religion, love, sex. I go through all the stuff that's roiling around in my mind, and she listens with complete attention. At the end of my spiel she breaks into a big grin and says, "I got it!"

I feel tremendously relieved, even though I know that "getting it" is part of the lingo of est. I don't care; I feel understood, unburdened, as if by dumping everything on another person — an attentive, listening person — I have taken it off my own back. I sleep well that night for the first time since all this began.

, , ,

We're greeted at the start of the second weekend by our new trainer. He introduces himself by saying sternly, as if we'd better get it straight right away:

"I'm not Ron — I'm Lon."

Theresa and I have to hold back giggles. Lon seems like the opposite image of Ron: a blond, tan, surfer type of guy who might have been a kid who cut class and caused trouble for Ron the high school principal. We wonder if it's part of the whole est strategy to give us this kind of one-two punch; brooding intellectual followed by swinger jock. Whatever, it's definitely not a good-cop-bad-cop scenario. Lon has the same jargon ("languaging" they call it) as Ron, the same tough, no-nonsense approach, making sure everyone toes the line, obeys the rules, knows their place ("You are all assholes"). There are, however, from both these guys, genuine acknowledgments (praise, recognition) for people who "share" and "get it."

By Saturday night we are moving our chairs apart again to prepare for another "process." This one is called — oh no — "the truth process." So I may plunge back in the pond with its snakes and sea monsters, or worse, what I imagine is the whole jungle of my unconscious, a swampy morass of threatening creatures I had sealed off long ago — maybe as far back as childhood — by sheer willpower.

The trainer relaxes us into a meditative state, describing a beautiful beach, blue sky, with white sand and palm trees, a breeze off the blue water — and from there we move on to our own places to find our own "truth." I pray for the power to survive whatever might come. I steel myself for monsters.

Cute little orange spaceships zip onto the screen of my mind, darting and circling in pretty patterns against a black background. It reminds me of the opening of a benign Disney movie. The lightness and charm of it is pleasantly surprising. But I can't help wondering what dark and tortuous demonic scenes lie behind such an innocent display.

A lovely landscape appears with a placid lake and sheltering trees. Blue, sunny skies with fluffy white clouds come into view, followed by aerial scenes of lush, beautiful landscapes, as if I'm looking down from a low-flying helicopter. Mountains and trees, rocks and streams, all in full natural color, charged with their own beauty (as in Gerard Manley Hopkins's poetry), roll along through my mind. I begin to relax. I feel myself smiling.

So is this what I feared to look into all those years? Is this what I feared was a nightmare landscape whose ugliness could envelop and destroy me? As more and more wondrous scenes pass across my mind's eye, I begin to laugh, with a joyful feeling of relief and release. All that worry for nothing! I'm OK! I'm filled with beauty, a living treasure house of the world's natural wonder!

I'm laughing so hard that tears start rolling down my cheeks. I'm not just laughing, I'm whooping, guffawing. I grab my stomach and try not to roll off my chair. All around me other people, deep in their own interior worlds, are crying, bawling like babies, sobbing with what sounds like pain and despair, some making awful moans, some even screaming. The idea that in the midst of all this anguish I'm having the time of my life strikes me as even more hilarious. I try to calm down by remembering I have to go get serious and start writing again on Monday morning, I'm only halfway through a novel I must finish to meet a fast-approaching deadline. I can't just get silly and hysterical, I have to be ready to go back to work.

Hi ho, hi ho, it's off to work we go . . .

The Seven Dwarfs are parading across the screen of my mind singing their trademark song! I slide off my chair in whooping laughter, holding my stomach as I fall to the floor, sobbing with wrenching spasms of hilarity. One of the program volunteers comes over and asks if I'm all right, handing me a Kleenex. I realize he thinks I'm crying and carrying on with some horrible past memory. This is even funnier. I manage to sputter "Yes, yes, okay," and nod through my tears and whoops of happy hysteria.

I haven't laughed like this since high school, when I used to go into just such seizures with my friends and fall on the floor as I'm doing now, doubling up into a fetal ball of joyous hilarity. I forgot how deep-down good it feels. When I finally pull myself up off the floor and onto my chair I feel like I've just been washed clean by some marvelous interior bath. I'm purged and refreshed and healed in the most thoroughly restorative, satisfying manner imaginable.

Now I'm actually looking forward to these "processes." There's one more. We're supposed to think back to an emotion that bothered us in childhood. I figure I'll go for broke and try "anger with my parents." I close my eyes to think about this, and suddenly in my inner vision I'm watching what looks like a videotape played on fast forward. There are scenes of me as a child and my parents looking as they did then. I see my mother and father from a child's-eye view — they loom above me, looking down with the youthful faces of their twenties, in the clothes they wore then in old photographs, as we zoom through a vacation we took to the mountains of North Carolina and I feared falling from a cliff outside the hotel where we stayed, imagining they were urging me toward it. I had a jar that I was using to catch lightning bugs, and I was running toward the cliff. Why didn't they pull me back? Here's a scene they told me about: my father is driving our car through a cemetery with my mother holding me on her lap as a baby, and when my father turned a corner, my mother fell out of the car and I hit the ground with her.

This fast-moving series of scenes all has the same theme: my parents are trying to get rid of me. I realize I must have thought that as a child, through these very scenes that are being played back. Now, from an adult point of view, I see these acts and events I interpreted as treachery were really innocent. I feel like something is "lifted" up out of me — the huge weight of that lifelong fear and its accompanying anger. I'm relieved and "lighter," deeply grateful for finally "getting it." This experience, in the capsule compression of twenty minutes, is just what I hoped would happen in Freudian psychoanalysis — a recalling of childhood traumas that led to an understanding of them and with that an unburdening and relief. Instead, I got hallucinatory waking nightmares. And here, with more than a hundred other people in the ballroom of a Boston hotel, I get in two weekends what I was looking for by lying alone on a black leather couch five days a week for six years. (The relative costs: psychoanalysis, $30,000; est training, $325.)

, , ,

The day after the est training is over, I'm flying. I go to Jordan Marsh and buy T-shirts for me and Theresa, giggling as I do — even buying underwear I need is fun. That night I visit a friend in the South End and refuse his offer of a glass of wine, feeling if I have even a sip I'll go through the roof. I'm already high — but no substances took me here. We sit on his stoop to talk after dinner as we often do, and I notice beautiful lights from long windows at the top of a brownstone across the street. When did they put in that penthouse? I ask. My friend laughs. It's always been there, he says. I never noticed. I'm seeing things I never saw before that were there all the time.

Getting up in the morning for me is usually like trying to rise from the protozoan slime, but now I "wake up feeling energy and life," I note in my journal a week after the training. I want my friends to experience this glow of good feeling and aliveness, so I "share the training" with them, urging them to come to an introductory evening (the "guest seminars" I used to scorn when Duncan invited me), but they back away in fear and trembling. They tell me I've been brainwashed!

I look up brainwashing in the dictionary: "intensive, forcible indoctrination aimed at replacing a person's basic convictions with an alternative set of beliefs." But I still have the same beliefs I started with! I'm still a Christian, an active member of my church, a writer, a member of the Beacon Hill Civic Association, a lover of Theresa. I'm all those things I was before, but even more deeply now.

In the course of the two weekends I was never asked to "believe" anything. When presented with new ideas or concepts, I was told, "Don't 'believe' this, but 'try it on,' " or " 'Hold it like a brick' to see what if any new insights or understanding it gives you." I was asked to participate in whatever positive work I was doing in my life before, but with greater commitment. I was urged to get involved in the life of my community, and the world, to contribute to it, to contribute to others, to be responsible for my actions and commitments. I was told that the only real satisfaction is through service to others.

I bring my friend Judith from church to one of the guest evenings, and a visiting trainer who reminds me of a preening peacock comes right up to her out of the whole crowd and starts yelling at her because she hasn't signed up. She is totally turned off, and I don't blame her. I apologize. She says she'll make me a deal: "If I see in a year that you've really changed for the better because of doing this thing, I'll sign up." I smile and thank her. Another friend I urge to sign up gets so angry at my insistence, he takes off his sportcoat in my living room, throws it on the floor, and stamps on it like a mad flamenco dancer!

Most of my friends want me to explain intellectually what this experience is and what you "learn" in it that makes such a difference, but it doesn't work that way. It's not something you "learn," it's not positive thinking or "tips" on how to succeed, or anything like that. It's "experiential" — that is, based on one's experience of it — but that doesn't cut any ice with the skeptics. The closest explanation I can find is in a book I come across entirely by chance called *Pillar of Fire*. The author, Karl Stern, in recounting his conversion to Christianity writes:

"There is a German word, *durchleiden*, for which there is no good English translation. It means to experience and get to know something by suffering. To 'suffer a thing through' with your entire being, rather than to 'figure it out.'"

I'm frustrated by trying to get this across to friends who don't trust anything if there's not a way intellectually to "figure it out." Still, this doesn't dilute my enthusiasm for "the work." The incredible high of the first few days after the training doesn't last, but I'm enjoying much greater energy and wakefulness, which I love, and surprising changes keep occurring. One day out of the blue I decide to get rid of my stash of marijuana. I wrap it up in a couple of brown paper bags, and under cover of darkness, stick it in the garbage can outside my building. When the garbage truck comes the next day, I take a picture of it hauling off my last supply of pot. I know I'm done with it, and I feel relief. It just didn't go with church and health and the whole kind of life I'm trying to live.

Not wanting to lose our edge, our newfound energy and good feeling, Theresa and I enroll in a follow-up seminar called "Be

Here Now" that meets one night a week for ten weeks. Some of our friends smile knowingly and say this is proof we're in a "cult." But we still have our same religion, our previous work and beliefs, and live in the same place; nor are we asked to alter any of those things.

Our complaint about the seminar is that it's often boring, even though we like the leader, a young woman volunteer named Julie. We all grouse that too much time is spent trying to urge us to get other people to enroll in the est training, and/or come to "guest seminars," where friends then often protest at being "pressured" to enroll, thus reinforcing the "brainwashing" and "cult" rumors. I don't like the recruitment methods of the kind that drove away my church friend, yet I know there's tremendous value in "the work," so I keep coming to the seminar.

I arrive early the night of the third session of the seminar, restless and wishing I'd gone to a movie instead. I look up at the blackboard at the front of the room, which says, "The purpose of the Be Here Now seminar is to live life with nothing added." Well, it's pretty simpleminded, I think. But there's nothing else to think about, so I start wondering what it means to live "with nothing added." I feel a little fuzzy from drinking two glasses of wine at a picnic the day before, and now that I don't drink very much, even this relatively minor effect bothers me. It comes to my mind that wine — or any kind of alcohol — is something "added" to life. It's as if a light bulb goes on.

The next thought is that I'm going on a short vacation trip to Maine in a couple weeks, and I decide I won't drink anything on the trip. This is a revolutionary idea for me, and it feels good. I've never in my adult life imagined taking a pleasure trip without drinking; but now the prospect of not drinking on such a trip is bringing pleasure. I have a sense I can feel the machinery of some little-used part of my brain cranking, like some rusty Rube Goldberg apparatus that hasn't been used in ages — and with another sort of grinding of the wheels, the next thought that comes is that I don't have to wait until the vacation not to drink — I can start not drinking now! A smile of relief and revelation comes over me. It feels as if the desire to drink has been "lifted." I was able to cut down and change my drinking pattern before by sheer willpower, and it sometimes felt as if it took all my energy just not to do it. Sometimes I lusted for it, especially in a restaurant where I saw someone order a kir and the light fell on the color and the bubbles in the glass and I could feel my throat parch and my insides yearn. But sitting in that seminar room at a Boston insurance office, I know that's gone now. And it is.

I don't make a vow to never have a drink again, because I know it's not necessary. For a few years after this I will have a glass of champagne or wine at the wedding or birthday of a friend, but the few times I do, I feel nauseous. I tell my doctor I feel as if I'm allergic to it, and he says that's possible, that pregnant women sometimes become allergic to alcohol, knowing it's damaging to them and their child. Now, fifteen years later, I still don't drink or smoke dope and have no desire to, though my twelve-step friends tell me I'm still "an alcoholic," which I thought was someone who couldn't do without alcohol. Whatever.

A year after I do the est training my friend from church who was yelled at by a trainer when I took her to a guest seminar says she wants to enroll in the est training. I'm shocked. Why? I ask.

"I told you if after a year I thought the experience had changed you for the better, I'd do it," she said. "Well, I think it has."

So people can change.

I would like to report that the demons left too.

No such luck.

I realize that even a genuine "breakthrough" like the one I got from the est training isn't going to solve everything, can't be a "cure-all" for life, whose conundrums are more complex than any program, whether of self-improvement or psychiatry — or even religion. This doesn't invalidate any of these ways of dealing with life; it simply means life is too immense and mysterious to be solved by any system.

Chapter 3

HOLLYWOOD
AGAIN?

———◆———

I'M SITTING ON A CUSHION ON THE FLOOR IN THERESA'S apartment in the North End. It's three small rooms in a row, the middle one a kitchen, with a table drawn up to the window that looks across a parking lot to Boston Harbor, with ships and sailboats moving like toys across the blue. Few people in high-priced condos have such a splendid view as I see from this funky old building, nor do they have the homey warmth and cozy feeling Theresa has created in these modest rooms, sanding the wood floors she found under layers of moldy linoleum, painting the walls, hanging her own imaginative photographs that capture the unexpected humor and poignancy of life, restoring thrift store furniture that now seems charming and original, making an attractive home of unpromising, low-ceilinged, box-like spaces. A freelance photographer who works at a picture-framing shop, Theresa more importantly is an artist of life, one who knows how to make people as well as places at ease, enlivening the ordinary with wit and imagination. She is the only person I know who lights candles for breakfast, making toast and oatmeal seem special. Some people see her outer beauty — the long brown hair, lovely face, and lithe body — and assume such physical attributes make her shallow, not knowing the spirit inside is far more beautiful, and solid as gold.

Waiting for Theresa to get dressed, I'm rested and at peace as I sit on the cushion on the floor, and then suddenly in my imagination I find myself in a scene that seems real as Theresa's apartment: I'm lying in a field of yellow-gold straw that grows wild like a weed, and around me are birds and sky, a vast and deep beauty. I sense I was here in this field as a child but was closed off from feeling the beauty and wonder of it fully, and now I do, in the fullness of my life now and being with Theresa. Experiences like this don't seem "mystic" to me, but a kind of heightened awareness that sometimes comes, always unexpectedly, pleasantly, never consciously intended or thought out beforehand, just given, like an insight that is "seen" rather than conveyed through the intellect. Back on the cushion on the floor again, I grab my notebook and scrawl a word to remind me of what I'm feeling:

Abundance.

Before we did the est training, Theresa and I seemed to be pulling and nagging at one another and falling into sulky silences. Now, a few months later, it feels like we both have blossomed and shed our prickles and are able to open and enjoy — and we do. I think of Yeats's line "Life overflows without ambitious pains" and Richard Wilbur's poem expressing the passionate joy to be found in everyday life, giving me goose bumps whenever I read it: "Love Calls Us to the Things of This World."

It's a Boston summer Saturday and white sails trim the blue of the Charles River and "reggae boats" and "jazz boats" go for sunset cruises in the harbor with music and drinks and food. Carts loaded green with lush leafy vegetables assemble in Copley Square for the farmer's market, with fresh corn from the countryside to go with lobsters you buy in the North End and plunge in a pot to boil at home. Sometimes we make a picnic and spread a blanket on the grass by the pond in the Public Garden, eating deviled eggs as the Swan Boats pass, but today we pack sandwiches and thermoses of iced tea to take on the train that goes to Singing Beach in Manchester, where the white sand squeaks ("sings") as you walk, and after swimming and sunning we lean against one another on the rocking train home as a sudden rain splatters the windows and the lights of the passing towns blur gold through the wet glass.

Back at North Station we run through the rain to Theresa's apartment, yowling and laughing as we charge through the old, narrow streets, getting soaked, wet clothes clinging fresh to our skin as we pass Paul Revere's house and the Old North Church. We make a dash up the slanty stairs of Theresa's building and into the small three-chambered space, the big bed in the last room, white blinds shutting out the street. We make love and take a shower and slather after-bath lotion onto each other. She drapes a towel around my neck and gently cleans my ears with cotton swabs. All this is bliss; then sleep, buried deep in bright dreams, rising next morning to rainy-clean air and hot coffee, all of it seeming some extra blessing of life, some priceless reward. Grace. The next morning we swelter through services at King's Chapel, giving thanks for the blessings of being here, with each other. My prayers are of gratitude.

Fullness comes not just in love but in work. I finish the novel I've worked on the last two years, a novel that like all the rest I've written is a kind of purging, a piece of the past transformed into story, essence of experience reimagined, molded into forms that life resisted, peopled with characters larger and more distinct in motive — as well as different in dress, habit, and hair style — than those one knows.

I think of the manuscript I give to my editor as "my Hollywood novel." *Selling Out* is the tale of an innocent writer from the East (in Hollywood terms, New England seems as exotic and remote as Damascus) who goes to La La Land to write a TV series and succumbs to all the standard temptations of glitter-glut, barely escaping with his life and wife. I feel relieved and clean when I finish the book, lighter not only from the load of responsibility lifted (contract fulfilled, payment on the way), but also from the sense of having wrapped up the Hollywood part of my life and stashed it, filed it, put it on the shelf. Transforming my experience there, I believe, has lifted my own private "Hollywood" curse — just as writing my first novel, *Going All the Way,* freed me from home, and *Starting Over* freed me from the angst of my first divorce and its chaotic aftermath.

So now that I've purged it, I'm free to go back to Hollywood, right?

But why would I want to?

I've sworn off the stuff as I once did bourbon, publicly proclaiming I'm cured of Hollywood. I've not been tempted to return, even by the one friendly caller from the Coast who drops in to see me in Boston a year or so after my return and recovery. This pleasant producer of TV movies and series whom I briefly worked with in my California incarnation seems incongruous on Beacon Hill — as does his proposal. He and his partner have wrapped up rights to a TV hit of the fifties that they propose to dust off and polish up with a zingy new story line for the eighties. They've acquired none other than "Mr. Ed" (the talking horse). Their idea is to give the nag a man for a partner who for some reason yet to be determined is on the run, just like "The Fugitive" of television series fame, man and steed traveling from town to town and city to city, with Mr. Ed providing the runaway human not only with transportation and companionship but also with advice. When asked if I'd be interested in writing a pilot for this potential new hit, I point out that I have no experience as a comedy writer and so am hardly qualified to land such a plum.

"Oh, but it's not a comedy," my producer friend hastens to explain. "It's going to be a weekly drama."

The talking horse, then, would not be mouthing comic lines, but offering sage (if not sagebrush) advice to his fugitive cohort.

This is an easy one to turn down.

I do take on a literary TV assignment — a dramatization of Mark Twain's *The Innocents Abroad* for PBS — with the understanding I don't have to go to L.A. for any reason, including meetings. So what could ever make me think of going back again?

Money.

Not that any L.A. moguls are dangling big deals — or any deals at all — in front of me. The idea comes from one of my closest writer friends, Sara Davidson, whom I got to know after I enthusiastically reviewed her book *Loose Change: Three Women of the Sixties*. She's one of the few who writes quality books and magazine pieces while living in Los Angeles and working successfully as a TV writer-producer. I tell her I've finished my novel, but I don't have any ideas for another book and I need some cash coming in.

Sara suggests we collaborate on a movie script. Both of us have earned writing and producing credits in television (Sarah created the series *Pat and Mike*) but neither of us has hit the feature-film jackpot. While I'd never have considered collaborating on a book, the idea of working together on a screenplay seems not only feasible but maybe even . . . fun! A screenplay is more like doing a puzzle than sculpting a work of art, and it's always nice to have help when you're stuck on a puzzle. And solving this kind of puzzle may get you big bucks. Hey — why not? Sara and I agree to collaborate, fifty-fifty. We'll split the millions! Our future is set.

Now all we need's the idea.

We brainstorm back and forth on the phone, make lists of topics and themes and plots we might spark to, kick around characters, ideas, situations, but neither of us comes up with anything we both feel we could work up enough interest in to invest the necessary time and energy. Then one day I'm walking down the street when I get an idea that excites me.

I've been trying to think of a love story, and imagine a "starving artist" painting away in his garret, wishing for love. So what else is new? Nothing more comes. Until this particular afternoon while ambling along Charles Street, the main drag of Beacon Hill, I "see" in my mind's eye the artist painting the image of the beautiful girl he wishes would appear in his life — and that night he goes out and meets her — a girl who looks just like the one he painted. To leap ahead, he realizes he can paint what he wishes for and he will get it! (Maybe the notion comes from those stories of the first cave paintings being made for the purpose of "getting" the animal the hunters wished to kill.) I'm excited by the possibilities of such a plot — a man has the power to get what he wants by painting it!

Sara is also turned on by the idea and we eagerly go to work on it over the phone. How does he get this power? Is it only when he uses a particular brush (the "magic brush" idea)? What if someone steals the brush (takes his power)? Is it only when he uses it for a good purpose that he can get what he wants by painting it? Can he "paint out" (kill, destroy) something or someone he doesn't like, someone who threatens him or his beloved? Can he create evil as well as good through his painting?

We feel we have a saleable idea somewhere in all this, something that would make a good movie and be fun to work on. As we get the plot and characters fleshed out, Sara says we'll soon be ready to pitch our idea to a studio or production company. She'll have her agent set up meetings, but also wants to suggest people she and I know in the business. One of the producers I'd met in my time out there seems an especially good idea to Sara, who's heard good reports about this man and his partner.

"So when can you come out?" she asks me.

"Are you kidding?"

She tells me how cheap it is to get a round-trip ticket from coast to coast.

, , ,

I decide to return to Hollywood — not to live there again, of course, but to make a deal for a script that will bring in some cash and then come home and write it. Now I'm going out there on my own terms. I'll use my hard-won knowledge and experience to make sure I don't get bushwhacked. As long as I'm going, I might as well set up more than one meeting — not just the project with Sara — and make sure I meet only with people I know and like. My old friend Don Devlin is a writer/producer who's always liked my much-shopped novel *Going All the Way,* and he offers to co-write a script of it with me for a feature film. He says if I'm coming out, he'll try to interest the actor/producer Tony Bill, who has a deal with Tri-Star, and maybe we can set up a meeting there. I call Martin Manulis, the classy executive producer I so enjoyed working with on the television series I created, *James at 15,* who'll be happy to see me and hear any ideas I have for TV. April Smith, whom I'd brought from Boston to L.A. to work on "James," is now a successful writer-producer and will set up meetings for me with her old boss on *Lou Grant,* the highly respected producer Gene Reynolds, who is known for his quality work in television. For good measure, April also arranges a lunch with a hot new young woman executive at ABC (hopefully, she'll still be hot by the time I arrive). Hey, I'm set. And I don't even need an agent to arrange things for me. If anyone wants to offer me a deal, they can do it through my cool New York entertainment lawyer, the guy who writes into my contracts that "services may be performed in Boston." This time I'm doing it my way, baby.

, , ,

I pray before going out there. I'm not praying for guidance about whether or not I should go — I've already made my mind up about it — I'm only asking for help in making the trip a smashing success. There are times I get apprehensive about it, but I reassure myself I'm a different person now — not the naive, hard-drinking cream puff who sauntered into the jaws of the lion the last time I came. (I picture the Hollywood beast like that MGM lion, snarling with ease as if he's just swallowed a writer as an hors d'oeuvre.) I'm savvy now and sober, centered in faith and integrated by est, ready to stare that MGM lion right in the jaw. Daniel goes into the lion's den, unafraid!

My return to the scene of the crime begins auspiciously. I walk on the stretch of beach I love between the piers of Venice and Santa Monica with April, one of my dearest friends, whom I've known since the days when she was city editor of the *B.U. News* at Boston University and at the same time (*quel precocious!*) managing editor of the *Cambridge Phoenix* (later the *Boston Phoenix*), the first of the influential alternative weeklies.

Walking in the breeze of the beach that first day of my return to L.A., I feel as together as I ever have in my life. I'm wearing a sharp red-and-white checked sport shirt and freshly pressed khaki pants whose waist measurement is four inches smaller than that of the ones I wore when I fled from Hollywood four years before. My body is clean of drugs or booze, my eyes and mind are clear, and I know no fear. April is impressed.

That night I have dinner with Martin Manulis at his gracious home in Bel-Air, just the two of us, served by his cook. I decline his offer of a fine red wine to go with our beef bourguignon, and opt for the Perrier. Martin expresses his amazement at my transformation. I beam. I tell him of my return to church, my new way of life — then pitch my idea for a TV series based on a minister. He warms to the idea. My hypothetical TV minister's a Protestant, denomination vague, and Martin suggests a priest and a rabbi who come once a week for a poker game with him. Why not? They can all share their troubles trying to keep their constituents happy. I speak of the daily problems that assault my real-life minister, and how we'll have a regular warehouse of such material to feature on each episode. Martin is enthusiastic, and wants to set up a meeting with his agent. We're getting serious, here. I leave with a sense of accomplishment, as well as a tiny touch of apprehension.

What if Martin's agent makes a deal for me to write a pilot of this minister story? Then if it's any good, the network will commission a series, and they'll want me to come out and work on it. But I won't do that again. Martin knows that, of course. He knows how disastrous that last period was for me out here and how I swore off Hollywood. He knows I wouldn't come back and live here. Doesn't he? Did I say that? Well, if I didn't say it in so many words, I surely implied it. It's obvious, isn't it? Surely it's obvious to a man as sophisticated and intelligent as Martin. Surely. What am I worried about?

The next day Don Devlin takes me to lunch with Tony Bill, a very hip guy. He's not only an actor, director, and producer, he owns his own hip restaurant in Venice, 72 Market Street, where I've met people for lunch and dinner. A good place to see people and be seen. But we can't have lunch there today because Tony is directing something at one of the studios in the Valley, so we need to eat at a restaurant in the Valley. Tony is actor-handsome, and cool, circumspect. Polite. He says he'll set up the meeting later this week at Tri-Star to pitch *Going All the Way*. This is my first novel and still the most personal, the one in which I poured out my deepest emotions, the one I'd give anything to finally bring to the screen. I tell Tony I don't really like to go to pitch meetings, I'm not very good at it, but since I'm in town I'll be glad to go if he wants me to be there. After all, I'm the author of the novel as well as the proposed coauthor of the script, along with Don. We shake hands and Tony says he'll get back to me.

That night I have dinner with my friend Eve Babitz, the talented L.A.-born artist turned writer who is known for her plain-speaking of the truth, a practice that is often shocking.

"What are you doing here?" she asks me. "I thought you didn't like it here. I thought this place almost did you in."

"I'm only here for a week," I say. "Just to make a deal and then go back to Boston and write."

"Ha. You think you can get off that easy? You think they'll let you do that?"

"They can't make me do anything I don't want to do."

Eve laughs.

"You're living in a fool's paradise," she says.

That's just Eve. That's just the way she talks to people. We laugh and have a great time.

That night I can't get to sleep. I wonder if I should call up Martin and tell him I only want to do the pilot script of that minister series, nothing more. Make it clear I'm not coming out here to live again. But that's silly. He must know that. I'd sound neurotic, making a call like that — not the together guy I'm presenting myself to be now. Who I really *am* now, dammit. And why am I feeling guilty all of a sudden? If I get a series on the air about a minister, I'd be spreading the word, not as a proselytizer but just raising people's consciousness, that there are ministers and churches and people who go to them trying to live a good life. But what about that other idea, the one I'm supposed to pitch with Sara about the artist who can make his wish come true by painting it and ends up destroying his enemy and then himself? What kind of message is that? Black magic? Voodoo? Where did it come from, anyway? What put such an idea in my head? God? What for? Why? Where else would I get such an idea? If not from God — who else? Who? Don't be ridiculous. Go to sleep. I try. Somewhere around first light, I do.

I go to the Valley to meet Gene Reynolds for lunch. He is as I imagined he'd be — a straight, clear, no-frills, no-nonsense, low-key kind of guy with no pretensions, no hype, nothing to sell, trying to do good work. I tell him how I admire his work, and he tells me of his respect for *James at 15*. I think how great it would be to work with him. I tell him I don't want to ever come live out here again, but I do have an idea for a pilot that I think would make a good series. He says there are plenty of writers who do pilots and don't continue on with the series. He understands the situation and he understands me, I can tell. Not only that, but he has such a great track record of success with quality series television like *M.A.S.H.* that he'd probably have the best chance of anyone in Hollywood to get a show like the one about the minister on the air and not only make it a success but maintain the high standards he's known for. In terms of respect and integrity, Gene Reynolds is like the Adlai Stevenson of television. I explain to him that I've told Martin Manulis about this idea I have for a series pilot, but we haven't done more than talk about it, we haven't committed to anything yet. I ask Gene if he'd be interested in hearing about it.

"You've pitched it to Marty already, haven't you?"

I look down into my iced tea.

"Yes," I say.

"I don't think you'd better tell me about it, then."

He says it casually, smoothly, not frowning or making a face of any kind, not even a slight squint, but I know I've made a gaffe, I've shown I'd betray my friend and colleague whom I worked with if I could make a deal with this man who might have a better chance of getting it on the air. I start off presenting myself as a fellow purist, and by the time we kill the quiche, I've tried to slither past my word as snakily as any of the Hollywood con men I despise — with one of the few people acknowledged in the business as an honorable man. I feel sick. I thank him for lunch, and for his time. Which I just wasted.

That night I have dinner with Don Devlin and he tells me the good news — Tony Bill has set up a meeting at Tri-Star for Friday afternoon. I try to act pleased. Hell, I should be pleased. Just because I blew it with Gene Reynolds — maybe it's a sign I shouldn't mess with television again, maybe television just sets off bad stuff in me, and I should stick to doing feature films. Don is expansive, telling me about Tony Bill, who has the power to set up a meeting at Tri-Star just like that. Tony is quite a guy — very particular about things, Don says. He's especially particular about how people dress. It doesn't have to be formal, it has to be . . . right. Tony might just wear a sweater to some-place dressy but it would be the precisely right sweater, and if he tied it around his neck it would be tied in just the right way. Funny guy. Amazing guy, really. Particular guy. Don shakes his head and laughs. He mentions, by the way, that Tony says I don't have to come to the meeting at Tri-Star. I say it's no trou-ble, I'm here in town anyway, I'm the author of the book, so . . . Don says Tony thinks it best if just he and Don do the pitch.

"Oh," I say. "Okay."

I shrug, acting like I don't give a damn. I try to remember what I was wearing when I had lunch with Tony. An old sport jacket and a summer, short-sleeved shirt. Wrong. I know I said I wasn't anxious to go to the meeting, how much I hate those meetings, but now that Tony Bill doesn't want me to go, I'm pissed. Him and his fucking clothes. Fucking Hollywood.

Welcome back.

"Welcome back, welcome back, welcome back . . ."

The theme song from the old series *Welcome Back, Kotter* rings through my head, taunting.

What have I done? What am I doing?

I just finished this novel about *Selling Out* in Hollywood, and now I'm trying to do it! I pitch my idea for a series about a min-ister (to bring issues of integrity and faith to the masses!) to my friend and colleague Martin, and then try to sleaze around him to give it to Gene Reynolds because he might have a better shot at getting it on the air! Hey, this could be another scene in the novel I just finished (or is it finished?), the one in which I've sup-posedly purged myself of Hollywood and all its grievous ways. And all I had to do was get on a plane and land here to be right back in it, with the whole thing pushing my pulse up again — I can feel my heart pounding.

Back at the Marmont, I drink a Diet Coke. I try to be quiet and pray, but I'm too jangled. I try to read Scripture, but I can't concentrate. I can't sleep. I pace, turn on TV, lie down, and pace again. Tomorrow I'm supposed to go to the meeting with Sara to pitch our story about the painter who can get what he wants just by painting it. What crap! What am I doing, trying to purvey the kind of junk I ridicule and put other people down for foisting on the public. I can't. I can't do it. I have to call Sara and tell her. I reach for the phone and realize it's four in the morning. I can't call her in the middle of the night. I have to wait till at least seven. Maybe I can sleep till then. Maybe. If only . . .

Light creeps into the room and I take a shower, then order a pot of coffee. I call Sara and tell her I can't do it. She tries to make me see reason. Just come to this one meeting with the producers you know and like. I can't, I say. (I'm afraid they'll say yes, here's some money, now go write this ridiculous story, and I'll have to do it — or feel I have to do it, or try to do it, or some damn thing, and I'll end up a basket case.) I say I'm sorry. I tell her I haven't slept all night. I ask forgiveness. She sighs. I've put her in a terrible position. She has to go to this meeting and pitch a story without her alleged partner, the person who made the contact for the meeting, who now seems to be having a nervous breakdown in his hotel room. Of course she can tell them anything she likes, or cancel the meeting, I don't care as long as I don't have to do it. Okay. She says okay but it's not okay.

Now I call April to tell her I don't want to come to lunch with the hot new young woman executive from ABC. April say it's too late to cancel. She wants to know what's wrong. I pour out all the angst, the whirlwind of confusion I'm causing. She says I don't have to pitch anything, just come and meet this young woman, she's perfectly nice, we don't even have to talk about television. Okay, I say.

I go to Century City to meet them for lunch. It's ABC Land. Sterile white towers. A sort of Dominican Republic of entertainment. I feel half sick. The young woman executive is very young and very perky. She says she loved my series *James at 15*. I thank her. She says she understands I'm out here to line up some projects, and I say "Not exactly, really." I'm suddenly afraid that if I throw out any idea she'll jump at it, want to buy it, want to offer me some megabuck deal that will lure me out here to live again — and die. I've now suddenly reversed the terror of the writer fearing no one will buy his ideas — now I'm afraid they will!

So, the executive asks, what do you hope to accomplish on this trip?

I put down my fork, unable to continue the pretense of eating. My hand is shaking, just like in the bad old drinking days.

"I hope to get back home in one piece," I say.

April stares into her Caesar salad. The hot young executive looks at her watch. It will soon be over.

But I've still got one day to go. I have to call Martin to tell him I don't feel ready yet to meet with his agent about setting up meetings for our pilot idea. Seeing the condition I'm in, April suggests I just come out to her house in Santa Monica and sit in her hot tub, and I eagerly accept. The sun is hot and so is the tub. I feel like I'm sitting in hell. And I chose it. I get out and dry off and go to the living room with a Diet Coke, trying to read. No use.

April and her husband, Doug, are going to a business dinner tonight and she has to get supper for her son and get dressed and pick up the babysitter, so she can't give me a ride clear back into Hollywood but calls me a cab. The driver is a brawny young guy with a hillbilly accent who's never heard of the Chateau Marmont, but I give him the address and he says he can get me there and that's all I care about. It's late afternoon and L.A. is choking in smog, the air thick and the sky a hot brown. I'm doing that day's crossword puzzle from the *New York Times*, a panic-suppression activity that keeps my mind absorbed, and I haven't looked to see where we are. When I feel a sudden lurch, I look up to see we're on some freeway I don't know about, certainly not one that takes you to Hollywood. I ask the driver what's going on, and he admits he's never driven to Hollywood before. I tell him to get off this freeway — I don't know where the hell it's going. I also tell him to slow down — we're careening around other cars at breakneck (my neck, I fear) speed. He tells me there's something wrong with his brakes. He's pumping the brakes and they aren't working. My God — this is it. This is what's happening because I came back. I look out the window at anonymous skyscrapers and palm trees against a yellowish haze of smog, and I think (not a prayer but a mental screech), Oh God, oh Jesus, please get me out of this one, if I get out of here alive I promise I'll never come back to Hollywood, really, I'm not kidding this time, shit shit shit! I remember the retreat and the woman wanting a "sign" to know if she should marry the man who was courting her, and I'm thinking if I ever wanted a sign from God to tell me whether I should go back to Hollywood again, this is it! I scream at the driver to get off the freeway, get off at any exit, just let me out, I'll pay him if he just gets the car to stop and let me out! We're racing past other cars like we're on the lam, it feels like a carnival ride that's out of control, and as I scream and point at an exit, he veers off, letting up on the gas and finally slowing to a halt at a gas station, and I pay him some monstrous tab — over fifty bucks — and go in and call Don Devlin and say, "Listen, can you come and get me, just come and pick me up? I don't know where I am but I'll ask —"

Don comes to the rescue, and I pour out the story of the harrowing wild ride on the freeways and how I've learned my lesson at last, I don't need any more of a "sign" than that to tell me I should stay away from Hollywood. I've learned my lesson; I'm not coming back.

Don laughs.

"Don't be so sure," he says. "Tony and I had our meeting at Tri-Star and it really went well. I have a feeling they're going to make a deal for us to write the script. We should hear on Monday."

On the plane back to Boston I'm praying that Tri-Star doesn't offer us a deal.

I feel like kissing the ground when I get back home. I swear I'll never leave it again, at least not for Hollywood. I walk up and down Charles Street as if to get grounded. I go to my bench in the Public Garden and pray. I pray the Twenty-third Psalm as I always do when I come here, and then I give thanks for getting back, for being back, alive and in one piece. I shiver as I think of my harrowing cab ride through the smog. I look at the ducks on the pond, gliding so surely and peacefully, making life seem easy and natural. I try to tune in to their wave length. The weeping willow that cascades down by my bench seems sheltering, protective. I think of a maiden whose long hair I can hide beneath. This spot is a haven. Add another "e" and it's heaven. Maybe that's what heaven is — a haven, a place of shelter from the earthly storm.

The next day the call comes from L.A. It's Don.

"Good news," he says. "They want to make the deal."

Damn.

Don says he made the pitch as I asked him to, saying that he and I would collaborate on the script. They're offering a modest first-draft screenplay payment, which Don and I would divide equally. Modest as it is by Hollywood standards — in fact, barely peanuts — it's a windfall in my world. The work on a first-draft screenplay wouldn't take more than three or four months, while a book advance that would pay as much could mean a couple of years of work. This could solve my immediate financial problems and give me a little breathing room.

But would I still be breathing at the end? Haven't I just vowed not to go back to Hollywood? Well, does that mean literally or figuratively?

I ask Don if we can write the script collaborating by phone. No. You need to be in the same room, he says, be able to kick ideas around, pace back and forth and spark one another's thoughts in the way it only happens when both people are present. I tell him Anne Sexton and Maxine Kumin used to have a phone line that only went to each other's study, and they worked on their poems together. Each of them won the Pulitzer Prize, so the method must have worked.

"That's poetry," Don says.

"Okay, then. Why don't you come to Boston and work here?"

He says he'll come to Boston if I'll come to L.A. We can take turns. A few weeks at each place, alternating until we're done. I say I have to think about it. Don says okay, but don't take too long — we have to give Tri-Star an answer.

When I hang up the phone my heart is pounding.

Isn't that enough of a "sign"? Or maybe it's just a sign that I'm chicken. Scared. Or self-defeating. Turning down money I need. So what do I want for a sign? What more do I want? Here's what I want: I want the voice of God to roar down like thunder, saying "Don't go to Hollywood!" or "Don't be a fool, take the money and run!"

How else am I going to make that kind of money? Shit. I have to calm down. I don't trust myself to make a decision. I try to pray but I can't sit still and concentrate. I decide to do something healthy. I make myself a dinner of steamed vegetables. After I eat, I go sit on my bed and take my pulse. It's 100.

I go to see good old Joe Brenner again, who helped me in my est crisis, and after I describe the situation, he tells me he thinks if I go to Hollywood I won't be "in significant jeopardy." I ask him what that means — "significant jeopardy." He puts it another way. He tells me if I go to Hollywood this time I'll be "bruised but not scarred."

Bruised but not scarred?

Everyone is beginning to sound like the Delphic oracle, their messages shrouded in mystery.

I go to a Bible study class at King's Chapel. Judith is leading it tonight, and she has us do an exercise in which we draw a line representing our life and showing the times that God has "broken through." I feel like that's what's happening in my life right now — God is breaking through. Or trying to break through. But I'm still not sure what his message is!

I make an appointment to see Sister Madeline. She advises me to pray about each alternative and see what comes to my mind. I'm in a state of high anxiety, but I go home and try to quiet myself and breathe deeply and pray. A picture comes to my mind. I see a candle — a single candle. I take it to mean that I should only work as a writer by myself and not collaborate with someone else.

That's clear — isn't it?

Or is it?

How do I know I'm making the correct interpretation of seeing a single candle?

I ask other people's opinion.

I have lunch with a woman who lives in my neighborhood and goes to Harvard Divinity School. She interprets my "sign" of the single candle in a different way. She sees the candle as an invitation to "go outward," and "putting soul at risk" in order to grow. "Don't hide," she says. "Christians are to go forth."

I have coffee with a writer friend who thinks I'm crazy to do anything involving Hollywood.

"It sounds like you're setting up the sequel to the novel you just wrote," he says.

Another writer friend says I'm crazy not to take the deal.

Theresa says I should stop asking people.

Of course I know she's right. I finally get up my nerve to call Don Devlin. I tell him I can't do it. He has my blessing to write the script himself.

"You're sure this is what you want?" he asks. "Because you won't be able to change your mind again."

"I'm sure," I say.

"Okay," says Don.

I hang up the phone and burst into tears. I bawl like a baby.

I'm plunged into despair at the thought of the money I gave up, and I tell Sister Madeline I might not be able to make that kind of "movie money" again. It could have eased my ongoing money problems, and I turned it down. What if no other deal comes along? What if I can't make a living anymore?

Sister Madeline asks how old I am.

"Fifty-two."

She points out that for all these years I've managed to make a living, so why don't I just relax and assume I'll continue to be able to do it? I tell her she doesn't understand. I'm upset. Now she is, too. When I get up to leave, I get the feeling she isn't looking forward to my return. She says she's "willing to hang in there" and makes a future appointment, but I know she's not enthusiastic about the prospect. I feel it even more clearly when, for the first time in our meetings, she doesn't walk down the stairs with me.

I write her that I understand her not wanting to hear about my discomfort, or pain, or whatever it might be called, which does not seem to have altered. I tell her I will continue to pray and to do all I know to do to be in touch with God. I thank her for her time and enclose a contribution for the center that I'm sorry is not more adequate. I say, "I am sorry to have put my depression on you, which I see now was not appropriate. I hope to see you in a happier time."

But something between us is broken. I never go back, nor do I ever hear from Sister Madeline again.

One of the hard lessons I learn from this repetitive "Hollywood" experience is that no matter what we learn from experience and truly *know* intellectually, we still may not be able to act on it. Gaining wisdom is one thing; acting on it is another. The fact that we "know" something may even make us think we are therefore safe from repeating it and lure us into letting down our guard. Confronting a situation we've muffed before should make us all the more alert when another one like it arises.

I realize these anguished decisions I later regret are not always so earthshaking after all, though they seem of life and death import at the time. Perhaps the true demonic element in it all is the torture of my heart and soul afterward. That's where the demons really do their job, waking me in the night in a sweat of regret, jabbing me with thoughts like barbs of what-might-have-been, lines I said that if only they could be retracted would rectify everything, gnawing fantasies of how wonderfully things would have worked out if I'd made the *other* decision. This unceasing inner teasing and diatribe is mentally and emotionally exhausting, and I think how relieving it would be just to blank it out with drugs or drink. For the first time since I stopped drinking, I desperately want to numb myself in some way, any way. It isn't alcohol or marijuana I long for but peace, surcease from the torture. This is before the advent of Prozac and its derivatives, and the one time I'd tried antidepressants — in the wake of my father's death and the end of the seven-year relationship I'd believed would last all my life — the medications available only depressed me more. But I am not going to turn back the clock, roll back my hard-won sobriety by drowning in a bottle of rum. I pray and clutch my fingers into tight fists, bite my lip, but don't give in to the siren song of instant blanking out by guzzling from a bottle or inhaling a weed. But I have to do something, I can't bear my own consciousness.

I pray, and read the Psalms and the Gospels. I pray for some nondestructive way to stop the hammering of regret, to turn down the noise of the squawking demons that break through any attempt at nonverbal meditation. I pray and I get an answer. It doesn't come in a booming voice from the heavens or a burning bush or prophetic dream. It just occurs to me one gray autumn afternoon while I'm standing on the platform of the Charles Street MBTA stop waiting for the Red Line subway to come. For some reason I start thinking of myself like a character in a novel: "Dan is standing on the MBTA platform waiting for the subway." Something clicks, and I continue, not quite knowing why: "The roar of the train comes and it pulls up to the station. Dan and several other people get in one of the cars and the doors shut behind them." I feel relief, a kind of lifting of the pain. I'm no longer "inside" myself but simply observing myself, which puts me outside the cage of my own mind and feelings. I am watching those thoughts and feelings now, "objectively," like a scientist or a novelist who gets to follow his character and observe his inner consciousness as well as his outer appearance. I smile. I use this technique, off and on — whenever the demons get too loud — for the next few months, until the squawking over this particular crisis subsides. I make it through, without booze or drugs or pills. I am grateful, and reassured, that some-how, some way, my prayer was answered, not in some big life reversal or anything at all dramatic, but a simple thought, given to me, a gift that makes all the difference.

Chapter 4

SIX DAYS OF HELL

———————◆———————

BY THE SPRING OF '85 I'M FULLY RECOVERED FROM MY nightmarish weeklong return to Hollywood the previous fall, and am happily enjoying life in the Boston slow lane with Theresa and my friends, neighbors, and fellow parishioners at King's Chapel. I am, if anything, even more active in the life of the church. I'm honored to be appointed a member at large on the parish council, one of the lay governing bodies of King's Chapel, and even though I no longer see Sister Madeline in spiritual direction, I continue the disciplines she helped me develop. I regularly meditate on the Gospels, as well as on a powerful free-verse poem by Thomas Merton called "He Is Risen." It's about Jesus being present in one's life, and I'm especially struck by the idea so powerfully conveyed in the verse that Jesus is with you; he is walking ahead of you on your path, in your life: "He is going before you to Galilee."

I think of Jesus appearing to the disciples on the road to Emmaus after the crucifixion, not in a blare of heavenly trumpets or a cone of divine light, but just as a fellow traveler on the way. I often meditate on John 21, in which Jesus appears to the disciples on the shore of Galilee after they have spent the night fishing in vain. Again he does not arrive in some rococo scene, surrounded by angels, but simply as a man on the shore who tells them to cast their net on the other side. And it comes up filled with fish. He makes a fire of coals and tells them to bring the fish, inviting them to "Come and dine."

I think of that as Jesus' invitation to the banquet of life, inviting us to partake, to taste and smell and see and hear and touch the wonders that are here, now, available to each of us if we only wake up, become aware, and see, as Jesus says in the apocryphal Gospel of Thomas, that "the father's kingdom is spread out upon the earth, and people do not see it." This Jesus I see is not a parsimonious puritan who preaches sin and damnation, but a life-giver, a life enricher, a guide to fullness, to savoring the simple, everyday glories, and using ourselves in service to the world, to contribute to it with our greatest capacity.

When my novel *Selling Out* is published, Theresa helps me celebrate and spread the word about the book. Her photograph of me for the book jacket magically makes me look better than I do when I look in the mirror, and she designs and produces pins with the title of the novel and a drawing of a palm tree that we pass out to friends and booksellers. She takes me to Filene's Basement to pick out a pinstriped suit that Nathan Detroit might have sported in his prime, but hey, we're living large! Two of my best friends in life, Jane Wylie Genth and Ted "the Horse" Steeg, cohost a lovely New York party at The Dairy in Central Park, with champagne and strawberries and a string trio playing Bach on a golden spring afternoon.

I take this occasion to publicly thank my friends who've stuck by me during the dark days, whose essence I've poured out in the novel *Selling Out* about my Hollywood daze and during the aftermath when I returned to Boston feeling hollow and broken.

These are friends whom I learned I can count on, whose friend-ship is not based on my literary, financial, or any other kind of status in the world. One of the great life lessons of the Holly-wood collapse the novel describes is that I learn for the first time a truth that's been recounted through the ages but had never hit me in the gut before — there really are people you think are friends who fade away when things go bad. And you value and honor all the more the ones who treat you the same no matter what your circumstances. These I dub at the party as "Friends Regardless of Ratings," and give them plaques with that inscription, as if I'm handing out Oscars or Emmys. My gener-ous Hoosier landsman, Kurt Vonnegut, draws the biggest laugh when I call his name and he shouts a term I haven't heard since the fifties (the last era when ocean liners were considered trans-portation as well as cruise hotels).

"Gangway!" he says, and pushes through the crowd to claim his award.

In all this Theresa and I become closer. In the lingo of "the work" of Werner Erhard and the est training, she "supports" me in the book's publication, designing and producing pins we give out. She listens sympathetically to all my complaints, disap-pointments, fears, and concerns, bringing her joy and humor and sense of fun to the celebrations, providing the love to share that makes accomplishment meaningful. With the fullness of my work at church, a new novel coming out, and Theresa, this is one of the best seasons of my life. So this is the next thought that enters my head:

If things are good, why can't they be better?

Theresa shares the same sentiment. She's had a few shows of her photographs at local venues, while she keeps up her regular job framing pictures. Both of us are feeling "empowered" by the est training we did a year ago, and the follow-up seminars we've taken together that are given by the same company, Werner Erhard and Associates. We believe that — as they phrase it in "the work" — we "have a say in the matter." That is, instead of sitting around waiting and hoping for life to improve, we can actually do something about it.

The idea that even if things are good they can be even better is of course not an invention of est or the self-help movement. It goes back at least as far as the Garden of Eden — with memorable consequences. (Could that story be a Divine hint to leave well enough alone?) It is also an article of American psychiatric faith, as expressed by one of the Drs. Menninger of Menninger Clinic fame, who said in an interview with *Time* magazine I read back in the fifties that people could not only get well but "weller than well." There is of course a homespun article of faith that offers different advice:

"If it ain't broke, don't fix it."

In the heady spring of '85 such a thought strikes me as "dis-empowering."

It is in this spirit that Theresa and I sign up to do the "Six Day Advanced Course" offered by Werner Erhard and Associates. This is the one I first heard about during the est training, where they tell you how "graduates" of that work can go on to an out-door, est-ian version of Outward Bound. It involves hanging by ropes from sides of mountains and all sorts of other feats of physical and psychological courage (or foolhardiness, depending on your point of view).

In our mood of high empowerment now, both Theresa and I are anxious to prove our mettle. Bring on Mount Everest. Bring on the "Six Day." We can hardly wait for August, when our time of testing finally arrives. We're giddy with anticipation, caught up in the excitement of challenge, and the opening of new possibilities — for growth, mastery, enlightenment; for the ever elusive, ever beckoning . . . more.

We get a ride with fellow participants from Boston to the site of the East Coast Six Day program in upstate New York (there is also one for the West Coast in California). We stay at a motel near the campsite the night before the program begins, and gorge ourselves on "the last meal," loading up on rich food and gooey desserts that we hear won't be part of our healthy, no-nonsense diet for the next week. Theresa is delighted to find that a local movie is showing "Pee-Wee's Big Adventure," which seems exactly right for our last chance at frivolity. We gorge on popcorn and laughs.

The next morning we check our frivolity at the Six Day registration desk, along with our wallets, cash, car keys, liquor and/or drugs of any kind, including prescriptions, unless medically authorized as necessary by a physician. I feel a tremor as I hand over my wallet. Now I have no identification. Do I still have an identity? Will I have it six days from now? If it's taken away, will it be returned, along with my credit cards, driver's license, and voter registration?

We go to another room to be photographed. First it's a still picture, which seems like a mug shot. All that's needed is someone holding a number under my face. Next we are videoed as we tell who we are — our name, what we do, where we live, whom we live with. I think of those tapes of hostages shown on television to prove they are alive and being treated well by their captors. We're assigned rooms, and Theresa and I ask to stay together. I'm vastly relieved that our request is granted.

That afternoon we gather for our first session. There's about fifty of us, ranging in age from early twenties to one or two mid-sixties, but mostly thirty- and forty-somethings. At fifty-three, I'm among the oldest. Now comes the crucial moment when we meet our "trainer" for the course, the person who will run things — and run *us* — for the next six days. The term "trainer" originated from Erhard's original program, "the est training." It brings to mind childhood scenes of the Barnum and Bailey circus's famous lion tamer Clyde Beatty cracking his whip to make the kingly beasts obediently leap to their chairs. When our trainer enters the room, I think he fits the Clyde Beatty image; all he needs is a whip and some chairs. We're the lions, but without claws, teeth, or power.

The man I'll call Gib comes growling to the front of the room with brisk, hell-bent strides, quickly establishing himself as numero uno, supreme commander, and minor demi-god for the ensuing six days. He wears a crisp white shirt open at the neck, no jacket, and dark slacks — exactly the outfit that Werner Erhard himself wears in a promotional video for this program. A glowering man in his early forties, Gib has black hair erupting in a curly, twisting tangle on top of his head, like an outward emanation of his thoughts and commands. As each of us goes to the front of the room to introduce ourselves to him and his minions (some are on staff, some volunteers), and our fellow campers, Gib critiques us on one or all of the aspects of our "presentation" (the way we are dressed and groomed, how we speak, what we say, how we live, who we are).

I say I'm a writer living in Boston and I'm here with Theresa, whom I've been going out with for more than two years. I say we did the est training together the year before, and, in what I hope will be a preemptive strike against attacks, I introduce the issue that Theresa and I have had to battle the world about since we first began going out. This issue makes no difference to us but often brings down the wrath or at least disapproval of people who don't know us: the big difference in our ages.

I am fifty-three; Theresa is twenty-six.

, , ,

When I meet Theresa at a party in Cambridge two years before and am struck by her beauty and wit and warmth, I know she is young. I also know I want to see her again. I hope she might be twenty-nine or possibly even thirty, which would put matters at least in the outer limits of social acceptance of male-female chronology in our culture, but no such luck. We've already gone out several times when I learn she's twenty-four, and I take a deep breath and admit to fifty-one (I am tempted to try forty-nine, but the lie seems sillier than the truth). Since it doesn't matter to her, it doesn't matter to me.

But what about Theresa's mother? What will she think about her twenty-four-year-old daughter going out with a twice-divorced man over fifty? A writer who doesn't even have a regular income. I'm apprehensive about the inevitable introduction. I've never been good at the nerve-racking ritual of "meeting the folks," and this time there are built-in objections for the family. Her mother, Mary, lives outside of the city in Brockton, where Theresa grew up, and her married older sister, Suellen (whom I also must meet), lives in Plymouth, in the same southerly direction from Boston. The night Mom and Sis come in to have dinner with me and Theresa, I'm so jittery I spill an entire pitcher of iced tea when the door buzzer rings. To my surprise and relief, both mother and sister are friendly and approving. At dinner, while Theresa and Suellen are engrossed in conversation, Mary and I speak of our love for Theresa, and her mother leans across the table toward me to express something special.

"Theresa has the Holy Spirit in her."

Yes. It is something I have sensed about her daughter but never would have had the imagination or insight to put into words. It is not about piety or formal religiosity. This quality or element her mother describes in these sacred words shines out in a kind of purity of intention, deed, and understanding, a heightened sense of joy and also pain that is rare and precious. Her mother knows I see this in Theresa, and that is important. Age is not important.

It turns out to be important to other people, though, primarily people who don't know us. Some young people Theresa recently met assume I play the role of sugar daddy. (Ha. I barely have enough sugar to pay my own rent, much less hers!) Why else, they must reason, would a beautiful young woman go out with a gray-haired old guy who has never been mistaken for Paul Newman? A literary couple who are friends of mine keep making excuses not to have dinner or go to events with me and Theresa, but a time finally comes when they can't get out of it.

Theresa is her usual delightful and witty self, and at the end of the evening the wife exclaims, "I never thought I'd have such a good time!" Isn't any attractive young woman who dates an older man a "dumb blond" (regardless of hair color) whose company is bound to be a bore?

Walking with Theresa through Faneuil Hall, the marketplace in Boston, two young guys brush against me and one of them says in a threatening tone, "That better be your daughter," and spits on the pavement. He is one of many freelance arbiters of social propriety we meet as we walk in the world. One of the few places where we are accepted, and understood, and respected, is church. Good old conservative King's Chapel. Another reason I will always love it. One of my favorite parishioners, the beautiful white-haired Harriet Parker, then in her seventies, asks me how old Theresa is, and when I tell her she pokes a finger in my chest, smiles, and says, in her Boston accent: "Cradle snatch-ah!" Then she laughs, and I laugh, and Harriet is our friend, mine and Theresa's, always welcoming, loving, true.

At a party of friends in Boston earlier this summer to celebrate the publication of *Selling Out*, I call for attention to say I want to give Theresa a token of thanks for her love and support. "We've been with each other for more than a year now," I say, "and I know some people are surprised we got together at all, because of the great difference —" I pause, and the place is hushed. I continue — "because of the great difference in our *beauty*."

There is laughter, smiles, and applause. Everyone knows I'm referring to age, and everyone here understands the genuine love we have for one another. After I make my toast, the younger wife of a distinguished Bostonian comes up to me and Theresa and says she and her husband also had to take crude remarks and put-downs because of the difference in their ages. She tells us not to take it personally; it happens whenever an older man goes out with a younger woman.

, , ,

I hope that prejudice won't surface here, now, at the beginning of the Six Day ordeal. In hopes of defusing the issue in this roomful of strangers, after telling our respective ages, I throw in what I intend to be a light comment in our defense. I point out that the great Russian writer Dostoyevsky fell in love with and married his young secretary, and the gap in their ages was the same as mine and Theresa's. Most of my fellow campers laugh or smile, seeming to take the situation with friendly acceptance.

Not Gib.

He growls and points. He calls me "dirty old man." The smiles of my fellow campers turn to frowns or blankness. I feel like a marked man.

The first day isn't even over.

That night we are taught a new "game." It's called "Stand up/sit down." When the trainer (or one of his deputies) tells you to stand up and sit down, you do just that. You do it time after time, minute after minute, hour after hour. You do it fast and you do it slow, however you are told. You do it until you think you're losing your mind. You do it without questioning. Yours not to reason why, yours but to stand up and/or sit down. As the night drones on, I question something in the procedure. The man in charge says my problem is "age." Too old. I want to strangle the son of a bitch.

There are also lectures by Gib that go on into the early hours of the morning. People have a hard time staying awake. If you think you're falling asleep, one of the assistants will give you a wooden log to hold. You stand at the side of the room holding your log. You have to stay awake to keep the log from dropping, and if you fall asleep and drop it, that wakes you up.

We finally get to bed at three in the morning, and we're wakened at seven for calisthenics. This is human potential movement boot camp. After calisthenics comes the uphill mile run.

We are told to go all out, to run faster than we've ever run before, and we're going to be timed. Volunteer assistants line the way, urging us on, yelling encouragement or insult, anything to keep us from slowing down, much less (God forbid) stopping. I run at full capacity, somewhere in the middle of the second half of the pack, and wince when I hear my time called (just under ten minutes) as I puff and heave across the finish line. I'm slow, as I have been all my life (I blame it on flat feet, not poor conditioning and lack of strength), and I can't believe I'll be able to make a significant reduction in my time before the end of these six days, though I'm promised that's the case, that it's only my mental perception of my limits that's holding me back. The old "It's all your mind" line. Sure, sure. Well, I believe in reality. Maybe I can get it down three or four seconds, but I know my own body, my own capacity, and that's it.

On the third day I cut one minute and thirty-two seconds off my time. I am astonished and elated.

We are divided up into teams of seven people each for all activities, and the times of each individual for the uphill mile run are added for a team score. The fastest and most-improved teams are announced every day at lunch. The day I make the big cut in my time, our team is the most improved. I've never been on a winning team before for anything, anywhere, and when the news is announced, I not only stand up and cheer with the rest of my team, I tear off my T-shirt and wave it wildly in the air, shouting at the top of my lungs. I am pumped anyway by cutting my own individual time in a way I'd never believed possible, and the added high of helping my team be the best sends me into hyper heaven. I get an adrenaline rush like I've never known, the kind I've witnessed only when basketball teams cut down the nets in triumph, and football heroes are carried off the field on their teammates' shoulders. Now it's me, it's my team, and I'm pumped, stoked, streaking through the stratosphere as I whip my T-shirt around like the flag signaling the winner at the Indy 500.

Surprisingly to me, I have no trouble with the physical feats, the "hanging from a cliff" sort of thing that makes the Six Day seem such a test of courage. I get into my rope harness tied by a volunteer and skitter down the side of a mountain (rappelling, it's called) with the rest of them. I climb to the flimsy top of the tall, thin ladder on the platform that seems the size of a postage stamp and make the leap into air and scenery that makes the "zip line" a toughie, and haul myself hand over hand across a deep ravine in the "Tyrolean Traverse."

I'm not even freaked out by the challenge of the "process" that requires us to stare at our body in a wall of full-length mirrors while wearing only a bathing suit and being watched by everyone else. We go up in rows of eight at a time, first facing the mirror while standing at attention, then turning to face our fellow campers, who stare at us in silence. Some people cry as they look at themselves or are looked at by the others. To my amazement, some people with perfectly good bodies are the ones who cry. A good-looking woman whose body bears no flaw that I can see looks at herself and bawls, tears coursing down her lovely cheeks. A fat guy looks at himself and smiles; a muscular man begins to tremble and looks as if he might faint. There's no way to know who will react how, or least of all, why.

I'm surprised at my own reaction. I paid almost no attention to my body until it revolted against my abuse of it with alcohol and inactivity five years before this at age forty-eight, when exercise and diet and cutting out booze got my pulse and weight down to normal range. I continue my daily exercycle workouts and diet, and I've recently taken up Tai Chi, but none of that has made me a jock or bodybuilder. My arms are still stringy, my shoulders aren't broad, there's a bit of flab at my waist. My legs are the only parts that look good and strong.

This unathletic image used to sadden and depress me in high school, stripping my hope of glory in sports and thus, I feared, the love of women. From college onward I simply stopped paying attention to my body, relying on my mind and what talent I have as a writer and talker to earn my share of money, attention, and love. My body was something I dragged along and covered with clothing to keep out the cold. I was neither ashamed nor proud of it, but hardly counted it among my assets.

After we stand in front of the mirror, and the eyes of our fellow campers, we have to make a list of all the things we've done to our body, part by part — all the abuse, neglect, accidents, and punishment we've given it, and all that it's done and does for us in spite of this. Damned if I don't begin to appreciate my body! Look how it's carried me around for more than half a century, never complaining until I pushed it to the brink and then sending clear warning signals (the accelerated heart rate) that give me a chance to fix it before a serious breakdown.

After all, my body's been through a lot — a broken and dislocated fifth cervical vertebra from a car wreck at age twenty-one that might have paralyzed me for life, as well as a broken thumb that never returned to its right position; cuts on the wrist from abortive suicide attempts in my early twenties; years of ingestion of booze; amphetamines, experiments with LSD, cocaine, hash, and a couple years of steady marijuana use; hospitalization from infectious arthritis after drunken swimming in polluted waters in Maine. There's been little physical activity beyond carrying cases of Almaden Chablis half gallons from the trunk of the car to the kitchen during my forties, and, I'm sure, other abuses that have faded into boozy forgetfulness. And here I am at age fifty-three, hanging from cliffs and pulling myself across ravines hand over hand. I thank my body. For the first time in my life, I appreciate it.

So my body is doing fine in this test of outward limits of endurance and survival. It's my mind that's cracking. It's become clear now that Gib, the trainer, has found favorites among the campers. He singles out a few men — and especially women — who give the right answers, come up with the right insights and revelations, and are held up as paragons of transformation, their words and ideas repeated, endorsed, their attitudes praised. They seem to grow taller and to glow in the affirmation of the leader, who in this self-enclosed world is God. His pronouncements are like thunderbolts hurled from the platform from whence he speaks. His wrath is terrible, spoken in shouts of rage and blistering contempt.

He not only has favorites among us, he also has favorite targets, objects of disdain, exemplars of transformational sloth. Theresa and I are prime among them. At one of the sessions he makes her stand up and shouts accusingly, "Theresa, what's all this shit about being with a man who's old enough to be your father? What the hell are you doing with Dan?"

I'm frightened for her. I grit my teeth and duck my head, praying. Please be strong, I pray, please don't let this bullying asshole hurt you.

"I love him," she says.

She looks at me, and instead of seeing support and love and pride in her own courage, she sees a frightened man with his head down. I'm in agony. I don't know how to defend her. I know that in this game we've agreed to play, this game in which a macho, blustery, rage-filled man plays God, there is no way to win, no way to go against his will. He has the power. I have no more power than Job. Less than Job. Job is a man who is known to his family and friends and has their sympathy. I don't know the people here. They see me as Gib (God) sees me, as his treatment of me, his attitude toward me, tells them who I am. I have none of my books with me that prove I have another identity; hell, I don't even have my driver's license and credit cards. I am no one. Except who Gib says I am. A dirty old man.

And Theresa is a "snake."

That is Gib's word for women with long hair. Gib says women with long hair use it as a weapon, to deceive and connive, to abdicate responsibility, and to hide behind. They are low. They are without honor. They are the kind of creature that would stoop so low as to be with a dirty old man. The other campers aren't as friendly to us as they were at first. Gib doesn't call on us. He calls on his favorites and praises them for their astute responses, their appropriate use of the lingo of "the work," their insights and revelations that bolster the theories he force-feeds us. When Theresa or I raise our hand, it's as if we're invisible, unless he wants to go after us to illustrate some unempowering example. I stop raising my hand, hoping simply to survive, to somehow get through this ordeal by being anonymous. And even more, hoping Theresa comes through it unscathed. It's not easy being a snake who goes out with a dirty old man.

The spotlight turns on Theresa when Gib announces he's providing an opportunity for all "snakes" to shed their skins, and become real people, get off their bellies and stand up and be counted as upstanding citizens. Professional barbers/hair stylists have arrived and free of charge will cut the long hair of any who wish to take advantage of this opportunity for salvation.

The hair police are here to strike, this time not from a feminist position but a sort of "human potential" Puritanism, though in each case long hair is regarded as a sin, whether it's the sin of "luring men" or "hiding out" behind a natural veil of beauty. Of course, being a dirty old man, I indeed find Theresa's long hair alluring, a part of her natural beauty. She knows I love it. She knows I wouldn't want her to cut it. What will she do? We're not allowed to sit together — no one can sit next to anyone they came with, or anyone they even knew before the Six Day. When the hair cutters are announced, the audience claps and cheers. The cutters take up positions in the corners of the room, ready to operate.

Several women with long hair immediately stand up and head for the shears, as if they can't wait to be shorn of their shameful locks. Cheers go up for these brave, liberated volunteers. Theresa sits tight, accruing more scorn. The pressure builds. She must be in agony. I'm in agony with her. As the night wears on, other women heed the call as Gib, like a revival preacher, peppers his sermons of self-realization with praise for those who are shorn, and scorn for those who keep their snake-y identity. I write a note to Theresa that she should do what she wants, not to resist the shearing for my sake. I can't stand to see her suffer. Still, she resists.

I'm fearful of what may come next. I'm getting paranoid. I worry that our room is bugged. I draw in, wanting to be as anonymous as possible now, wanting Theresa to do the same. I just want to get through this, I just want to survive with my mind and body intact and Theresa intact, as well as our relationship. Our love. Yes, I love her. But who would believe that here, now?

There's an evening devoted to sex. When I say "an evening," I mean from late afternoon until about midway into the next morning. Like three or four A.M. Somewhere in there we break for dinner, and there are bathroom breaks about every four hours, but aside from that, it's a marathon of attention. Ordinarily it would be no trouble to stay awake for discussions and confessions and movies about sex, but on the sleep we are getting — or not getting — consciousness is an accomplishment no matter what the subject. Ordinarily this is a subject I would be not only engrossed in but also commenting on, telling stories about, trying to get my words in edgewise into any discussion. But now I sit mute, hoping to be anonymous. I am afraid that Gib will pounce on me and Theresa, try to expose the sexual practices of a dirty old man and a snake, make a further example of us, and I don't utter a sound. For once I am glad to be unnoticed.

There is no lack of stories in the room. Confession is not only encouraged but urged, the more detailed the better; the more graphic and lurid, the more approval you win. This is like a community Oprah, in which everyone in the audience gets to have a turn at the mike. Everyone is encouraged to "get it out," confess the awful truth, lay bare for laughter the hang-ups and fetishes, delights and obsessions that you never told your best friend, much less your priest or parents. Women tell of smearing butter between their legs for their Great Dane or Irish setter to lick off. Techniques are compared. Men tell of circle jerks and daisy chains, of doing it with sheep and goats, of masturbating while imagining freight trains crushing their privates, of being tied to bedposts with silk stockings while a girlfriend dances to Gregorian chants. You name it, we got it. The idea is to get rid of it, get rid of the fear and guilt of it by getting it out in the open, expose it to the light and be able to laugh at it. Listen to other people's stories and see that whatever you did or imagined, not only has somebody else done it, they have probably gone you one better, added a banana cream pie to your most elaborate fantasy. Gib cheers on the confessional, praising his favorites and anointing new ones.

We watch a movie marathon of sex as well, some of it porn, some of it documentary stuff that looks like it came from old *National Geographic* archives, or Margaret Mead's outtakes of Fiji Islanders in grainy black-and-white ritual dances of fertility; animals humping one another in zoos and on farms, horses and dogs and grasshoppers mating, the whole world doing it. Funniest of all to the audience is the coupling that draws the most hoots and hollers of hilarity and derision — some home movie–quality footage of an elderly couple doing it, a man with gray hair and wrinkles and pot belly getting it on with a saggy-skinned woman with drooping breasts. Oh, this is rich to the largely twenty-to-forty-something audience; they whistle and cheer and jeer as we gray-haired participants scattered among them smile and laugh at the right times and try to blend in with the crowd so our age isn't noticed, so we're not associated with the saggy-droopy partners on the screen whose sexual activity is seen here as subject for ridicule.

I keep thinking this too shall pass. I pray that Theresa and I just get through the sexathon without being singled out, and somehow we do. We get to our beds for a blessed few hours of conked-out sleep and I'm relieved and glad to get to the morning calisthenics and the uphill run because it means we've survived another day and night. I think there are only two to go. Or is it three?

I keep on because I think there may still be some benefit I can't imagine or foresee, because there always *has* been in this work. I think how shaken up I was after the first weekend of the est training, how tempted I was to quit, and how much I would have missed, how much I would have lost, if I hadn't returned and finished the course. I know the est training and the work I did that followed it with Erhard's programs played a key part in releasing me from my alcohol habit and opened me up to a much wider and deeper experience of my own spirituality, my church experience, the enjoyment of my writing — and even in sustaining and deepening my relationship with Theresa. So I keep thinking I must hang on, hang in; if I split, I may be missing something crucial.

And underneath all that is my determination to stop my pattern of running. I have too often run when things got tough, going back to childhood, when I cried and left my first camp halfway through at age ten because I was homesick; when I transferred to another school in my freshman year in high school, and transferred again in college; when I twice got divorced; when I backed out of business deals, opportunities, like writing the script of my own novel with Don Devlin; when I left the perfectly good literary agents . . . I have to stop the pattern, I have to stick things out, and no matter how awful this experience is, I keep thinking I may gain something just by stick-ing to it, running the course, crossing the finish line. So I grit my teeth and pray, and I stay.

One night — I don't even know which it is anymore, they are running together — we are given some rubber bats and instructed to bash them on gymnastic "horses" to let our aggression out, to purge ourselves of the accumulated hatreds, antipathies, angers, and rage that we've stored up over the years, the bile that is festering in us and blocking us, preventing us from reach-ing our human potential, from becoming the people we think we can be, the free spirits who dance and create and love and live large. Imagine that gymnastics horse is your enemy, but give it a face, make it your abusive mother, father, babysitter, brother, the lover who betrayed you, the boss who fired you, the rival who cheated and deprived you of the prize, the snob who scorned you, all of the condescending creeps who overlooked you or didn't even notice you, see them all as you smash that bat on their imagined bodies. Scream and yell as you give it to them, let yourself go and really lay into them, forget your civilized veneer and flail away.

Noises of pounding, grunts, shouts, screams fill the air as staff and volunteer assistants urge us on, whooping us into greater fury as we pound, pound, until the arms are tired, until the throat is sore from shouting, until we can lift the bat no more and finally let it fall as we fold ourselves to the floor, gasping, clean, purified. Yet I don't feel like I know I should, the relief that should come isn't there, perhaps because I forget about all my past issues and put all my venomous strength into smash-ing Gib, imagining him as I bring down the bat, over and over, harder and harder, until my arms are drooping like limp spaghetti, my throat shouted dry and scratchy as a roll of sand-paper.

But there he is, unfazed, at the front of the room, cocky as ever, preening and posing as master of us all, numero uno, dictator-jefe-tsar-top sergeant-tyrant ruling this roost I'm trapped in for six hellish days — and nights, don't forget the nights, though it all runs together into one long endless stretch of nerve and body, mind and soul.

One night when Gib and his minions are really pouring it on, with harangues and accusations of wimpiness and cowardice and irresponsibility, combined with stand-up/sit-down exercises till you think your mind will fall out and your muscles atrophy, as dawn begins to smudge the windows and we still haven't slept since the three or four hours of the night and day before, each of us is given a sheet of paper with a passage from a book called *The Way of Transformation,* by Karlfried Graf von Durckheim. In his scratchy, attack-dog voice, Gib reads it aloud as we try to focus on the words on the paper:

> The man who, being really on the Way, falls upon hard times in the world will not, as a consequence, turn to the friend who offers him refuge and comfort and encourages his old self to survive. Rather, he will seek out someone who will faithfully and inexorably help him to risk himself, so that he may endure the suffering and pass courageously through it, thus making of it a raft that leads to the far shore. Only to the extent that man exposes himself over and over again to annihilation, can that which is indestructible arise within him. In this lies the dignity of daring. Thus, the aim of practice is not to develop an attitude which allows a man to acquire a state of harmony and peace wherein nothing can ever trouble him. On the contrary, practice should teach him to let himself be assaulted, perturbed, moved, insulted, broken and battered — that is to say, it should enable him to dare to let go his futile hankering after harmony, surcease from

pain, and a comfortable life, in order that he may discover, in doing battle with the forces that oppose him, that which awaits him beyond the world of opposites. The first necessity is that we should have the courage to face life, and to encounter all that is most perilous in the world. When this is possible, meditation itself becomes the means by which we accept and welcome the demons which arise from the unconscious — a process very different from the practice of concentration on some object as a protection against such forces. Only if we venture repeatedly through zones of annihilation can our contact with Divine Being, which is beyond annihilation, become firm and stable. The more a man learns wholeheartedly to confront the world that threatens him with isolation, the more are the depths of the Ground of Being revealed and the possibilities of new life and Becoming opened.

I wonder if there is any truth to this. I wonder if this affirms my desperate hope that if I endure this six days I will in fact be stronger, that going through this hell will be worth it? I hate the part of me I know is "soft," the part that wants to flee from difficulty and pain and confrontation, so I can't help wondering if maybe there is something of value in this dark advice, something I need to learn. On the other hand, I wonder if it isn't just a justification for the shit we're having to take at the Six Day!

Then we are read a letter from Werner Erhard — a letter addressed to us, the people who have passed through some of the "annihilation" described by the passage we just heard and read, and survived. Werner says we are being tested, we are purposely having everything thrown at us, put through the most severe circumstances he can conjure up, not as punishment, but as preparation for what we will inevitably face in life. He tells us that nothing he could put together here, no series of physical or mental or emotional challenges could be as rigorous or difficult as the things we will have to undergo in the course of our lives.

Maybe because this message is not so eloquently worded as the one by the German guy, or maybe because I know it was Erhard who invented this Six Day thing, I get angry at him and his theories. Who the hell does this Werner guy think he's addressing — a roomful of Japanese kamikaze pilots? Marines recruits at Parris Island preparing for a wartime invasion?

Years later I will think of those words and feel that Erhard was right in addressing them to a bunch of middle-class, over-privileged Americans, for even we pampered sons and daughters of an affluent society will face in our time the death of loved ones, the betrayal of friends, the unexpected vagaries of jobs and career in a changing economy that threatens imagined security, the "slings and arrows of outrageous fortune" that are part of the human condition, from Shakespeare's time to our own and before and after, ending with the ravages of age and finally our own extinction, the snuffing of our own brief candle.

But I will also come to think Werner was right when he said there was no way he really could toughen us for that, not by depriving us of sleep or getting us to dangle from clifftops on ropes held by ninety-pound schoolteachers and stringy-armed accountants. I also come to believe, after being in a number of workshops Erhard led, and getting to know him through several long interviews I conduct with him, that his intention is benefi-cent; that he wanted like hell to prepare people for what life was going to throw at them, knowing from his own experience how unexpected and powerful such blows would be, and how frus-trating and demoralizing it is when you have no means of coun-tering them.

This theory of preparing people for the blows of life by shak-ing them up may or may not be useful, may in fact be more harmful to some people, but it's not something Erhard originated. The respected Buddhist nun and author Pema Chodron says in an interview in *Tricycle: The Buddhist Review* when asked about students' concerns for "safe" places to practice and learn, "A situation where no one rocks the boat and the whole thing is smooth creates a very weak understanding and feeds into the avoidance of pain, which is the major cause of suffering. . . ." The technique of challenging the student, of purposely causing discomfort in order to bring enlightenment, has been practiced by controversial gurus throughout history, most notably by the mystic Gurdjieff, and Chodron's own teacher, Trungpa Rinpoche, who was known for his drinking and sexual relations with students yet was revered by followers like Allen Ginsberg as well as celibate Buddhist monks and nuns.

But all such philosophical considerations are far in the future that night. All I want to know is if I'm going to make it till morning, and through another day and night, to get out of here. I'm angry and scared and disoriented. Who am I? Who was I when I came in? Can I prove it? They have my ID, driver's license, every last shred of documentary evidence of who I am or think I am or was and thought I was. And who will I be when I leave, if I ever get out? I'm losing it. I think the red light at the top of our bedroom ceiling that is some kind of fire alarm thing may really be a listening device, or even a hidden video camera, and I tell Theresa to whisper, not to speak of what we really feel while in the room. I think They are after me, us.

My fears get specifically sexual. I fear for Theresa, who failed to cut her hair, and it shines forth now like a badge of dishonor, the mark of the snake, illicit lover of the dirty old man, me. I fear for her safety, fear she will somehow be physically violated, abused, although there is no evidence or hint of such a possibility. Perhaps because I feel it is happening mentally, emotionally, it may happen physically too. It seems like anything can happen now if Gib decides to orchestrate it, for the crowd is with him, under his sway, whooping to his leadership, sucking his favor. Only Theresa and I and a couple of other malcontent misfits are out of the flow.

, , ,

On the last night there's some kind of group free dancing, movement to express yourself, to wave arms and throw legs and gyrate around the room. My sexual fears kick in again, imagining some kind of orgiastic exploitation of our weakened condition, keeping an eye on Theresa, wanting to protect her from any harm, ready to hurl myself in the path of any attackers, wanting to attack Gib as he barks his commands, wanting to rip out his throat with a rusty razor blade. My heart swells at the thought. Ah, the joys of enlightenment. But the "dance" is completely benign, most people flowing and glowing with looks of peace and love. We are thistles, thorns, in their garden of earthly delight.

We are herded on to the night's final process, in which our original "presentation" — that is, the video introducing ourselves at the opening of camp — is shown again and critiqued by Gib with kibitzing from staff, volunteers, and favored campers. Much attention and concern is given to the stars of the week, Gib's favorites, on earthshaking issues such as whether they look better (or make a better "presentation") with or without glasses. (Those deemed better without glasses are urged to get contact lenses when they get back home.) When my own image is flashed on the screen, Gib says nothing, and when one friendly camper, taking pity on me for the lack of interest, tries to drum up some curiosity at least about whether I come across better with or without glasses, Gib says in a bored voice, "Whatever," and clicks on to the next image. If he deems you a nonperson, such niceties are irrelevant. Who cares if a leper wears horn-rims or contacts?

The next morning is devoted to a basic training–type inspection of our quarters, and Theresa and I labor mightily to be perfect in order to be released. We won't be given back our identity until an inspection team of Six Day graduates okays our quarters. First we flunk when dust is found on a light bulb. Next time around there's a hair on the underside of the toilet seat. We scrub again for dear life, beginning to fear we'll never get out, that we'll be incarcerated here incognito like inmates in a Mexican prison.

Finally release comes, and there is one last gathering to say goodbye to Gib — and also to sign up for further programs and seminars. I don't want to register for anything, ever again, I just want to get home and pull the covers up over my head. Except for me and Theresa and the few other lepers, people are jumping around like they're on helium, beaming with eager enthusiasm, crowding around to give Gib a hug, tears of gratitude in their eyes, praise and thanks foaming from their lips. I feel like a Jew at a Nazi rally, hoping to escape unnoticed.

Back home in Boston, Theresa and I sleep for twelve hours. I've never been so drained and exhausted in my life. We don't say much. We drag ourselves to the Public Garden and lie down on a blanket. We thought we'd come out of this experience flying, like we were after the est training, only maybe even higher. Instead, we're crawling. Or worse. Sinking.

In a few days I get my sleep back on track and my malaise turns to anger. I'm enraged at Gib, at est, at Werner Erhard, the whole show. I don't want to have anything to do with them, with it, with seminars or workshops or transformation. I want to bolt the doors and lock the windows and never hear from those assholes again. I refuse to go to the follow-up seminar.

I get angry at Theresa because she goes anyway. She still thinks "the work" has value. I've just moved to another apartment a few blocks up Mt. Vernon Street — a plan that was in the works at the start of the summer — and I get even angrier at Theresa when I hear she has given my new address and phone to the people I now call by the favorite name of their many critics: "est-holes." I don't want them to know where I am.

All this deepens the rupture between me and Theresa from the whole Six-Day experience. While I was feeling guilty and scared that I couldn't protect her, it looked to her like I was retreating from supporting her, not being proud of our love in the face of the attack on it. We continue together, but it doesn't seem as strong in the aftermath of this debacle. It's as if some mutual trust is lost. Still, Theresa patiently and gently urges me over the next few months to "complete" my feelings about the Six Day by finally going with her to a meeting of our "team," the group of others in camp we were assigned to for carrying out tasks, competitions, and discussions. Part of the program is to keep in touch with your team afterward in order to keep the transformation alive. Theresa has told the others how I feel, and they welcome me warmly but gently when I finally go to one of their get-togethers in November. They suggest I get my complaints off my chest, that I write to Gib and ask for an apology, and send a copy of the letter to Werner Erhard. In "the work" this is called "completion," and I know from experience that completion is good for the soul. Like all anger held inside, this rage is poisoning my system. I want to pour it out. I do.

I write to Gib "to protest your arrogantly insensitive conduct of the course in general, and for your insulting, condescending treatment of me and the woman I came with in particular . . . ," detailing all my resentments with the eloquence of outrage. Oh, how good it feels to beat up on the man, if only on paper.

A week later, I receive a letter from Werner Erhard's office assuring me I will have a reply from Gib, and indeed a handwritten letter arrives from Gib himself, in which he "deeply" apologizes "to you and Theresa for the insensitivity and insults you experienced." He regrets "having gotten in the way of the opportunity" the Six Day experience is supposed to provide, and offers to arrange "scholarships" for me and Theresa — to do the whole thing again! I read this letter to a meeting of my Six Day team, and when I come to Gib's offer to me and Theresa to do the course again, everyone breaks out laughing. The laughter is healing. But it doesn't heal the wound I feel my relationship with Theresa has suffered.

I hear a rumor that Gib was going through a divorce when he was leading our course. I don't know if it's true, but it might explain his hostility to me and Theresa, the special fury he seemed to bring to that week in his dealings with the people he didn't like. It suggests to me the inherent dangers of courses like this, presented and operated with the best will in the world for the hope of helping people reach their highest human potential, enjoy their God-given gifts to the fullest; all the bright goals of such programs. Yet there is always the unpredictable, the human factor that might throw off either leader or participant engaging in some such experiential exercise at some especially vulnerable point in their life and cause unintended pain or damage.

Engaging in any such program is a risk; but so is life.

The year after Theresa and I do the Six Day Advanced Course, that program is "retired," in the lingo of Werner Erhard and Associates, along with the est training. The est training is replaced by a modernized, briefer, less confrontational, more Socratic sort of program called "the Forum," in which the person in charge is no longer called "the trainer," but "the Forum leader." The Six Day course has never been revived.

Despite our horrendous Six Day experience, Theresa and I go on to do more of "the work" of Werner Erhard and Associates, because we feel from our own experience that Gib's treatment of us was an aberration of "the work" rather than a typical expression of it, and we still value the benefits of the est training as a genuine transformational experience that enhanced our lives and continues to do so. Out of the "openings" we got from the est training, Theresa was able to heal longtime breaches within her own family relationships that brought her deep relief and satisfaction, and I was relieved of some of my old conflicts with my parents that still rankled, and for the first time allowed my deep love for them to surface, a love I held locked inside for most of my adult life. One of my greatest regrets is that I didn't do the est training while my parents were still alive, because I know I could have shown my love for them in a far more open way than I could during their lifetime. One of the most common and positive results of the est training as well as the Forum, the program that succeeds it, is the healing of relationships with parents. Countering the current vogue of seeing oneself as "victim," this program urges participants to stop blaming their parents for their woes, and express the natural love for them that is buried beneath the layers of resentments accumulated over the years. I also believe that getting rid of some of my self-consciousness and fear of criticism during the est training opened me up to leading my workshops in spiritual autobiography and creativity, a source of deep satisfaction for me as well as a way to contribute to others, to give back some of the gifts I've received.

Theresa and I take the Forum and other seminars, and continue to find value and uplift and camaraderie in "the work," which rather than the cliché criticisms of it as "selfish" and "aggressive" opens us to opportunities for service. The high point of our "High Performance" seminar comes when our group of eight people plans, prepares, cooks, and entertains at a Christmas party and dinner for a homeless shelter in Cambridge. We come away with the gift of knowing we are them and they are us, homeless or sheltered, employed or out of work, broke or salaried; we recognize ourselves in their eyes and in their plight.

In the years to come I take four seminars led by Werner Erhard himself, and I find them valuable and inspiring. I hear him speak to large groups and am not that impressed — in those kind of settings he sounds more like the pitchman his critics accuse him of being. But in the seminars, which are based on a give and take between the leader and participants, Erhard is at his best. His "inquiries" go to the heart of the matter at issue, sometimes bringing tears, and then later, almost inevitably, evoking relief, self-recognition, and a sense of restored vitality. While it's true, as his critics complain, that Erhard often "tears people down" in trying to get to the nub of their hang-ups, it is also true — but rarely noted — that he builds those people up again, often to a new self-esteem that surprises as well as delights them. Erhard seems to take his greatest pleasure in leading a participant to a "space" of greater opportunity. As a journalist, I observe him as he leads a seminar in Dublin for twenty-eight Irish priests and nuns, leaving them, by their own testimony, more committed to their work and faith than they were before. Some who have done his "work" find Erhard infuriating; others, like me, find him enlivening and stimulating, illustrating again that one person's inspiring teacher is another's despotic antagonist.

, , ,

Perhaps the greatest challenge and problem — and the greatest potential pitfall — for the seeker on a spiritual path, the person looking for "enlightenment" or "awakening," is how to discern when a teacher, minister, rabbi, any kind of guru, or any kind of program of religion, spirituality, transformation, "self-help," or "personal growth" has become a negative force and is likely to end as such rather than lead to any desired or desirable goal. Serious spiritual practitioners like Pema Chodron believe in the theory of her teacher Trungpa Rinpoche that "the job of the spiritual friend is to insult the student . . . if things got too smooth he'd create chaos. . . . And I wanted my foundations rocked. I wanted to actually be free of habitual patterns which keep the ground under my feet and maintain that false security which denies death."

But how do you know whether the teacher is tearing you down for your own benefit or for his own egotistical, masochistic kicks? How do you know whether painful lessons are "good for you" and lead to enlightenment and spiritual maturity or are damaging your own psyche and emotional stability? In other words, it gets back to the basic question: "How do we know when it's God?" There is no easy answer.

Sara Davidson tells me that on one of her visits to a spiritual guide who has helped her enormously, she felt the advice she was being given was not at all in tune with her own "truth," and she simply ignored it. "There are times," she says, "when you have to stand in your own truth." No other person can tell you how to discern those times, nor is there any set rule for doing so except to pray and go as deeply as you can within your own center and try to feel the message your own body as well as your mind is telling you. I've learned there are times when my body, in its distress, is giving me the message of my heart; that my body knows more than my mind, and I've ignored its message at my peril.

Dr. Spock's great message to mothers was simply to trust their own instincts, assuring them they know more than they think they know. The same wisdom applies to all of us as we try to understand God's will, to discern the right path. We continue to look for experts and gurus, psychiatrists and seers and ministers, even channelers who claim to bring us advice from ancient Egyptian royalty or figures from past lives. And all the time the answers are where we fear most of all to search: our own body (more than our mind), the "still small voice" inside we forget is there or won't take the time to listen to and often disregard when we hear it. In one of her essays Annie Dillard says if she could only give her daughter one piece of advice, just a single thing to live by, she'd tell her: "Listen to no one." She means, of course, no one else — no one except the person most likely to know, and least likely to be consulted: yourself.

Chapter 5

BRAIN-WASHING, "POST-CHRISTIAN" STYLE

SIX MONTHS AFTER THE SIX DAY DEBACLE, IN THE EARLY spring of '86, my relationship with Theresa feels held together with Band-Aids, but not really healed. We continue as before, but without the euphoria, the sense of being in synch that we enjoyed before the Six Day. We snap at one another, and retreat into sighs and silences. Out of the blue an old girlfriend I haven't seen for a decade writes to say she's coming to Boston on a visit and wants to get together. I met Lilly on a trip to Mexico in '71, and later went to see her in Seattle, where she lives. We've taken several romantic vacations together, and I find her extremely erotic as well as good company. We share a sense of humor as well as physical attraction, yet the question of long-term commitment never comes up because of geography — Seattle is her home, Boston mine. We speak frankly about other partners and dates on our home grounds, without jealousy, since we aren't a part of one another's daily or "regular" life; when together, it's as if we inhabit a parallel universe disconnected from the one we usually live in, a circumstance both liberating and erotic. Then in 1973 I meet the woman for whom I forsake all others for seven years of domestic stability, and a few years later I hear Lilly is stabilized herself, married and has a child.

Now she reports that she's getting a divorce and is coming with her mother and little boy to visit relatives in Boston. Since I'm still in the relationship with Theresa, shaky or not, I don't feel free to make a "real date" with Lilly; but tea at the Ritz sounds proper and safe. I imagine a nostalgic talk about old times, lending a sympathetic ear to the story of her divorce, and exchanging a friendly peck on the cheek. It's almost ten years since I've seen her, and I'm prepared for an older, more sedate, motherly version (after all, she is a mother now) of the sexy, carefree, careless girl I knew in the height of the hippie era. I'm vaguely imagining a milk-and-cookies version of the old, wild Lilly.

Wrong.

She's dynamite.

Lilly is wearing a beautiful white silk blouse with a maroon suit and matching high heels, her hair lush and loose, her eyes bright and clear. Gone is the blowsy, unstrung look of her hippie days, as well as the giggly aura of irresponsibility. This is a confident, attractive woman who has got herself together and is radiating lust like the glow from an atomic energy plant.

"My God," I say, "you look great."

"So do you," she says.

I, too, have gotten it together since we last met, when I staggered off from a Caribbean weekend with a crushing hangover, weaving my way through JFK. I'm twenty pounds lighter now, and a whole lot steadier of hand and clearer of eye. We toast with our teacups in mutual admiration, wanting to jump across the table and into bed (or just onto the table), but I have to meet

Theresa — who knows I'm having tea with an old girlfriend and is on possessiveness alert. When we leave the Ritz, Lilly and I embrace, and it's electric. I feel singed. But there's no way I can break my plans that night with Theresa without ending the whole thing, and Lilly is leaving the next afternoon. There's no way to make a hotel-room tryst because her son is in the same room with her and her mother is in an adjoining room. We promise to talk — to make a plan — when she gets back home to Seattle.

Fantasy and scheming heat the phone lines over the next few months. At the same time my lust is rising, my deception begins to bother me. I read Scripture passages every day and the passage about everything hidden coming to light keeps popping into my mind, causing little jolts of discomfort. I'm trying to live without guile or guilt, and I feel I have to come clean with Theresa. My Christian teaching is bolstered from another direction by the concepts of est-ian Forum seminars that encourage "sharing," not keeping secrets they call "with-holds." A therapist who's also done est and believes in the pragmatism of its tenets urges me to tell all to Theresa. So I confess, or unload my with-hold, and utter hell breaks loose; chaos and crying, regret and recrimination . . . the most wrenching man-woman kind of angst like this I've ever been through. But out of it comes a kind of understanding, a recognition that things have changed between us since the Six Day, and a mutual agreement that we won't pledge to be exclusive over the summer and will see how we feel again in the fall. Now I feel free to finally rendezvous with Lilly. I'm hot on the phone to Seattle with her making plans, panting like a bulldog in heat.

How's this for irony — we can meet in San Francisco on my way to a Jungian seminar on the life of Jesus! My minister has recommended this in-depth program, sponsored by a San Francisco Jungian group called the Guild for Psychological Studies, at a place called Four Springs in northern California. And hey, it fits right in with planning a rendezvous with Lilly, who can come down from Seattle to meet me at me at a romantic hide-away on the northern California coast! Is that God's will, Divine coincidence, serendipity, Jungian synchronicity — or not? I'll soon find out. I make reservations in a northern California lodge with hot tub and Jacuzzi, and go to sleep imagining Lilly slowly, sensuously, stripping off the elegant suit with the luscious silk blouse and slipping into the hot tub, with me plunging in after. Ecstasy! Bliss!

So at the same time I'm preparing for my Bible study seminar, the next big rocket boost on my journey to enlightenment, I'm coincidentally planning my rocket launch into sexual bliss with Lilly in that hotly fantasized hot tub. I begin to wonder if the rockets I'm about to launch are going off in opposite directions, but I shake off the thought. Too distracting, like an annoying gnat. But other gnat-like thoughts begin buzzing, as I learn more about Lilly's situation. She mentions that she doesn't want her husband to know about our rendezvous. Wait — isn't she divorced? Oh, well, she's *getting* a divorce. She and her husband are separated, and they've agreed to a divorce, but it hasn't happened yet. So you're still married? I ask. Well, she supposes she is, "technically," but if it's just a technicality, I wonder, what does it matter if her husband knows she's going on a trip with an old boyfriend? Well, why make him feel bad if she doesn't have to?

I'm trying to get this straight. On my way to a Bible study seminar on the life of Jesus, I'm meeting a married woman who is lying to her husband and child in order to meet me for a romantic rendezvous. Sure, I know the statistics about how most of us screw around before and after and during marriage in this age of enlightenment and equality. But trying to get this to jibe with leading a spiritual life and going to a Bible study seminar to discern and follow the will of God is a bit much.

I lay it all out to my current spiritual director, a sincere woman with a husband and family who has gone to seminary in her fifties to become a minister, and she asks me, "Do you really want to get involved with a married woman?" The prospect reeks of complications and conundrums, just when I'm trying to clean up and clarify my life. I pray. I lose sleep. I call Lilly and tell her I can't do it; I say I'm trying to live as a Christian as best I understand that, which doesn't allow for doing things undercover and having to get involved in lies. I want to wait until she's really divorced to get together with her. She screams at me, cursing me, saying I've ruined her summer, her plans, maybe her life. She calls me a miserable shit and writes a letter elaborating her charges, demanding I pay for the nonrefundable plane ticket she now has to cancel. I send her a check.

Okay, a change of plans for the summer — now it's just me, Jesus, and the Jungians. It was just a year ago I went off to summer camp with est for the fabulous Six Day Advanced Course and ended up a blubbering bowl of jelly, nearly broken in spirit, my cherished relationship with Theresa torn in some crucial way. This program I'm going to now sounds like the opposite kind of experience. What could be more healing than spending sixteen days with Jungians studying the life of Jesus? If you said spend sixteen days with Freudians studying Jesus, I'd fear that such an experience might be, for a believing Christian, more like the est Six Day ordeal was for me. But unlike Freud, who wrote about religion as *The Future of an Illusion,* Jung was a Christian and believed that most people's psychological problems after midlife were "spiritual" problems. A Jungian seminar on Jesus, then, sounds like a way of integrating psychological and religious understanding in a way that will enhance my whole life.

I don't say to anyone I think it's "God's will" that I go to this program, but I believe it. I don't mean I heard a thundering voice say, "Dan, I want you to go to this Jungian seminar on Jesus this summer," but there are certain "synchronicities" as Jung would say — or "signs" as some of my friends and I from church retreats might put it (sounding not unlike our Old Testament ancestors). For one thing, I've been serving for several years now as cochair of my church's adult religious education committee, planning retreats, classes, "silent days" of meditation at the parish house, and anything else we can conjure up to provide spiritual sustenance. Our minister, who's done this indepth seminar himself, thinks it will give me new ideas and enrich my own spiritual experience. My old friend Norm Eddy, the minister from the East Harlem Protestant Parish, and Walter Wink, the dynamic Bible study leader, have also done the program and think it's worthwhile.

As an added cap to this whole bonanza, like an angel for the highest branch of the Christmas tree, or a cherry to top an icecream sundae of spiritual delectation, the catalogue describing this workshop says, "The life and teachings of Jesus, the foundation of Guild seminars, offer a paradigm of a life fully and vitally lived in relation to a central value and an inexhaustible source for the clarification of choice-making." The clarification of choice-making! Is that not the very heart of my search, another way of finding the answer to the question my fellow seekers and I express in our simple lay persons' terms as "How do we know when it's God?" How can I question that this very seminar, then, is the next right step in my own journey?

, , ,

As I fly west, I smile as I think of the life symmetry of this trip — how I came to California to write the *James at 15* television series on NBC in 1977, left in the depths of my midlife crisis in 1980, and returned to health and to church in Boston. Then, four years later, feeling fresh, clean, cleaned out, geared up, and at the top of my form after getting a blast of psychic energy from the est training, I returned to L.A. with the heady self-assurance that this time I can do it my way — only to flee back to Boston a week later, a basket case of twitching trauma, indecision, and insecurity.

What a relief that I've learned my lesson! Now as I head to California, it's not for the mirage of movie-land fame and fortune, but an almost opposite mission — immersion in the life of Jesus. Despite my mistakes and wrong turns and self-inflicted traumas, here I am at age fifty-four recovered in body and mind from the state I was in six years ago in the depth of my midlife crisis, which was capped by the death of my father in May and my mother six months later. Oh, how I wish my parents were alive now to see me sober, healthy, not smoking or doing any drugs, committed to daily exercise and prayer. Is this not a miracle? My parents would surely say yes, and I'm sorry they're not here to share it. I think of them in prayer — I *see* them in prayer.

I see my father smiling, dressed nicely as always in a well-fitting suit, white shirt, and tie, good brown shoes polished to a shine my own never attain, his brown eyes glinting behind his glasses, smiling, and then breaking into song, a hearty hymn or a choral piece he might have sung with the Scottish Rite choir that gave him such pleasure, allowing his musical talent to flourish, a talent that was manifested through the violin in his youth and later the pedal organ my mother bought him that sat in our living room during the years of my growing up. I see my mother smiling, too, enjoying "the gang," my high school friends she loved and loved to feed, serving home-made goodies she baked between selling houses and befriending her clients, whom she also fed, taking meals to those who had just moved to town, a walking one-woman, unofficial Welcome Wagon to the world. As I "see" my mother and father in my mind and think of them, I wish I could express my love directly, physically, in the way I shrank from, muting my feelings with booze when they still were here.

These are the mellow if bittersweet thoughts of my journey, with gratitude for my blessings of health and work and spirit, and now this new chance to expand my spiritual horizons — to learn more and experience more of God, in a setting that sounds from the catalogue description ideal, even idyllic: "Located on three hundred forested acres, eighty-five miles north of San Francisco. . . . In the 1500 foot high hills of Lake County, CA, the site provides a main lodge, seminar room, meditation room, library, art rooms, cabins, swimming pool, grape arbor, orchards, and trails."

When I get there, it strikes me as a bit ironically reminiscent of my Boy Scout rookie days at Camp Chank-tun-un-gi. I wake up freezing in a cabin that seems open to all outdoors, and go down the trail to the latrine, clutching my shaving kit, thinking of the handout we were given with a quote from Thomas Mann that seems especially pertinent: ". . . one served a God whose nature was not repose and abiding comfort but a God of design for the future, in whose will, inscrutable, great far-reaching things were in process of becoming, and this was a God . . . who must be sought for, for whom one must at all times keep oneself free, mobile, and in readiness."

Hey, as an old Eagle Scout and refurbished Christian, I'm ready to get my next instructions, as eager as if I'm about to earn my merit badge in Jesus! The coleaders of this particular sixteen-day session are a handsome, graying Protestant minister in his late forties named Del and a matronly woman therapist called Betsy. In addition to fourteen of us "campers" here for the first time — most of them ministers or former ministers as well as lay leaders, churchgoers, and religious dropouts seeking a new connection or understanding — there are four "returning veterans" who serve as assistants to the coleaders and take part in Bible study and discussions, helping the leaders keep things on track. Not present at our initial session are the three guiding muses of the enterprise, the trio of women in their seventies who established and carry on this work: Elizabeth Boyden Howes, the formidable founding mother and guiding spirit of the place, and her faithful cohorts, Louella Sibbald and Sheila Moon, all of whom will make presentations in their own particular fields of interest during the course of the session, joining us for meals and occasionally sitting in on our daily Bible study classes.

I'm caught up excitedly as we engage in a lively discussion of John baptizing Jesus, and the significance of this moment in beginning Jesus' ministry. After reading the accounts and talking about them, and relating such experience to our own lives, we are sent to the art room to try to portray this great moment by drawing or painting or modeling in clay or making collages, using whatever materials we need or want to exemplify the meaning of this story. The aim is to make it more tangible to us than the usual intellectualizing and to discover deeper layers of meaning the story reveals in our own psyches.

At the end of the period we lay our works on the floor, and I'm fascinated and moved by what is called forth, by what amazing variety and inventiveness are displayed in our disparate group. None of us are professional artists, but all are touched in some way that brings forth an original response. The work that most strikes me, in fact inspires me, is a collage made by a woman in her thirties who has worked as a chef and masseuse. Her collage combines photos from magazines showing a form emerging from water, a great sunburst, and, most riveting of all, a message of the new power gained by the experience of the one baptized, emblazoned in words cut from newspaper headlines that combine to read: "Now You Can Really Move."

I get goose bumps, not only from appreciation of the deep understanding the collage with its message reflects, but also from what transformation has meant to me; and what it might mean again. Perhaps it will happen at this workshop, like discovering some sure new way of "knowing when it's God." I want that headline bannered across a collage of my own life:

Now You Can Really Move.

, , ,

The next morning we plunge deeply into the hard intellectual study of the synoptic Gospels, Matthew, Mark, and Luke ("synoptic" simply means "similar in order, content, and statement"), using a book that is the basis of this course, *Records of the Life of Jesus,* by Henry Burton Sharman, Ph.D., identified in the volume only as "Honorary Lecturer in the Department of History, Yenching University, Peking, China." There are three columns on each page, quoting from each of the Gospels on the same events, arranged in sections such as "Beginnings of the Public Activity of Jesus" with subjects such as "Jesus Begins at Nazareth," "Jesus Teaches Throughout Galilee," and "Growth in Fame of Jesus."

We settle onto pillows and cushions in a circle on the floor in the seminar room, where all Bible study sessions are held, with copies of Sharman's book (the *Records* is how we refer to it) on our lap or at our side, along with our notebooks that we write in as studiously as if we were taking an honors course at Oxford. Our leaders have made a big point of telling us that scholars have "proved" that the original version of Mark did not contain the Resurrection story, which they say was "added on later." Our leader in Bible study today is Betsy, the therapist, who asks us slyly why we think Mark left out of his Gospel the stories of Jesus' birth and Resurrection. It's suggested by Betsy and endorsed by Del and some of the resident veterans (who serve as a kind of Greek chorus of affirmation to whoever is the leader, especially if members of the class don't pick up on the leader's view) that the stories of Jesus being born of a virgin and later returning from death to appear to the disciples weren't known when Mark was written, but were "made up" and "added on" later. Why else would Mark have left them out? Betsy suggests, and most everyone seems to agree, that the only logical answer is that Mark didn't know about them, and they were added later not because others had knowledge of such events, but because they created the Christian "myth" that was necessary for creating the church.

I have my own answer, though I realize it's not the "correct" one. But I say it anyway, admitting I am not a theologian and this is only my personal speculation: What if Mark chose not to include these stories because he was trying to gain credibility with an audience far beyond his own geographical and cultural boundaries, and he didn't think the masses of people who weren't on the scene would believe such miraculous events? What if he knew all about these events but didn't want to appear "sensational" or be laughed at or discredited by the scoffers of the day — the Pharisees and scribes who asked for "proof" of such happenings? What if he felt by sticking to the purely mortal stories he would win more believers? What if those accounts were actually in the documents he was using as source, but he felt they were too difficult for those who didn't have direct experience of them to understand, and so decided he would simply describe the rest of the teachings and message of Jesus?

I don't suggest these possibilities as the truth, but in response to Betsy's questions. Most of my fellow seminarians join Betsy in smiling at me with benign tolerance, as if I'm a student in a calculus class who hasn't even mastered his childhood multiplication tables, or a transfer kid from another school who just doesn't know yet how we do things here. Of course, I'm new to their teaching. It's only the first day.

, , ,

My roommate snores louder than a truck grinding into second gear. He's a handsome, enigmatic man in his forties, not a minister, but a seeker, like me — yet I feel no rapport with him. I try to be friendly, but he responds only minimally, exuding a barely subdued hostility, a kind of smoldering resentment — of me in particular and life in general. Maybe he'll loosen up. A lot of us seem jarred, or thrown off, as this whole "journey" is beginning.

In a session on the Nativity story, we are asked to identify with the characters as elements "within us" — the babe, Joseph, Mary, the shepherds, the wise men, and Herod, who is trying to kill the newborn. One of our women campers seems especially disgruntled today, explaining she has "Herod in my head, holding me back, saying this experience won't be very good." Leader Del has warned us that in this new approach to studying the life of Jesus, we are likely to encounter "resistances," and now we have an example of how such a resistance may be embodied in the context of a Bible story. He points out that "the Herod in us" is the force that is trying to resist the "new view" of Jesus that is being presented here. We are told to "work on" the "Herod in us."

The woman who confesses having "Herod in her head" says she is bothered by all the "nature" here — "there are trees, everywhere you turn." I find that's one of the comforts. That and silence. I love eating breakfast in silence. There are also periods of silence every day, an hour after the morning seminar and before lunch, another hour after the afternoon seminar and before dinner, and unless there's an evening talk, from after dinner until 8:20 the next morning, when breakfast is over. The silence is nurturing, calming, a chance to reflect that gives a different perspective so far from home, out of the usual daily routines. Unlike the "Herod lady," I enjoy the trees, birds, hills, and sky as a relief from the intensity of the seminars.

We are encouraged at the midday meal break to turn our lunch into a "stoa," which the leaders tell us is a Greek custom of discussion over a meal (my *American Heritage* dictionary defines it simply as "an ancient Greek covered walk or colonnade," but perhaps the ancient Greeks had discussions there as they munched on grape leaf lunches). The "stoa" the leaders describe is meant to continue the discussion of the morning's biblical studies, and at least one leader or assistant is at each table to steer the discussion into an affirmation of the Four Springs viewpoint. If that view isn't endorsed, lunch becomes an argument. In the interest of digestion, I suggest at my "stoa" that it seems to me each of us is our own Gospel writer — we select and edit and omit and add according to our own beliefs and preferences. Another "camper" agrees with me, but the veterans and leaders look at us both blankly, as if they simply don't hear us.

The next day Del leads us in a study of the "miracle" stories of Jesus. We focus on the story told in Matthew, Mark, and Luke of Jesus calming the storm at sea with his disciples in the boat. As recounted in Mark 4:37–41:

> And there arose a great storm of wind, and the waves beat into the boat, so that it was now full. And he was in the hinder part of the ship, asleep on a pillow: and they awake him, and say unto him, Master, carest not that we perish?
> And he arose, and rebuked the wind, and said unto the sea, Peace, be still. And the wind ceased, and there was a great calm.

In Matthew's version the disciples wake Jesus.

> And he saith unto them, Why are ye fearful, O ye of little faith? Then he arose, and rebuked the winds and the sea; and there was a great calm.

The Luke account says:

> Then he arose, and rebuked the wind and the raging of the water: and they ceased, and there was a calm.

After we look at these passages, Del asks us, "What might explain the storm ending?"

After some discussion of weather patterns, Del says we must distinguish between events that are "supernatural" and those that are "supra-natural." He says that "supernatural" would imply Divine intervention and thus be a miracle, whereas "supra-natural" would be "seeing the extraordinary in the ordinary," which is "an event within the realm of the natural that hasn't been able to be explained rationally." In this way, a natural event is made into a legend; what couldn't be explained becomes symbolic, and thus "myth."

But to return to Del's original question, what indeed might explain the storm ending?

Del's answer to what "really might have happened" is that Jesus "calmed down the men in the boat."

Had Jesus calmed the actual storm, it would have seemed a supernatural event and given him supernatural powers, while his simply calming the men in the boat and soothing their fears until the storm passed would be a rational explanation. This leaves Jesus a charismatic man, but not one with supernatural powers, not one who might be the Messiah, or savior, or Christ.

I want to debate this view, but I realize I'm naively innocent of any theology beyond what I've learned in Sunday school as a boy in Indiana, plus what I've crammed in my catch-up course on religion since returning to church. I'm not equipped to debate the meanings of the Scriptures with the trained theologians, ministers, and analysts I find myself among here. I am, though, getting their message. Just to make sure we're all getting it, after this morning's lesson on the "supra-natural" nature of Jesus calming the disciples rather than the storm, the "quote of the day" on the dining hall reads: "If we relate to the spirit, there is no need to look for miracles."

The need for miracles is connected here to the "need" for belief in Jesus as Christ (the Messiah), and next we are presented with the "Jungian" aspect of the seminar, based on a snippet extracted from a letter Jung wrote to a minister in an ongoing debate with her about Christian theology. The context is not referred to, though, when Del reads this passage from Jung's letter:

> ". . . like little lambs we follow the shepherd, naturally to good pastures. . . . Christ and his cross deliver us from our conflict, which we simply leave alone. . . . Instead of bearing ourselves, i.e., our own cross, ourselves, we load Christ with our unresolved conflicts. We 'place ourselves under his cross,' but by golly, not under our own. Anyone who does this is a heretic, self-redeemer, 'psychoanalyst' and God knows what. . . ."

This brief extract from a letter that amounts to an essay of more than fifteen hundred words in response to complex issues of criticism of Jung for trying to use "myth" in a positive way is the underpinning of the "Jungian" aspect of this seminar. When I look it up back home in the library, I find that Jung also says in the same letter, "The fact that I as a Christian struggle to unite Catholicism and Protestantism within myself is chalked up against me in true Pharisaic fashion as blatant proof of lack of character." This is not mentioned at our seminar.

That Jung is a Christian is surely relevant when we learn that the three founders and leaders of this Guild sponsoring our study of the life of Jesus are not. We learn this at an evening in which the three women therapists who founded and carry on the work of the Guild for Psychological Studies tell us about its history.

Elizabeth Boyden Howes, the principal founding mother, explains it all began when she graduated from college in 1930 and went to a seminar a friend told her about in Canada, led by Dr. Sharman, the author or "compiler" of *The Records of the Life of Jesus.* "He had left the University of Chicago, resigning because he felt too many of his colleagues began their studies with the assumption that Jesus was Christ, and that hurt their objectivity," Howes tells us. "He felt he had to separate Jesus and Christ. I studied with him four summers and then for a whole year. He knew I was grabbed by it, that it was answering a quest in my life — and it has ever since. The study turned over my life, I knew this is what I wanted to do with the rest of my life. We've tried to stay faithful to what he taught, and [enlarge] it, adding to it — silence, art, movement, and music."

Sheila Moon was a student at UCLA, trying to finish a Ph.D. in psychology, when she met Elizabeth Howes: "She gave me a whole picture of a psychological and religious knowledge — I walked out of church and was in a family. I went to the *Records* and everything flipped over for me in a positive way. I had a sense of where I was going. I realized how Jesus was using mythic things from inside himself to help people — in 1945 I led my first myth seminar."

Louella Sibbald says, "I was teaching in San Francisco at the time when I went to a seminar at the Pines and it changed the whole direction of my life. Elizabeth and Sheila asked me to stay, and we've lived and worked together for forty years now. I had begun a Jungian analysis, and we all went to Zurich to the opening of the Jung Institute. We had our analyses there — though none of us with Jung himself. I had my analysis with Mrs. Jung — for my money Mrs. Jung was the most integrated person in Zurich. We were at the first banquet and Sheila sat next to Jung himself."

Sheila says, "I walked with him along the lake; he was so gracious, generous."

Elizabeth adds, "We each had some time with Jung — immensely valuable. Jung knew nothing of Jesus the man, he was interested in 'the dogmatic Christ'" (in other words, Jesus Christ, the Christ of the Christian Scriptures).

Louella Sibbald warmly recalls the time when "we were waiting for Jung on the patio. He came from the garden with a hoe, and he was wearing a straw hat. He came and greeted us all, and with sparkling eyes, he started talking about how the arche-type of God changes."

As well as these nostalgic memories of the Guild's founding and the founders' meetings with Jung in Zurich, Elizabeth Howes frankly admits what she calls "the negative side," acknowl-edging, "We have not been accepted by the San Francisco Jung group — we were refused admission to the Institute. But creativ-ity wouldn't have come if we weren't kicked out of the Jungian cradle — although that was painful."

Speaking of the Guild seminars on Jesus, she says, "Now, two thousand years later, we may be really getting to what Jesus said — not just the church dogma. We have been so blind — through belief — we haven't had a chance to experience the real Jesus."

Asked if she's a Christian, Elizabeth answers, "Do I call myself a Christian now? I say no, but I'm deeply involved in the whole Christian development. In no way do I want to belittle Christianity."

Louella Sibbald explains: "We are *post-Christians.*"

The next day I meet privately with Louella for a session of one-on-one consultation. At the beginning of our "journey" here, we are told that for an extra fee we can have a consult with one of the founding therapists, and I sign up for one with Ms. Sibbald. I stick to my personal rather than theological issues. I speak of my confusion about Theresa, whom I love, and yet fear I can't fully defend and support. I also tell of my confusion about Lilly and canceling the rendezvous with her.

"God is amoral," the elderly post-Christian therapist says.

Oh no, I think. If this is true, I needn't have canceled my illicit, erotic vacation with Lilly!

God is amoral.

The sentence rings in my ears, taunting me. That one pro-nouncement repeats itself over and over in my brain, a challenge to the very life I am trying to lead as a Christian. But then, this founding mother is a *post*-Christian. Maybe that explains her view. Maybe if you tack a "post" onto your Christianity, you don't have to try to live by all those stodgy old rules of morality. If God is really amoral, why not do whatever you want? Damn the torpedoes, full speed ahead! But I'm not ready to adopt this new creed. If you want to go "post," why bother with Christianity at all? The question seems increasingly relevant as we delve further into the Four Springs interpretation of the New Testament.

The next morning our Bible study hones in on "discovering from the *Records*" that Jesus is not the Messiah, a major point we've been led toward. A stumbling block to this view is Peter, who has to be dealt with now. Betsy the therapist kicks off the discussion by phrasing a "Socratic" question loaded for bear: "What might be Peter's meaning now when he says to Jesus, 'Thou art the Christ'?"

A camper answers, "He means, 'You are the expected one.'"

Betsy presses that, asking, "The one to do what?"

Since none of the campers come up with the right answer, coleader Del pitches in to give it: "You are connected to God in a way that will deliver us."

Betsy, smiling: "And if that's behind the words of Peter, out of what need is that statement coming?"

"Peter's need to be relieved of responsibility," answers a camper with the brightness of a student who's come up with the answer that the teacher is looking for.

Betsy nods, smiling, and says, "And behind that is the necessity to view Jesus in a certain way — what is the necessity?"

Del says, "Peter is connected to the source but he doesn't know it, and is projecting it out on Jesus."

I write down "projection" in my notes — alert to the Jungian terminology.

A camper who still seems confused points out that Peter made his statement "with great certitude."

Now Betsy tries to get the point across: "And what is behind the need to be certain? Obviously there's a deep yearning here — for salvation, for redemption, for healing. Do we know something of this yearning, have we experienced it ourselves?"

A camper who's interpreted the clues correctly now comes up with the approved answer: "Peter is looking as I have looked in the past for someone to rescue me, make it all well."

"Yes," another camper chimes in, "Peter is 'projecting' onto Jesus to make him the source."

The "lesson" here seems to be that we who believe in Jesus as Christ are being weaklings, children, "projecting" onto Jesus to be God so he can save us, since we aren't mature and healthy enough to do it ourselves, pull ourselves up by our own bootstraps, but let Jesus "carry our cross" as Jung accuses some of his clerical critics of doing, in the little piece of his letter we were read.

At lunch I suggest to Del that there are many different ways to interpret the Gospels and come out with many different points of view. Why can't he and the other leaders acknowledge that theirs is but one out of many possible interpretations? Del says that the Bible study they use here is the same "method" that is used now in all seminaries and divinity schools, and that anyone using it would come to the same conclusions.

"You mean that if we were here with a group of Jesuits as leaders, or Pentecostals, or Southern Baptists," I ask, "they would all come up with the same answers as you do?"

"Yes," he says flatly.

Several camp assistants at my table (or "stoa") with Del are obviously irritated by my questioning "the method" and the infallibility of its use. Jan, an assistant who has previously been friendly to me now says with obvious irritation, "Some people who come here evidently don't read the catalogue that says we are going to engage in a new way of looking at the life of Jesus from a Jungian perspective."

I excuse myself and go to my cabin to read the catalogue to see if anywhere it says that this program is presented by "post-Christians" whose study concludes that Jesus was a mortal man but not the Christ. I find nothing that explains that. What I do see is the statement that what is required of the student is "the willingness to see new truth" and that "it is this willingness to put truth, no matter what the truth may turn out to be, above cherished ideas, that marks the attitude of this study."

I think of Pilate's question to Jesus: *What is truth?*

Jesus is too smart to answer.

I'm sure the "post-Christian" view of the Gospels is going to prevail here, and I wonder now how wise it is, or how fruitful it will be, for a "plain" Christian to stay. I'm tempted to go back to Boston, take in a Sunday service at King's Chapel, and go to the beach. Yet I don't want to "chicken out," and I have another consideration as well. I have taken voluminous notes on our proceedings here, knowing that some day I want to write about this experience, and if I leave before it's over, then whatever I write can be discounted or second-guessed or undermined for not being complete. It can be charged that I missed some kind of ameliorative, positive ending that at this point I can't foresee. If I'm going to stay, though, I have to tell my fellow campers how I feel, and I request a chance to speak about it at a meeting that afternoon.

I say simply that I am a believing Christian, and I feel isolated and even intimidated in what seems to me a program designed to counter that belief. Since the founding leaders have told us they are not Christians but consider themselves "post-Christians," that belief seems to be the approved one and the basis of the Bible study and exercises we are doing.

A fellow "camper" speaks up to say that her husband came here a year ago and said that four people left before the session was over because they were Christians who felt uncomfortable with this program's theology. I look at one of the leaders for a response to this, and am told, "The reason those people left was they didn't understand what we were doing."

I am told by the leaders that I, like the four Christians who left a year ago, am failing to understand the process we are engaged in. After the meeting breaks up, two other campers come up to me and say they feel as I do, but they also feel intimidated and don't want to speak about it in front of the leaders. One woman starts crying and says she is afraid. The woman who told about the four Christians who left a year ago now says nervously that maybe she shouldn't have said that in front of the group; she hopes the leaders won't be mad at her.

I seek out Jan, who until the "stoa" today has seemed friendly to me. I ask her if I get to the point where I feel I should leave, how can I get back to San Francisco? She says quite coolly she thinks there's a bus that leaves from the nearest town, several miles away through the woods and hills. I ask how I can get to the town. She shrugs and walks away.

At the next stoa one of the returning veteran assistants criticizes me for questioning the program, and others join in the attack.

Posted on the wall of the main building is the new quote of the day: "If the energy of evil is to be deflected or transformed, something or someone must suffer the impact. — Charles Willard."

I do not feel comfortable.

My discomfort grows at an afternoon session in the grape arbor, a lovely outdoor spot on our "campus," in which Elizabeth Howes delivers a talk on Jesus' journey to Jerusalem. My special discomfort is not about the subject matter or content or point of view, but rather the way in which each of us is coerced into the speaker's point of view by being required to finish certain key sentences in our own words. These sentences are so designed that by completing them you're acknowledging the validity of beliefs that may not be your own — or in my case, may be counter to your own. The effect is like having to answer the question "When did you stop beating your wife?"

One of the sentences we are asked to complete — aloud, in front of the rest of the class — is based on the snippet extracted from Jung's letter that some people "let Jesus carry their cross for them" — thus abdicating their own responsibility. The concept is translated into the idea of Jesus "carrying your journey for you" — since we're talking about his journey to Jerusalem — and the sentence we are asked to finish is "I have let Jesus carry my journey for me by . . ."

I know that the "right answers" would be ones such as "I have let Jesus carry my journey for me by believing if I prayed for his help everything would be all right and I wouldn't have to be responsible for myself." But I don't believe I've done that. I don't believe I've let Jesus "carry my cross" or "carry my journey," but rather see him as part of the journey, beside me on the journey as he is with the disciples after the crucifixion when he walks with them on the dusty road to Emmaus; or walking ahead of me as he is in Merton's poem "He Is Risen" that says, "He is going before you to Galilee."

But I don't want to get into a whole brouhaha by bringing up what I feel is the coercion built into the question, so I give an answer that is true for me, whether it is approved by these "post-Christians" or not. I say, "I have let Jesus carry my journey by shutting him out of my life for a long time, by turning away from Christ and Christianity when I became an intellectual atheist in college, by not being a cocreator with Him in my own journey for so many years."

No one speaks or comments. Elizabeth Howes moves on to the next person.

At a ceremony the next evening each of us is asked to light a candle and finish aloud (another) sentence, one that begins, "I bring light to the darkness of . . ." Some of the statements are: "I bring light to the darkness of the church . . . I bring light to the darkness of the military . . . I bring light to the darkness of a church that thinks it needs Jesus to save it . . . I bring light to the darkness that looks for a savior." When it comes my turn, I light my candle and say, "I bring light to the darkness of those who can't see the light of those they disagree with . . ."

I begin to understand the appeal of this program to the majority of my fellow campers, those with the exception of the handful of other Christians (current rather than "post"). Many of them are clergy or lay people who are disillusioned with the church as church, have been turned off by the hierarchy or orthodoxy or dogma or personal travail they've encountered in whatever their own religious community happens to be — or has been. Along with that they have lost their faith and are trying to find a new way back to some kind of spirituality.

At one of the stoas a returning veteran camper who is a disaffected nun is surprised to learn that two of my fellow Christian campers and I are active in our respective churches. "But you must surely be on the fringe of your churches, isn't it so?" She assumes anyone who's come to this seminar is at least a "fringe Christian" if not yet a complete "post-Christian."

The few of us who are "plain Christians" ask before the second Sunday if we can hold a communion service among ourselves. We are told that here communion will be observed as an individual exercise, each person going alone into the "meditation room" and making up his own communion service. I point out that since "communion" involves community, those of us Christians who wish to celebrate the Eucharist would appreciate being able to do it together, though we ask no one else to join us who doesn't want to do that.

Our request is denied.

One of the final Bible study sessions finally gets to the point of "establishing" according to the *Records* that Jesus is not the Messiah, and it's announced there will be a party that night by the swimming pool. We'll be served dinner outdoors, with candles on the tables, and everyone is to dress up in their best clothes. A delighted fellow camper claps her hands and says, "Now that we've decided there's no Messiah, we might as well celebrate!"

It's no surprise that in later Bible studies we "establish" that there was no Resurrection, and that, as one now well trained camper puts it, "It's the child within me that wants to believe in the Resurrection."

At the banquet on the last evening, the wine flows in celebration and each person gets to speak and make a toast. A minister who came with a bad case of burnout says this experience has changed his life, though he seems as angry as he is grateful. "I've been out in the world and had my ass burned," he says. A woman tells of not getting accepted for an administrative position at her church "because I didn't worship Jesus enough." This gets big laughs and cheers of sympathy. Another woman tells how this seminar has freed her "from the need for the Jesus image." One woman tipsily reveals that in a private counseling session with one of the therapists here, she's been advised to divorce her husband, and she's going to go home and do it! Cheers! A woman minister sitting next to me smiles and asks with heavy theological condescension, "Have you survived the threat to your Christology?" I assure her that my Christology and I are intact.

When I get home I write to one of my fellow Christian campers who was feeling as shaken I was by the experience, to ask how she's doing. She reports that "the first 4 days afterwards were very weepy, I felt fragile and even more as if I'm from another planet than usual. I called a friend who was there two years ago and after a few minutes he said, 'Shall I come over?' I ended up bursting into tears. . . . I realized that although they stirred up all kinds of things in me, there was really no safe place to go to share quietly and integrate it carefully."

When I get back to Boston, the first thing I do is head for Glastonbury Abbey, where I take communion every day and join the monks in song and prayer at each of the daily offices.

The sacred music and prayer, the quiet, the Eucharist, are like balm to the soul. Being here is like "spiritual recovery." When I speak of my experience to one of the Benedictine brothers, he says, "You sound battered." I am.

The work of est and Werner Erhard is accused of "brain-washing," but never once in those programs — not even in the nightmarish Six Day Advanced Course, with its leader's personal bullying — was I asked to believe something I didn't believe, was I told that there was only one answer and theirs was the right one. I was asked, rather, to "try on" their answer, never to take it as "the truth" but to see if it fit, if it seemed to work for you, was suitable and right for your own life and experience. Otherwise, throw it away. Only at what was advertised as a Jungian view of the life of Jesus was I told there was but one way to believe and asked in public to repeat something implying a belief I didn't hold. Having people finish sentences based on a belief in which they don't believe (like "I let Jesus carry my cross for me because . . .") is immoral, and seems to me a prime example of what is meant by "brain-washing."

I learn that labels are not reliable. I presumed that anything called "Jungian" would be "liberal" or "open" in its approach. But anyone can label themselves however they want — as "Jungian," "Freudian," "liberal," "conservative," "free-thinking," "humanist," or whatever — and then do whatever that means to *them,* which may not be what it means to you, or even to the world at large. I learn to ask more questions before committing to a program, especially ones away from home — and to ask lay people as well as professionals about it. My own minister and my two minister friends who felt they had benefited from this program are graduates of theological seminaries, knowledgeable and sophisticated about the latest methods and theories of Bible study, and so were able to put the Four Springs viewpoint into perspective, uphold their own beliefs in debates, perhaps even test them, and take what they wanted from the experience.

"The multimedia exercises at Four Springs, using art, music, collage, and writing to give a deeper personal experience of the Bible stories helped me 'get into scripture,'" the Reverend Carl Scovel tells me, and he brought those kinds of techniques to his classes at King's Chapel. "My reservations about Four Springs," he adds, "were that their scriptural scholarship — what you found so disturbing — was hopelessly outdated, and on top of that, dogmatic. But I was willing to set that aside for what I got out of the 'experiential' exercises." The Bible workshop leader and minister Walter Wink says, "I owe a huge debt to Four Springs for putting together techniques for experiencing Bible study. I had to swallow some of the leaders telling me to think for myself and then jumping all over me when I came to different conclusions than they did, but I put up with the bad aspects of it because the good parts were so valuable to me."

In my own naïvete and lack of theological grounding, I wasn't able to set aside that "post-Christian" Biblical scholarship and benefit from the kinds of exercises at Four Springs I'd enjoyed before in classes given by the Reverends Carl Scovel and Walter Wink. I had no idea that the kind of "post-Christian" Biblical scholarship taught at Four Springs was considered outdated by people as knowledgeable as Carl Scovel. At Four Springs it was presented as the latest thing, as well as the "truth."

From all this I learn *again* something else I had learned before — that just because something is "religious" or "about religion" doesn't necessarily mean it's going to be the right thing for you in your own spiritual quest.

Although these are uncomfortable lessons, I'm happy to learn that my religious faith cannot be "brain-washed" out of me. I also confirm my journalistic feeling that to write about such an experience you need to stay the course and keep extensive notes, and I feel in this sense it was worth it, to serve as a warning to seekers, not in the abstract but with a specific personal experience of such an ordeal. Now that I've done it, I don't feel I have to subject myself to such an experience again. This also teaches me how crucial it is in my own talks and workshops to be as sensitive as possible to the beliefs of others and never to attack the core spirit of a sincere believer in order to try to impose your own views. Trying to bully someone into a belief opposed to their own faith is a kind of theological sadism, a form of spiritual rape.

Chapter 6

THE WEDDING

———◆———

AFTER MY TWO SUMMER-CAMP-FROM-HELL SESSIONS — the est-ian Six Day, and then a year later the post-Christian Jungians — I must have filled my quota for drama for a while. That fall of 1986, life settles into a blessedly regular routine of writing, church, and friends. Now that my nonaffair with Lilly is over, I'm back with Theresa, both of us seeming more at ease and comfortable with one another after surviving the Six Day and Lilly (or the threat of Lilly).

Neither Theresa or I talk about "commitment," that loaded word that makes men panic, and I assume she's content to go along as we always have, "commuting" between her apartment and mine on foot or by bicycle, enjoying each other and the city and church and friends and est seminars at the Forum offices just as we always have, but now that there's less tension between us, everything seems more relaxed.

The mood of harmony continues into the New Year of '87, and we're getting along so smoothly now I wonder if this post-Six Day, post-Lilly era is echoing a time in my own parents' relationship. After twenty-five years of marriage they were divorced, and a year later got married again — to each other. Their "second marriage" was as peaceful, harmonious, and mutually supportive as their earlier years were fractious. It was as if they had finally accepted one another, with all their faults and virtues, and they lived together with mutual satisfaction.

Is a miniature version of that kind of "second time around" acceptance happening now with me and Theresa? I'm pretty much taking our relationship for granted, concentrating fully on writing the book that began with the article "Returning to Church," which was published in the *New York Times Magazine* in Christmas week of '85. At Christmas a year later, I realize a whole year has passed and I've only written fragments of the book that's supposed to continue and enlarge the story. I've justified delaying the real writing by telling myself events like the Jungian Jesus seminar are essential "research," but now I realize I have to hunker down to work, the disciplined daily routine that writers will find any reason in the world to put off until they feel they have to start now or they haven't a prayer of meeting their deadline (and prayers, no matter how fervent, won't do it).

Finishing the book is my New Year's resolution for '87, and knowing I have no more excuses to put it off, I finally get into that wonderful rhythm of writing every day and feeling the whole thing coming together. Now that I've got in the groove of working, the last thing I want is to rock the boat with any big life change. Even so, I'm beginning to think about a subject that is usually farthest from my mind: marriage.

Suddenly it's in the air, as I hear about upcoming marriages of friends. The oldest son of my oldest friends in Boston, Shaun and Dorothy O'Connell, is getting married in April, and Robert Manning, the former editor of the *Atlantic Monthly*, who's been a good friend since the days of my writing there, is planning to remarry after the painful loss of his wife, Margaret, who died of cancer several years before. The lovely woman he is planning to marry is named, coincidentally, Theresa.

So what's the matter with me? Why don't I marry my own Theresa? We've survived some pretty big personal earthquakes now, and we're going into the fourth year of our relationship. She's never been married, and though I know she wants to be, she's stopped talking about it, which, in my perverse male psyche, seems to make me feel free to consider it. I have such a terrible record with marriage — two brief failures — I've sworn never to do it again.

But hey, I'm not the same person now. Am I? At least I don't drink anymore, which surely gives me a better chance, and besides, I'm a Christian who not only goes to church but takes an active part in it, studying and even writing about religion and God. Isn't marriage with a woman I love the logical consequence of this spiritual journey I'm on, that I'm writing about? I'll be fifty-five years old in May. What am I waiting for? The effects of the Six Day debacle have receded, and now that Theresa and I are back on our home ground, into our familiar routines, neither of us seem as vulnerable as we did in that hostile kingdom ruled by Gib.

This whole conversation is only taking place in my own head, however. I haven't mentioned such thoughts to Theresa yet, much less the scary word *marriage*. I'm waiting till I've got it sorted out, and I'm absolutely sure it's the right thing to do, for both of us. I know, I know, I'm deciding what's "the right thing" for her without bothering to consult her about it. But listen, hold on a minute, I'm about to broach the subject.

I almost brought it up a few weeks ago. When she's leaving for work in the morning with her backpack after spending the night, the whole situation of our living between her place and mine and carrying our clothes and belongings back and forth seems absurd. But all I say is, "Listen, we've got to talk about our lives."

She laughs.

"This *is* our lives!" she says.

Several thousand years of Zen wisdom are summed up in that sentence. Theresa is wiser, as usual, than me.

So maybe I'll bring it up tonight — how maybe we should live together, even think about getting married sometime. We weren't going to see each other till the weekend, but she called this afternoon to say she has something she wants to talk to me about. Sure, I say, come over after work. Won't she be shocked if she brings up the subject of commitment, maybe even living together, and instead of blowing it off, I'm even willing to talk about *marriage!*

I sit on the couch in the living room, but Theresa doesn't sit down beside me. She takes a seat in a chair across the room, facing me. She says she has met a man from her past, and she's decided to have an affair with him. She knows I don't want to get married again, and she doesn't want to just keep going back and forth between apartments the rest of her life, without even having a commitment.

"Okay," I say.

It seems ordained, like a piece falling into place. I don't tell her I've just started thinking about the possibility of marriage, because I'm not even sure I can make the commitment and stick to it. I feel I owe her this freedom, this chance to strike out on her own. I still love her, as I always will, but besides feeling shock at her announcement, I feel relief, which makes me think I might not have had the courage to do it after all. Though it sounds completely contradictory, I'm relieved because I couldn't bear to disappoint her, to find that whatever kept me from staying in a marriage twice before would still prevent me from doing it now. Given my record, I believe that deep down, I love her too much to marry her.

Silently, as if in a sacred ritual, we make love that night for the last time.

Our relationship continues much as it was before, but without the physical intimacy. Since the man Theresa is seeing now lives in another city, she and I continue to spend a lot of time together, doing pretty much all the things we always have, except we are no longer physically intimate. Others have misunderstood our relationship, which I know now is lifelong, lasting beyond romance, deeper than geographic distance. Those who know us well honor the bond we have, while some have been jealous or suspicious of it, judging it by the standards of the world, as expressed by Gib when he labeled me a dirty old man.

I think of a passage from a beautiful book by the late John Williams, a writer and friend whose novel *Stoner* tells of a love affair between a man in his forties and a woman in her twenties. When the man is told he's old enough to be the young woman's father, these are his thoughts:

> It had not occurred to him how he must appear to an outsider, to the world. For a moment he saw himself as he must thus appear. . . . He had a glimpse of a figure that flitted through smoking room anecdotes, and through the pages of cheap fiction — a pitiable fellow going into his middle age, misunderstood by his wife, seeking to renew his youth, taking up with a girl years younger than himself, awkwardly and apishly reaching for the youth he could not have, a fatuous, garishly got up clown at whom the world laughed out of discomfort, pity and contempt. He looked at this figure as closely as he could; but the longer he looked, the less familiar it became. It was not himself that he saw, and he knew suddenly that it was no one.

, , ,

Working on the book *Returning* continually consumes a bigger part of my life. I am in the rhythm of the writing now and I love it. This nearly trancelike state comes at a certain point in every book, and it's as if the book itself takes over and you are simply following it, recording what it's telling you. It's a rhythm I recognize in sports sometimes; I saw it when Tom Seaver pitched for the Red Sox, a purity and precision of form, a regular delivery that flows, like a leap and dunk of Michael Jordan, or the symmetry of a pure shooter like Glen Rice connecting on a three.

In writing and art as well as in sports there's a "zone," and finding it is bliss, a blessing. It's wonderfully described when I interview the San Francisco sculptor Ann Honig Nadel about the "miracle" of creation. "You have to work to learn the skills first," she says, "but then you come to a point where something else takes over, where something is coming out of you that's not you. . . . In my heart of hearts, I know 'I' don't do it. This is a miracle. It's the only reason I believe in God."

When I finish writing a book I am usually exhausted, mentally and psychically, and want to just look out the window for hours on end, or get on a plane to some exotic destination. When I reach the end of *Returning,* though, and send the manuscript to the publisher at the end of summer of '87, I have a different reaction. Like a light coming on in my head, the thought occurs that the book was born in the minister's course on religious autobiography at King's Chapel, and I have an impulse to "give it back," to offer such a class for people who have no church or synagogue but still are seeking, wanting to explore the spiritual dimension of their own experience.

I propose a course in "spiritual autobiography" to the Boston Center for Adult Education, which is housed in a beautiful old mansion on Commonwealth Avenue in the Back Bay. There's a warm, traditional atmosphere of community and learning in the high-ceilinged rooms and the graceful stairways. I've taken courses there myself, in Tai Chi, and French cooking (a friend says "Those cancel each other out!"). The Center accepts my proposal and puts it in the catalogue. I say I'd like to have a long table and chairs for about fifteen people, the ideal maximum for such a class. On the night the first session is held, I walk into the room and find fifteen people sitting at the table.

It begins. Several people from the class invite me to give a talk or a course at their own church or adult ed center in a neighboring town. I have no idea that leading such workshops will take me throughout the country and to Mexico and Northern Ireland in the coming years. As always, what you give is given back, more abundantly than you could ever imagine.

, , ,

The book *Returning* is scheduled for publication in April of '88, and a month or so before that I am honored to deliver a sermon at King's Chapel. The church is full, and so am I, feeling a holy connection with my grandfather, a Baptist minister in Shelbyville, Kentucky, and Columbia, South Carolina, who died when my father was twelve years old. I am named after him — William Daniel Wakefield — and I wear his signet ring, have worn it ever since my father gave it to me when I was twelve.

There's a time in my childhood when I want to be a minister myself, after those inspiring Bible study classes given by the young couple from Kentucky, and feeling even then some connection with this grandfather whom I never knew, but whose spirit I feel informing me, even coming through me. Standing at the minister's lectern in this hallowed, historic church and speaking to the assembled congregation that includes Theresa as well as friends from outside the church who, like Shaun and Dorothy O'Connell, have come to wish me well, I feel I am linked to my grandfather's spirit, that I am here at this place and time fulfilling not only my own destiny but also his, who was cut short by an early death.

Across the street from the church and down a few blocks on Tremont is the historic Old Granary Burying Ground, where a simple slate marker bears the name of John Wakefield, a shipwright, of Boston, who died in 1667. According to family records he is the first Wakefield who came to America, migrating from England. When I started going to King's Chapel, I made it a practice to stop by his grave on my way back home and spend a moment in silence, feeling somehow his proximity to it helped me find the church to which I returned. Bones and spirit, family and history, all seem to be part of the movement in my own life that brings me to stand in the pulpit of King's Chapel.

When *Returning* is published, I'm asked to speak and lead more workshops at other churches and also synagogues and adult education centers around the country, and in doing so I feel, as Annie Nadel put it in speaking of her sculpting, that "something is coming through me that is not me." I am simply the transmittal machine, the instrument, the empty pipe through which the spirit flows to others. This is another kind of service — being the servant of the word, the Spirit — and is genuinely humbling as well as exhilarating.

Though I don't consider myself a minister — and I have no desire to become a "real" minister by going to divinity school and following that career path — the service of speaking and teaching seems a kind of ministry. Doing it, I know the feeling George Bernard Shaw described when he said, "This is the true joy of life, the being used for a purpose recognized by yourself as a mighty one. . . ." The "purpose" I recognize in such work is not to convert people to my belief, but to help them find their own, which may be linked to mine or to some other tradition, to come awake to the spirit within them, the great quest.

, , ,

Kicking through red and gold leaves on my way up Mt. Vernon Street that autumn of '88, I feel filled, warmed by the soft October sun and childhood memories of Indiana afternoons suffused with similar golden light and a sense of peace and promise. Everything seems more alive and glowing in the light of faith, and now it seems strange how long it lay dormant, slipping away in adolescence and seemingly snuffed in college and the literary life of Greenwich Village in the fifties, when Hemingway's "Nada, who art in nada" replaced the Lord's Prayer in my private dogma. Sacramental spirits of alcohol were poured in the name of Papa Hemingway and F. Scott Fitzgerald, the deities who preached — with Dylan Thomas, our drunken poet priest — to not go gentle, there are no second acts, and so we beat on, boats against the current. . . . This was the dogma of despair I proudly subscribed to, creed of enlightened intellectuals, the Enlightenment's leftover liturgy. Now it all seems unreal to me in a time when I no longer numb myself with booze as I did for a quarter of a century, write about faith, and give workshops in spiritual autobiography. (F. Scott and Papa roll in their graves, contemporary colleagues' eyeballs roll upward.)

I'm teaching a creative writing seminar at Emerson College in the Back Bay, easy walking distance from my apartment on the Hill, traveling to give the spiritual autobiography workshops several weekends a month, and teaching another evening session of it during the week at the Boston Center for Adult Education. I lead a new group there whose work inspires me with the idea for another book, *The Story of Your Life: Writing a Spiritual Autobiography.* I'm also writing essays, articles, and book reviews and enjoying friends and neighbors, but there's no new woman in my life.

Since Theresa announced her decision to begin a relationship with another man in the spring of '87, I haven't been involved in any sexual relations. Perhaps because my comfortable companionship with Theresa continues much as it was before but without the physical intimacy, I don't feel pressured to run around and try to find a new girlfriend. The few times I go on "dates," I don't have any desire to go farther. It dawns on me now that without any conscious intention to do so, I've been celibate for a year and a half, which feels like the right and natural thing for this period.

Rather than feeling frantic about not being in a relationship, I feel relaxed and trusting, willing to let things unfold instead of trying to rush off in search of some grand new adventure. More than I ever have in my life, I feel in tune, with God and the universe, as if I am really on "the Way," following the path. And now it leads me home again to Indiana.

In a few days I go to give a workshop at a church in Terre Haute and then on to Indianapolis for a hometown visit. I'll see the good friends of my high school gang as I always do, and also catch up with a girl (as I knew her then and still think of her now) who graduated a year after I did, and left to live on the West Coast when I headed East.

I met Sally again at a reunion of three high school classes ('50, '51, and '52) a few years ago, and we pledged a hometown meeting if we ever got back at the same time. She calls now to ask if by chance I'll be out in Indy next week, and by chance I will! Is it just coincidence (or the more intellectually respectable term "synchronicity" coined by Jung) or is it fate, destiny, karma, kismet? Surely it is part of the path I am on, the spiritual journey I write about — The Way, God's Plan — that leads me to Sally, putting us both, from our opposite coasts, back in the middle of the map in our old hometown at the same time.

When I look at her, I see first the mid-fifties woman who still has a great body, thick dark hair brushed just below her neck, only a few wrinkles around the mouth (for God's sake she isn't a kid anymore), and those big almond eyes, wondrous deep eyes; and then I see superimposed on her the image I carry of the girl I met the summer before the seventh grade.

Just thirteen she was, but seemed — as young girls do — older and wiser than any boy, glamorous beyond any boy's expectations, with glossy rich hair hanging straight to just below her shoulders as she walked toward me in shorts and a halter top, barefoot, long tan legs like a model or movie star. My breath came swifter and shorter as she smiled, friendly, but of course she had a boyfriend already, a year or two older, a football star on his way to high school and glory ("Natch," as we say then). Such a prize was way out of reach for a flat-footed, uncoordinated kid her own age whose own highest high school fame (such as it was) came from recording the exploits of bigger and stronger boys on the field and the court, the diamond and track.

But as A. E. Housman predicted, many of the lightfoot lads now lay by brooks too broad for leaping; yet some of the slow ones, the turtles, are still crawling on in their unwieldy way, survivors, accomplishers, accumulators, recognized and even respected at last for waddling up to some minor summit of their own small world — or political peaks of power, like Kissinger, bombing whole nations to bits and winning a classy society gal! The ultimate revenge of the nerds: getting the right girl.

As well as romantic attraction, we share an understanding beyond the imagining of strangers, the intimacy of two who grew up just a few neighborhoods away from one another on the same side of town, went to the same high school, and later left, in different directions but far, each making a mark of some merit in our work.

The idea that all this is fated and right takes root and grows after just the one meeting (pristine at first, only eyes messaging), and romance blooms with distance as we write and call across the continent all that fall and into the winter. Her voice sets me spinning fantasies of lifelong (however much is left of it, anyway) partnership, a joining together of like minds and experienced bodies, of spirit and flesh combined and melded the way it ideally can be, how God intended. I hang up after her phone calls smiling, then whistling, walking out onto the bricks of Mt. Vernon Street light as air, floating with the promise of awaited fulfillment. We make plans to meet again in the New Year of '89 in what we both feel is the sacred space of the old hometown.

She's arrived first and meets me at the airport, wearing gray sweats and her hair pulled back to a ponytail, looking to me as lovely as a storybook princess. We cling to one another and kiss,

kiss, kiss, smiling and laughing as we clutch each on the way to the luggage.

In a hotel room in the city we were born in, loving and making love, we exchange favorite lines of songs and poems, stories of childhood peopled with places and characters both of us know. In the joy of it all I say I want her to come and live with me, but I know she's a good girl from Indiana so we probably ought to get married, and she agrees. We laugh with delight, loving.

We've come so far, in years and miles, accomplishment and experience, disillusionment personal and professional, past marriages for me and for her the death of the husband a few years before who fathered her now grown children. We still harbor the mutual hope of all good grownups to "find the right person" for sharing a life, or what's left at last to people in their fifties, the golden time. Surely it's golden for people like us who keep in shape in the modern manner with conscious good diet and exercise, programs to prolong time itself at peak performance level; marathoners of maturity. She's wrapping up her own fine career in the coming months, and I just want to keep on writing, which surely can only benefit from being happily mated. Married people even live longer!

In the clean cold air of those precious days we drive out to places we love from childhood — Lilly's apple orchard, where the cider that flowed each fall was a golden brown elixir for natives, the wine of the gods. We drink from the paper cups held below spigots of oaken barrels and feel how lucky we are to live in this place, this "land of milk and honey, in the central west" we sang of in our high school anthem, a sacred hymn of adolescence, sung while standing still, hats off, cold breath blowing clouds before the start of a football game.

We giggle as we tromp the old streets of our Broad Ripple neighborhood, where hip new restaurants with nouvelle cuisine have replaced old hamburger joints, and five-and-ten stores

given way to espresso bars. We giggle over cappuccinos, thinking how perplexed our parents would be to witness such unfamiliar "foreign" potions served in our own hometown, our very
neighborhood. We hold hands and go visit high school friends,
surprising them by our being together, our obvious joy in one
another, not hiding our love as we hug and smooch. Yes, we
have rediscovered each other from the past and now we want a
future together.

Why wait?

"I guess at your age, you know what you want," says one of
her younger relatives, believing wisdom comes with longevity,
and trying to rationalize our bombshell announcement of plans
to get married after only three days of being together. It's January; we'll do it in June. Other relatives are not so sanguine, signaled by their short responses and scowls. Killjoys we think,
people who don't know the flash of revelation, the dynamite
blast of truth.

Sally says she's the luckiest woman in the world.

I smile, boasting my own good fortune at the same time my
bloated ego is boosted.

My many dear friends — whom I think of as family, having
none left by blood besides scattered cousins — greet the news
with a mixture of winsome wishes for happiness and loving
relief (at last, maybe he's finally settling down, and at his age,
none too soon!). Only one friend responds with questions
instead of congratulations.

"How long have you known her?" this fellow Nieman Fellow
and friend of many years is bold enough to ask.

"Like I told you, all my life — since grade school, for God's
sake! Isn't that long enough?"

"I mean, how much time have you been together — since you
met again?"

"Long enough to know it's great. She's a beautiful woman —
she always was, even in seventh grade."

But still that pesky Nieman Fellow friend is on the line with his picky, journalistic probing. What does he think he's doing, treating a beautiful love story like it's Watergate! What kind of friend is he, anyway?

"I thought you were never getting married again," he bores on. "What makes you think this will be any different than the others?"

Oh, that bastard is twisting the knife. The others. Plural. Only a few close friends like this newspaper character know there've been two. One of them I don't count. I learned that kind of counting from a novelist friend who after a decade of heart-to-heart talk of his past let slip he had also been married before World War II — in addition to the current wife and the two before her, which added up to four, not three — but when confronted on his math, he explained of his earliest matrimony, "I don't count that one." He was young; it was brief.

In like manner I discount my second — a wholly impulsive city hall marriage, even though I lack the excuse of youth (thirty-six is "old enough to know better"), but I do have brevity on the side of my argument for cancellation — we passionate, lust-driven lovers start arguing on the way from the courthouse to the celebration lunch and never stop, finally exhausting ourselves a little more than six months later and calling it quits — a draw, no victor, losers in both corners. The woman friend who stood up with us in the civil ceremony hears of our travail toward the end and advises, "Maybe you should cut your losses." Loss was all we had.

Becoming uneasy and irritated with my journalistic friend's investigative questioning, I cut short the conversation, say goodbye, and don't call this Watergating pal back till after the wedding, after it all is done. Why tune in to negativity? That becomes my excuse (unconscious policy?) in the trancelike days and months ahead; only seek advice from those who are likely to feed back positive reinforcement. No need to call the therapist I've consulted off and on in times of crisis over the past five years; she'd probably start some professional probing, a psychiatric version of my newsman friend's investigative journalism style. Besides, I tell myself, psychiatry is part of my past, the wisdom of the Old Way, and now I'm launched on the spiritual journey, the wisdom of the heart and more deeply the soul: "the sequence that culminates in faith" as Eliot's "religious quest" was described by biographer Lyndall Gordon; it's being on the path, "on the gleaming way" as the Navajos beautifully put it. Let's not tarnish the shine with psychological jargon, I tell myself, nor darken the way with negative tones.

After all, I'm in spiritual direction with a brilliant Episcopal priest, which means that every two weeks or so I meet with this articulate youngish man and talk about prayer, reading Scripture, looking for the movements of the Spirit in daily life, discerning the path within the thicket of possibilities, choices, temptations, wrong turns. Discernment. That's the key, the mystery, the subject that so entrances and baffles me.

How do we know when it's God?

I feel sure when I meet Sally and declare my love that I've arrived where I started and know the place for the first time. No further discernment is necessary. It's obvious this is the way, this marriage that will heal the past, mend my old collegiate-through-middle-age rebellion against my own roots, and most of all maybe please my parents at last — even though they're no longer alive. I know they'd be happy to see me settled, with a Nice Girl yet, and from the old hometown, a "girl next door" grown to a Good Woman. Wherever and however my parents are — somewhere, in whatever form they take — somehow, they'll know.

Everyone agrees with the wisdom of my choice, celebrates my good fortune — at least all those I tell. After the discomforting conversation with my skeptical journalistic friend, I become more careful whom I share the good news with, not wanting any more questioning to shade the brightness of my upward path, treading as I am in seven-league boots through clouds; I'm high.

Enthusiasm grows when Sally comes to Boston and wins my friends with her genuine charm — or anyway, all but one is won. The exception is understandable, but still troubling — an awkward situation with my former lover and still dear friend Theresa. She is shocked and disturbed when I tell how I met this high school sweetheart (for that's what Sally has now become in the growing myth, though in fact we never dated back then) and found this bond that seems "the right thing," the inevitable thing, in the rocky (now smoothing out) path of my already twice divorced life.

After breakfast and church with Theresa, I take her to a Brigham's on Boylston, a lonely, echoing, godforsaken place on a Sunday, and over cups of cooling coffee she says I shouldn't do it, not because she thinks that she and I will ever be together again as we were before, but I shouldn't do it for my own sake. Antsy now, I shift in my seat, consult my watch, and pay the check. Before we leave, Theresa says something that sticks in my mind, no matter how hard I try to push it out.

"I'm afraid," she says.

Jittery now, I hurry home, throw off my coat, and dial up Sally, hitting at once the high pitch of elation we strike in our long distance love calls, like singers performing grand opera arias, going higher and higher.

, , ,

Flickers of doubt come like shadows quickly cast by a fire, then are gone. Questions arise and are pushed away. O ye of little faith! A date is set — the minister is busy in June so May is chosen. No time for delay. No one is getting any younger — read the obituaries. People I knew, in public or personal life, not only older but sometimes younger, are gone in a poof, not only of AIDS but of "natural causes" like strokes and cancer, failure of lungs and liver and heart. Even with bypasses, triple, quadruple, you can't bypass the end forever, so why not grab what's left, together?

It's still hard to believe I'll really die, and if I live to ninety (as planned), I have thirty-three years left (a lifetime!) and yet — and yet — sometimes a fact of mortality slips past my ego-shield. When I read the obit of a beautiful actress just a few years older than me (one whose image had once been an object of my single-handed lust), I notice none of the write-ups say she was cut down prematurely, in the flower of her youth, or even suggest she's gone before her time. Oh no, it seems understood her time had come, she'd had her run. Curtain. Could it be this quick? This soon to be over? Are the credits about to roll? Whatever you're going to do — hurry!

I fly to Sally's West Coast for three or four days, then she to my Boston, making plans; a party for the hometown crowd — show them I'm stable at last, finally doing the right thing, not only marrying, but to one of them, one they know and like and admire, one with brains and beauty who's made it in the world beyond. Approval — at last! Weighed besides such considerations, man-woman misunderstandings seemed small, and whenever they occur (as they more and more do), I reassure myself this is my path, this holy rite, ordained by God, fate, circumstance, mother, country, church, the very path of Spirit I now speak about in public, write about, help others find. (How much more clearly could God set out the signs for me? What do I want, an itinerary, traced on a map by some angelic Triple-A?)

An author I've never met sends me a new book whose subject she thinks will interest me now that I'm writing and speaking about such matters as God and faith. It's called *Shiloh,* and it is not about the Civil War battle but a cult named after the biblical site at a turn-of-the-century town in Maine. The leader is a well-intentioned, charismatic minister who hears the voice of God — he deeply believes this — and following sincerely what he takes to be instructions from the Divine, leads hundreds of people to a dire assortment of disasters, deaths, deprivations, a whole tragic history, a fatal footnote to divine misguidance, all in the name of God, Jesus, Christianity, Light, and Truth.

I start reading the book on a brief vacation with Sally, and seeing in fifty-some pages that it's going to recount and document the true life story of someone who believes with all his heart he is hearing the voice of God and in fact is deluded, deceives himself and in doing so deceives others, causing great hurt and pain to many — all with the best intentions in the world — I close the book and put it down. I don't want to read such a story, a story that raises possible doubts about my own belief that I am following a "spiritual path" to the altar. The lesson of this true story seems to be that intelligent, devout people, with the best will in the world may in fact be totally lacking in discernment, may actually be deceiving themselves and bringing pain to those around them, people they care about and love. The implications are too upsetting.

I try to forget about *Shiloh*, like I try to forget about the woman I meet at a conference who is soon to be married but whose very presence anyway strikes me in the gut like a cannon blast of love and desire and lust, a knowledge that if she'd turn and say, "Follow me," I'd walk away from everything else, as surely (but hardly as nobly) as Peter and Andrew put down their nets and followed Jesus, forsaking all else. If that woman can affect me that way, should I be getting married to another? Well, aren't all men prey to such feelings, didn't even Jimmy Carter lust in his heart? The trick is simply to keep it in your heart (or, as one of America's great writers advised me in one such circumstance, drawing on the lore of men's wisdom through the ages, "Keep it in your pants").

Wedding plans progress as both Sally and I admit deep doubts to one another, fall into painful silences and yet keep going, as if we've boarded some powerful express train that's carrying us inevitably, surely, down the track to the altar, without any stops, picking up speed and momentum with each passing day so the very thought of getting off seems increasingly impossible the closer it comes to the reckoning. Invitations sit on a table in my kitchen for more than a week as I stare at them, pass them, neglect them, realizing as long as they sit there a choice is still possible, a leap from the hurtling train; but one bright day, robotlike, I pick them up with blanked-out mind and shove them in a mailbox, done. What the hell, it will be a great party, a chance to see the old gang from high school again.

While plans are being made for catering, music, luncheons, and dinners, for the big event, even a European honeymoon, little if anything is said about life after vows, or living arrangements, except an agreement that she will come to my city, live in my crowded apartment, a two-bedroom with one overstuffed as an office and workspace, the other a smallish, low-ceilinged cave with the basics: bed, chest of drawers, TV. When gently asked by a wondering friend what plans I've made for Sally's coming to live there, I say I'm planning to get another chest of drawers. Sally tells the curious friend and his wife she knows there's lots to be done; I don't even have tea towels! I confessed to not knowing what they are. Okay, then, drawers and tea towels; that ought to do it.

"Do you want the kind of woman who wears little dresses with spaghetti straps?" Sally teasingly asks as the date draws near, and I smile and shake my head, denying such frivolous taste, knowing I am lying (mostly to myself), just another victim of the old male American madonna-and-whore split, wondering again why America can't be as sensible as France, at least the France of history and literature, where mistress and wife are honorable categories, acknowledged and accepted; but thoughts like that at the close of the eighties are not just politically incorrect but border on the culturally criminal. Besides, such thoughts lead down the twisting paths of my sexual fantasies, the last territory I want to explore now. I want to close the door on it now, get this marriage thing done.

On her last visit before coming back for It, the Big Day (which is only two weeks away), Sally and I fight, cry, express our doubts, make up, go on, pray together, yet still neither of us seeks any outside professional help, advice, counsel. When I see my spiritual director, I find myself sliding over the rough parts (wanting his approval), playing to the Father's own genuine pleasure in my plan to settle down, tie the sacred knot, join with a fine woman of my own age and background in what should surely be a mutually rewarding path, a proper and fitting finale to the journey.

But one morning I wake so troubled I tell Sally I have to seek advice, talk to someone about all this. Unable to reach my spiritual director, I bolt out the door and down the street to my minister's house (the idea of calling the therapist I've worked with off and on the past few years doesn't even enter my mind), catch him in the kitchen, say I must talk, and the sheer panic in my voice is so obvious he takes me back to his study, cancelling other plans. This looks like an emergency.

The minister is also a friend as well as a spiritual mentor and teacher, and a good neighbor a few blocks away on Beacon Hill. In the sanctity of his study, I bawl. I cry like I haven't cried in years, a flood of tears, a pouring out of the dammed-up fears I haven't acknowledged about the upcoming vows (which the Rev has agreed to officiate at) and about my divorces, the failures to live successfully in such a state as matrimony. My love and concern and fear for Theresa spill out as well; her "I'm afraid" still rings in my head like a knell of doom. I lament having hurt her for not even knowing she once had wanted us to marry, for being so blind and hurting other women I loved in the past, either because I didn't marry them or (even worse) because I did! What a burden, what a mess, what a maze, a bottomless conundrum that no amount of early (in my twenties) Freudian psychoanalysis or later (mostly positive) therapy has helped to heal (so why return to it now, I reason), nor evidently, in recent years, genuinely uplifting, energizing programs of human potential and personal growth, nor prayer or faith, retreats of silence or community, nor spiritual direction or physical disciplines like Tai Chi or yoga, nor exercise and abstinence from alcohol. I've tried it all and feel much better and stronger and alive and filled than I ever have, yet I'm still in the dark when it comes to this crucial issue, this challenge or opportunity or trap, this scheduled marriage to which I'm hurtling at breakneck, breathtaking speed.

It's not the Rev's style to give advice, to tell parishioners to do this or that, but rather to listen, to ask questions, be present to their pain, and pray, with them and for them, not with ostentation or dramatic hoopla but quietly, plainly, sincerely. All this he does as I pour out my fear and confusion, and in his presence, after almost an hour, I grow calm, pull myself together, feel better for letting it out, and return to Sally to say "It's okay. I'm over whatever it was." She's skeptical at first, then glad. A similar session that night with the Rev solidifies my resolve.

I have another idea, too, a further way to seek some spiritual confirmation of the forthcoming vows. I take Sally to the Benedictine monastery where I've gone on retreat to wrestle with the question of discernment that now looms so personal and large.

"How do we know when it's God?"

Do I think we'll find a sign, a splash of sunlight poured over us like a blessing, a voice booming down from on high saying, "Get thee to the altar, slacker," or "Turn back before it's too late, you fool!" I don't expect such specific guidance (too easy, we have to discern for ourselves), but I hope that in this sacred space of chapel and woods I love, a place that's been a true sanctuary for me in the past, where I find solace and comfort of soul on solitary overnight retreats as well as weekends with members of my church, that Sally and I might find some ease in our growing tumult, some light might be shed on the murky path that was once so clear.

We sit on the ground and pray. Our emotions soar, fall, settle, slide. Everything is clear. Nothing is clear. We laugh at our own torment. A couple of loons, she says. Oh well. Let's keep going where we're headed. We'll see.

Both of us are assured that prewedding jitters are par for the course, a standard rite of passage, yes, for people past fifty as well as for teens, it shows you're still young at heart, and the heart has its reasons. (What are they?) Still, with days counting down the week of the wedding, a factor more frightening than mere anxiety or nerves rocks me. Sally and I return from a theater evening in Cambridge and play the answering machine, hearing a pained and painful message from Theresa saying I'm no longer her friend. There is fear in her voice. I feel numb, say nothing, and get undressed for bed. Sally's there reading a book.

I try reading a book of my own, but can't concentrate. I say something to Sally — nothing with any particular import, but my voice doesn't sound like my own. It's deeper, darker, sonorous, as if coming out of some echo chamber. Sally puts down her book and asks, "What's wrong? You don't sound like yourself." When I answer, it's still not my voice but "the other," as if someone else's voice is coming out of my mouth. I speak again to make sure I'm hearing the same scary, unfamiliar sound, seemingly coming from the depths of — where? And it's still there. Sally is staring at me. She asks if I'm all right. I nod, not wanting to hear it again, and turn over and close my eyes. The voice that was coming from me sounds like the voice that comes out of people in movies about demonic possession, the voice of one possessed before the exorcism takes place. Is that what I need — an exorcism? How do you find a priest who conducts such rites? The wedding is only four days away. There isn't time. And what use would it be to call my old therapist — what does psychiatry know about demonic possession and exorcism? Besides, I have an appointment to see my spiritual director the afternoon before the wedding.

The wise young Father listens carefully to my fears and says that just before ordination, many young men are torn by doubts and shaken by disbelief, but these distractions and negative thoughts are likely to be, indeed, the work of the devil. But after the vows are read, the rite performed, the newly minted monk is free of such fears and able to follow his calling. Marriage might follow a similar path, with the vows themselves dispelling the fears and anxieties that rack the candidate before betrothal. When I continue to speak my panic, the Father seems puzzled and asks if I haven't worked through these questions with my minister in the classes preparatory to marriage. I explain that in my own denomination and church there are no such classes; you simply tell the minister your intent, and if he approves, set a date when he and the church are free.

Now the Father is indeed concerned, and yet — well, it's the day before, the late afternoon before the wedding. He leans forward. Sometimes, he says, the vows themselves can dispel doubts and fears, can heal and bind. The vows are sacred, and have real power. I nod, respectfully, but I'm wondering if words can create such a miracle. I remember the magic word in the comics that transformed a mere mortal into Captain Marvel — *Shazam*. The Father rises. We shake hands.

With my mind careening like the Tilt-a-Whirl at the state fair, I realize as I walk to the subway in Harvard Square that I've boxed myself in, created a situation in which my minister and my spiritual director — both bright, perceptive men — each think the other is handling the nitty-gritty, the hard questions and explorations preparing a person for the marriage rites. If I'd made it clear — if I still could talk those things out, maybe even talk to my old therapist as well — but hey, let's be practical! The wedding guests are already assembling, relatives and friends from as far as California, this very night, when they all will gather at the dining room of a friend's Boston club for the "rehearsal dinner," traditional wedding-eve feast of fellowship and toasts.

Neither Sally nor I notice that the excellent plans we've worked out so well are all about marrying, but not about marriage. What will we do when we return from our fabulous

European honeymoon? What will we do in our daily life? Neither of us has a clue; or rather, the clues we begin to get from one another in the few days before the ceremony are not what the other imagined or wants at all. But what can be done at this late date? Hey — it's time to get dressed for the rehearsal dinner.

I get in the mood of celebration, happy to see old friends, enjoy the camaraderie, the good-natured roastlike toasts and jokes, the old club dining room, the coming together of so many parts of my past into one warm room, cozy with cheer and well-wishing. This is the part I like, the approval from peers, the feeling of being part of the world's way, God's plan, soon to be grown-up at last, settled and serene. Fears and doubts are lost in the fog of congratulation, of loved ones expressing love.

Best man honors this time go to one of my oldest friends, the famous high school football star known as "Horse" as well as "Gunner." The role has been played in the past by a lawyer pal from college and then a pair of writer friends from the literary world of New York in the fifties. The new casting carries out the hometown high school motif of the wedding itself, set by Sally and me, the soon-to-be bride and groom. On the wedding morning I of course don't see the bride (everyone knows that a pre-altar view is bad luck, which Sally and I are prudently avoiding at all costs), so my best man comes by to buck me up. By now, in the cold light of day, I need it.

"Horse, I'm afraid this whole thing is crazy," I confess.

The Horse's approach to his duties is jocular, having been through so many of my ups and downs and ins and outs over the years (nearly four decades by now), it's hard to predict what's next and how to take it, so lightly seems perhaps the safest.

"You can't stop now, everyone's here," says my veteran pal. "How can you refund all those plane tickets? Besides, there's a cake being delivered. What are you going to do if there's no wedding, give it to the homeless?"

"Come on, Horse, I'm serious."

But the Horse, trying to keep things on an even keel, keeps me smiling, even laughing at myself, and gets me to the church on time. Isn't that the best man's job description? The Horse is famous for getting the job done.

It isn't the actual church itself, but the parish house, which is even more sacred to me, being the scene of so much that's meaningful; that first Bible study when only three people showed up on a stormy night and found a power they hadn't known before in Scripture; meetings of the religious education committee to plan those memorable retreats, the minister's class in religious autobiography that begins my book about "Returning," sessions of the parish council, after-church lunches and brunches, talks and seminars, the big kitchen where I happily make my "Iowa Chili" recipe for forty, "quiet days" for reflection and meditation, and during the past few years a prayer group of five or six people who show up for an hour on Monday nights at six o'clock, taking turns to share a passage from the Bible or a book that means something special to them or a piece of music, and then a time of silence, followed by whatever concerns anyone wishes to express, and a final prayer. These gatherings are special, a source of strength and peace, a knowing of fellow seekers on a very deep level, a dimension of unspoken understanding that is precious and rare.

The parish house itself is special, once a family's four-story townhouse on Beacon Hill, with wild nineteenth-century wallpaper depicting scenes of imagined Paradise and casement windows looking out on the Boston Common. This is the place I choose as the most perfect spot for marriage, and Sally agrees, taking an immediate liking to Boston and the Hill and the church itself, feeling it all speaks more of tradition and sanctity than her own West Coast, wanting to share its old-fashioned, rooted, faith-filled aura.

Bolstered with caffeine instead of booze, and the best man's staunch if lighthearted presence, I find when I enter that loved, familiar home, filled now with friends from across the country and the years as well as the warm memories of my new life of faith, loving faces from all the disparate parts of my life, I am calm, peaceful, assured, serenely sailing to my destiny. Sally is lovely, a radiant presence, and we stand solidly side by side as the Rev reads the vows, the words that the spiritual director believes have special powers of blessing and healing, and then comes the kiss to seal the pact. The cake is cut and champagne poured, then come congratulations and toasts, which I love to give as well as receive, and I stand on a chair and make one in tribute to my bride, new wife, companion for life.

The only jarring note of the celebration comes when my spiritual director grips my hand in one swift downward shake and says firmly, "Done." Then leaves. Is he relieved, angry, happy, distraught, concerned? The room begins to drain of people and warmth, and I feel my energy draining as well, after the high of the ceremony and celebration, the culmination of the story, the dream; and now it's fading. Fast. There are empty glasses, crumb-filled plates, balled-up napkins. The light outside is growing dim.

By the time I walk out the parish house door with Sally, it feels as if a shroud has come over me, one that tightens my throat and my breath and presses on my mind with a fearful ache. There is one thing I know, with a certainty as deep as anything I've known in my life, know it in the pit and core of my being: there is no way on God's earth I can be married to this woman.

, , ,

Nothing I have ever done, no mistake of the countless ones I've made through the roller-coaster course of a dizzying life seem as deadly as this one, and to make it more frightening and hopeless, this time I have no excuse: I have done it without drinking or being on drugs, I have done it as a mature man (at least in years and experience), a faithful believer and church member, a

Christian who thought I was making a spiritual journey on a path of enlightened understanding, leading to fulfillment of God's plan, fate, destiny, the dream of wholeness and health. As we walk across the Boston Public Garden to the fine hotel where we've chosen to spend our wedding night, I feel I am drowning in darkness. It's hard to breathe or think. I have finally, conclusively done myself in, burning behind me the symbols and spirits I loved, bringing an innocent person into this self-created nightmare.

I think of turning back right then to the parish house, banging on the door, and asking the Rev to annul or simply tear up the document we signed, yet it seems too outrageous, too crazy. I tell myself that when we get on that plane tomorrow it might be all right, or when we touch down in a foreign country some blessing or new perspective or insight or transformation will come over me and the sun will come out and the birds sing and everything will unroll like the storybook ending it is all supposed to be.

Sally is aware at once of the dark that comes over me, and in the course of several days I choke out my awful confession of mistake, yet somehow it seems unseemly to stop, even when we get back home (my pad still lacks another chest of drawers, not to speak of tea towels), so we try to pretend it will be all right, we're doing okay, at least pretending to the outside world, yet she sums it up after several weeks with the bitter truth: "What's so horrible is, it seems like we don't even like each other anymore." We are prisoners of one another, of our own fantasy of fulfillment, gone empty. Somehow we struggle and stumble through the summer, trying to be polite to each other, having some sessions with the therapist I refused to consult before, but nothing changes, nothing lifts the tension of failure, and it winds down to the autumn, when she goes back to her own home. When the great romance begins, I give her a hand-carved wooden apple, a symbol of the fullness of what we think we have found. She leaves on my mantel another small, hand-carved wooden apple, no doubt one of a series the first one came from. But this one is different. This one looks chewed down to the core, the round red fruit reduced to a brown stem.

, , ,

Shortly after Sally moves back to her own home in southern California, I have coffee with Harold Kushner, the rabbi and writer who went to college at Columbia when I did. Like other friends, he has met and liked Sally, and hoped that this marriage would be a happy ending for both of us. When I tell him what's happened, he is sorry, of course, and in a rabbinical effort at healing he asks me, "What have you learned from this?"

"Nothing," I say.

All I can see at this point is loss, debris. Later, I come across a few ideas that seem to shed some light on this dark experience, though of course, like Monday morning quarterbacking, they can't alter or ameliorate the outcome. At least they might serve as warning signs for the future.

The wisest thing I read about man-woman relations does not concern Venus and Mars, nor any recent New Age sage's prescriptions, but a book called *Parallel Lives: Five Victorian Marriages,* by Phyllis Rose. Ms. Rose writes, "To the extent that we impose some narrative form onto our lives, each of us in the ordinary process of living is a fitful novelist. . . . Every marriage seems to me a subjectivist fiction with two points of view often deeply in conflict, sometimes fortuitously congruent."

I am sure the woman I call "Sally" would write the story in a completely different way. My version is as true as I know how to tell it, but it is only one side of what Rose rightly calls "a subjectivist fiction with two points of view."

Rose helps me understand my own experience when she says, "The plots we choose to impose on our own lives are limited and limiting. And in no area are they so banal and sterile as in . . . love and marriage. Nothing else being available to our imaginations, we will filter our experience through the romantic clichés with which popular culture bombards us."

What greater romantic cliché do we have than "man in his fifties meets old high school sweetheart and they fall in love and marry." This heartwarming plot fits Rose's belief that "easy stories drive out hard ones. Simple paradigms prevail over complicated ones."

My story with Sally was a real O. Henry job, hard to resist, which may be one of the reasons we stuck to it so long, suppressing all indications against it. Not only did it appeal to us, but perhaps more insidiously important, it was so predictably popular with other people — friends, acquaintances, strangers. "Bless you," people beamed, showering affection on us, which, being human, we gulped and swallowed with glee. We were loved — if not by each other, as it turned out, at least by people we knew! At least for the duration of our story. Of course our real friends love us and forgive us anyway. That, I believe, includes Jesus Christ.

As a child one of my favorite hymns was "What a Friend I Have in Jesus." I still think of him as a friend, and think that his most crucial message is forgiveness. This is the great gift of Christianity.

Later I realize — when my mind is clear enough to entertain such concepts — that even if I'm loved by Jesus, and my dear friends of a lifetime, I can't be loved by everyone, and no matter how hard I try, I can't be all things to all people. I can't be the itinerant writer I've been ever since I left home to go to Columbia and live in New York, and at the same time be the settled-down good boy from Indiana with a suitable wife, a white picket fence, and a stable occupation. I can't be approved by everyone. I can't be something I've tried to be but failed every time (a husband). That's another lesson I should have learned from painful experience but wouldn't admit to myself.

This is a turning point. Nothing will ever seem as simple again. The rest of my life will flow from this, taking a different course — geographically, even spiritually, and in other ways both obvious and subtle. But now, in the frozen aftermath of the marriage's dissolution, I don't know that.

Now I know nothing.

Chapter 7

WORDS FAIL ME

———◆———

IT'S DARK NOW. DEATH IS IN MY HEAD.

I'm relieved that the awful tension is over from trying to pretend, from living what we both came to know so painfully and quickly was a lie, but now that she's gone, and agreed to a divorce, I'm left with the consequences.

Debris.

I'm free.

Falling.

The Lord is my shepherd. I shall not want . . .

But I do.

I want to feel something. I'm numb. Nothing sounds good. Not even drink. Not even ice cream. Everything I thought I'd been working toward for nearly a decade — the peace, integration, fulfillment, maturity — all of it seems collapsed within me, like a tent brought down in a high wind. What's left is the empty sound of the wind, and darkness. In desperation I call the therapist I didn't consult before getting married and demand to know, What shall I do? My voice wavers, as if it might fade or scream. She asks if there isn't anything I want to do, anywhere I want to go, that sounds good to me, that seems like it might provide healing or relief or just distraction. I say the only thing I can think of is sex.

How original! What a great idea! Sure, I'll have some mind-numbing sex, blanking out all my problems with temporary ecstasy; what Anne Sexton called, with the poet's genius for accuracy, "the brief bright bridge of the raucous bed."

I call an old girlfriend and tell her my story and state of mind. She's in between men and says to come over. I do. I do what I thought I wanted to do, what I thought would cure me, and wake up feeling worse than before. The pit opens wider beneath me, the darkness deeper, more menacing.

The therapist recommends I try this new medication called Prozac. Once in the past I tried antidepressants, and all they did was depress me further. She says this stuff is different, works on a different principle. I say I'll try it. The way I'm feeling, I'll try anything. I take it for a week, but all it does is make me jangly and hyper and I can't sleep. I throw the rest away.

, , ,

Our Father, who art . . .

The Lord is my . . .

No.

Words no longer work. This is the worst part. Words are my solace, salvation, sacred connection. But I've ripped the connection out, sullied the words, stripped them of meaning. I stood in the place most sacred to me, the King's Chapel parish house, and said in response to my minister, in the presence of my friends, in the reverence of God and Jesus Christ, that I take this woman to be my wife, for better or for worse, in sickness and in health, forsaking all others; and two hours later walk out the door and realize the words I so earnestly spoke are simply not true, that I lack the strength or capacity or character or will to make them true. Maybe "technically" they aren't really lies because at the time I speak them, in the trance or state of illusion or madness I'm in, I believe them, but that doesn't make them true. The words of the ceremony don't turn out to have the special (magic) power my spiritual director suggested (hoped) they might. There's no theological "Shazam" that transforms me into the sort of person I had tried and failed to be before — a husband, an upright citizen living by the rules of my community, respecting its mores. I say I will do and be all that but I can't. I can't even begin. The words were only words.

Now all words are empty. I can't use them to pray.

All the same, I go to my prayer group at the parish house on Monday night at six. I go by habit, faith, and love. I've been going since it began with a notice in the church newsletter five years ago. I love the quiet of the room where we meet, the view from the old casement windows of this former Beacon Hill townhouse that looks out over the Boston Common. I read the seasons through the windows where the lush green foliage of trees nearly fills the summer scene, then burns to gold and red in autumn, becomes a sketch of delicate pen strokes etched on a silver sky by Thanksgiving, and shines through dark December with the lights of Christmas glowing in garlands of red, yellow, blue, green, white, festooning the night.

Most of all I love the people and what we bring to this room to share, in readings, music, discussion, and the twenty-minute period of silence that's part of each hour-long session. There are only five or six of us regulars, and the only other man is Charles Perry, who's become my best friend in the church community. Charles works for a think tank on international affairs in Cambridge and also lives on the Hill. I read a passage of Scripture at his wedding to Adelaide Ketchum, and I'm proud to be the godfather of their first son, Nicholas. Charles and I have our own ritual of going to dinner after prayer group to the Montien, a Vietnamese restaurant across the Common, where we like to share "the whole fish" and talk about our lives with the freedom of intimate trust. Except for Charles, I know little about the others in the group except what comes from sharing the hour together every Monday at the parish house.

There's a woman banker, an interim minister who serves another church but belongs to this one, a librarian, a housewife, and a graduate of Harvard Business School who is trying to find her niche in the corporate world. Ginger, the MBA graduate, doesn't belong to King's Chapel, but heard about the prayer group from attending the church's Wednesday noontime service for people in the business district. When she first comes, we're a little put off by her theology, which seems "fundamentalist" to our Unitarian Christian sensibilities, but her faith is so tangible, and so natural, we come to appreciate and rely on her.

Charles Perry and I both travel a lot, and whenever we announce we have to miss a meeting because of a trip — perhaps I am flying to Chicago or San Francisco to give a workshop, or Charles to his office in Washington or a conference in Paris or Brussels — Ginger whips out her notebook and writes down the dates. When we ask at first why she wants to know, she explains that she wants to pray for us to have a safe trip. Now everyone in the group makes a point of telling Ginger whenever they're traveling, to ask for her prayers. We all pray for Ginger about her work, her jobs, for she seems to have a hard time fitting in to the corporate world. (I'm relieved and happy when I learn a few years later she has joined an order of Roman Catholic nuns and lives in a convent. Yes. The information clicks into place, like an obvious outcome of the purity and passion of her search and her faith. I think of her with thanks, and the blessing of her presence among us.)

When nothing is left of my marriage but the apple's rotten core, I confess to the prayer group I can't pray. The Psalms and passages of Scripture that once meant so much to me now seem hollow — not because I don't "believe" them anymore, but rather that I myself seem hollow. I haven't lost faith in God, or Jesus Christ — in the midst of this time of anguish, that never occurs to me — but I've lost faith in words, or at least in words as communication with the Holy Spirit. I am still a writer, I am still writing and reading others' writing; I believe in words as literature and poetry and journalism, but not as prayer — at least for me, at least for now. The words I used, the vows I spoke in public, in the sacred space of the parish house, and the next day at Glastonbury Abbey, where I went with Sally for a blessing of our marriage, were rendered meaningless by my actions, my breaking and betraying them. So now the language — the words — of faith seem empty for me, because my actions have drained them of meaning.

I want to pray, but I need to find other ways than words. I've had a sense of prayer through the body since the first time I took a class in Tai Chi five years before at the Boston Center for Adult Education. All I knew about Tai Chi before the class was a brief mention in *Esquire* recommending this noncombative martial art as a good exercise for developing better coordination and mastery of the body. It sounds like a good "next step" for me after the program of exercise and diet I've incorporated into my post-Hollywood life. When we stand straight with feet firmly planted, chin lifted, and slowly lift our hands, palms upward, in the first movement of the sequence known as "the form" of Tai Chi, with Albinoni's "Adagio" playing in the background, a smile spontaneously comes to my face as I realize this is prayer. My two years of Tai Chi study with David Zucker, a master teacher, deepen that appreciation of the body as an instrument of prayer, and I find it next in yoga classes while moving into the age-old asanas and holding them in silence as I focus all on the still point of the posture. I'm thankful I know about these silent, physical ways of prayer, for they seem like my lifeline now.

There's a yoga class with a teacher I know and respect in Brookline at the same time the prayer group meets, and I tell the group I want to go there for a while. I ask their forgiveness and understanding. I ask for their prayers.

When I leave the parish house that night I want to cry, yet the tears feel frozen.

In going to yoga, in trying to pray through flesh rather than words, I feel like I'm going back to basics — going back to the body to find the spirit. In this dark period when I fear I've lost my way, when I feel disconnected from the spirit, I think of the card that Sister Mary Hennessy gave me when she read *Returning*. One side of the card has a picture of a door leading to a garden and on the other side is a quote from the Book of Revelation: "Behold, a door has been opened to you that no one can close." That declaration has a resonance to it that strikes me as true when I first hear it, like the deep peal of a great bell, and I still feel its truth. So the door must be there, it must still be open, but I just can't see it anymore. I remind myself I can't see New Jersey, either, but that doesn't mean it isn't there. I can't find the door with words now, and that's why I'm going to the body. Going to yoga.

, , ,

Late on Monday afternoons now I walk down Charles toward Beacon Street, but instead of turning left to go to the parish house, I turn right and walk through the Public Garden to the Arlington Street subway stop. I take the Green Line trolley to Coolidge Corner in Brookline, and from there it's only a few blocks' walk to Creative Yoga, a low-ceilinged, loftlike space covered with green carpet that occupies the top floor of a three-story walk-up. There's only enough room for a few more than a dozen students, and the place is almost always filled for the evening classes. A chart of the human anatomy at the front of the room is the only art or decoration — no paintings of ancient Indian holy men or photos of contemporary gurus with beards and blazing eyes. There's a small bookcase with a few books on yoga practice and pamphlets or brochures about classes and yoga vacations. The teacher, Carol Nelson, is a tall, attractive woman with a bell-like clarity in her voice, and the kind of calm, centered presence that comes from long discipline of body and mind.

I've learned that like anything else you may study, yoga depends on the teacher, no matter what the style. When people ask me, "Should I take a writing class?" I ask, "Who's teaching it?" When I encourage Carl Scovel to take a Tai Chi class with David Zucker at the Boston Center for Adult Education, he finds David's class time isn't convenient, so he studies with another teacher. When he tells me he isn't getting much out of it, I urge him again to take David's class, and after he does, he gives a sermon about the difference a teacher makes in any kind of study. His first teacher was perfectly adequate, Carl says, but the difference is that "he taught Tai Chi. But David Zucker *is* Tai Chi. He embodies the practice in the way he walks, speaks, and conducts the class."

The teacher makes all the difference in yoga, too. And you don't know how you respond to a particular teacher until you work with her. Carol Nelson tells me that her own style derives from studying with a teacher in Paris who was a disciple of B. K. S. Iyengar, but "softens" the method of this master teacher known for the strictness of his teaching, the striving for exactness in the posture. That "softening" must be what makes it more accessible to me, for I've taken Iyengar classes that were too exacting for my taste and capabilities. It all depends on who's teaching.

Carol teaches with the kind of awareness and attention that lets you know she is fully present to each student, and she corrects with gentle, light instruction that feels helpful rather than disciplinary. She sticks to the basics of the physical postures and does not use chanting or ritual of any kind — no Sanskrit words or candles.

For my own mood and needs of the moment, the lack of any overt spiritual trimmings is a blessing. I don't want words of any kind, whether Sanskrit or English, Hindu or Christian. I want to be baptized in silence, let silence wash over me, immerse myself in it. Perhaps the greatest thing yoga provides — at any rate the greatest of its blessings for me right now — is the silence of the mind, the shutting down of the continuous racket and chatter in the head, the endless static of life's disappointments, fears, and desires, the if-only-I-did-that-or-maybe-I-should-do-this percussion of past and future obsessions, trials and trivia that never lets us rest. Holding a yoga pose in which I have to concentrate all my attention on keeping my arms and legs, head and neck, feet and shoulders, in the proper position, focuses my mind as well as my physical energy and obliterates the chatter of what Buddhists call the "monkey mind." This is for me an easier form of quieting the mind than "sitting meditation," in which you simply sit in silence and try to let the thoughts pass through the mind until it stills. It's easier to control the body than the mind, and the best way of getting the mind to settle down is by making the body still. And there lies peace — the peace of emptiness and emptying, the peace of cleansing the clutter, the peace that not only passeth understanding but requires no understanding, only being. This is the peace that lets us be. This is the peace that frees.

It's not like thunder and lightning, it's not achieving nirvana or experiencing satori. It's nothing that earth-shattering or soul-shaking. It's small, but it's real. It comes in increments, small pieces of peace, carved out of the riot of the mind, torn from the chaos of the day, the tumult of being alive. I walk from the class and my body feels tuned, I'm imperceptibly lighter. I meet a friend after class at a Chinese restaurant and savor the food, the tastes tingling through me. At home I do a shoulder stand before going to bed — a far more relaxing and less neck-stressing pose than the head stand. You lie down and kick your legs up into the air, propping your hands against your lower back, and stretching your feet as high as you can, as if pressing them against the ceiling. It's a kind of upside-down posture that gives your body, your organs, a reversal of position that's supposed to be a relief for them, and at any rate feels good to do. Afterward I crawl into bed and fall into deep, slow-breathing sleep.

Yoga isn't a cure-all but it helps. It brings relief, provides a place to go out of the storm, a welcome shutting down of the psychic pain without resort to drugs or booze, enlivening and awakening the body instead of numbing it, and I think then the soul is revived as well. I sense that my soul most of all is in need of healing, and yoga seems to act as a kind of artificial respiration to revive it.

I don't regard it as a mystic Eastern art that is off the path of my own Christian way, but as a gift of God to my own body and soul. I know there's a fear among some sincere Christians that yoga is kind of rival religion that leads onto an alien path; even one of my important Christian guides, the Dutch theologian and Catholic priest Henri Nouwen, writes me a gently cautionary letter about my emphasis on yoga. I'm happy to find a book called *A New Christian Yoga* by the Reverend Nancy Roth, a former dancer who became an Episcopal priest, affirming the value of yoga for Christians. She sets the words to the Lord's Prayer to the movements of the classic yoga series called Salute to the Sun, observing that "in an uncanny way which helps to convince me that we all seek one God, this sequence of movements — which originated in the Hindu tradition — expresses the petition of the Lord's Prayer and could very appropriately be called "Salute to the Son."

I think people of all faiths can find their own message in the universal body language of yoga, a language of silent affirmation. In yoga I neither find nor seek some exotic new God, but the God addressed in my favorite Psalm, 139, that says "I will praise thee; for I am fearfully and wonderfully made: marvelous are thy works; and that my soul knoweth right well."

This is the same Psalm that reassures me when it asks:

> Whither shall I go from thy spirit? or whither
> shall I flee from thy presence?

If I ascend up into heaven, thou art there: if I
make my bed in hell, behold, thou art there.

If I take the wings of the morning, and dwell in
the uttermost parts of the sea;

Even there shall thy hand lead me, and thy right
hand shall hold me.

If I say, Surely the darkness shall cover me; even
the night shall be light about me

Yea, the darkness hideth not from thee; but the
night shineth as the day: the darkness and the light
are both alike to thee.

⌐ ⌐ ⌐

I'm still not out of the dark, but at least I'm not thinking of
death all the time. I even try going to church. I haven't been
since Sally left. We went sometimes when she was still here, out
of duty and hope, the kind of hope my spiritual director was
groping for when he said maybe the marriage ceremony itself
would relieve me of my fears and make the vows real; the kind
of childish hope that whispers in your ear that if you're good,
God will reward you, if you do all the things you're supposed to
do, nothing bad will happen to you. It's the kind of naive hope
that Rabbi Kushner helped us grow out of when he laid it on the
line in simple language, out of his own experience, that bad
things do happen to good people, so we might as well become
adults and deal with it.

I go to church and sit toward the back now, one of the two or
three pews farthest from the pulpit and communion rail. I feel
uneasy here now, as if I might be exposed as unworthy, a fallen
man. My childish fear is the one where the sinner is struck down
by lightning for daring to stand in the Holy Place, surely a fit
punishment for one who has broken its sacred vows, yet dares
to enter its gates again as if qualified, or deserving, or legitimate.
I see the greatest sin as hypocrisy, and the sinner I most despise
is the one I dread I've become — the hypocrite. I still see the

world through the fifties values of Holden Caulfield, the spiritual arbiter of the era for secular seekers, who brands such sinners with the hot zeal of his righteous condemnation as "phonies." Mouthing the words of the Prayer Book, intoning the hymns, I'm oppressed by the fear that I've become what I most despise — a phony. The liturgy rings in my ears like reproach, the hymns sound funereal, matching my mood.

My calendar tells me I face an obligation I'd forgotten about that I look on now with apprehension. It seems like a public test of my integrity — that is, if I have any left. I agreed a year ago to give a workshop on spiritual autobiography at Interface, an adult education center of New Age orientation in Cambridge. When I gave the course first at the Boston Center for Adult Education, I began by thinking of it as "service," but I soon came to realize that like any such enterprise it's just as enriching to me as to those I'm trying to serve.

Giving the workshop is fun, lively, enlivening, and a source of renewed connection with the world, as opposed to the isolation of the act of writing, my main activity. I meet bright, interesting people engaged in the quest that most interests me in life, and am privileged through the work to facilitate and share their discoveries, insights, moments of grace, and the genuine sense of community that grows and flowers in a room of people telling their own deepest stories. I always share my own story of returning to faith, and finding the narrative of my spiritual journey through the exercises of the course in religious autobiography I took at King's Chapel and offer now in some slightly altered forms in this workshop. Before I ask participants to tell their own stories, I tell them my own, as honestly as I can.

So what do I tell them now?

It's all very rosy and cozy to tell them about my bad old days in Hollywood when I was swilling down the Almaden Chablis by the case, and how I fled back to Boston and recovered my health and then the spiritual impulse I'd numbed with booze for a quarter of a century, and how (now comes the chorus of "Amazing Grace" in the background) I no longer long for the alcohol that fueled me since college and am living a productive, healthy life, blessed by return to church and the faith of my fathers (I cite here my father's father, the Baptist minister who I'm named after), the faith of my own childhood.

So how about an update?

Do I stand there smiling in front of a new group of trusting strangers looking for spiritual experience and maybe even uplift and tell how I got married in the church and faith I love six months ago and have already broken my vows and am getting a divorce? Can I stand in front of them now and leave out that rather crucial information? Do I try to pretend it never happened? Do I hide it?

"Phony!"

I wake in the middle of the night the week before the workshop with Holden's accusation ringing in my ears.

I decide I should cancel. I'll call up the Interface office and tell them I no longer lead such workshops. I'll tell them I've quit. But that seems cowardly as well as phony. To hell with it. I'll tell the truth. I'll simply stand up on the first evening, when I give my introduction, and tell my (formerly) inspiring story, but this time it won't have a happy ending, and the people who come will probably want their money back and leave. They'll be justified, I think. So that will be that, ending my two-year career as a leader of workshops on spiritual autobiography, but at least I won't have added "coward" or "phony" to my new identity as breaker of sacred vows, betrayer of the faith.

It's early December and snowing in Boston that Friday night when I go to what feels like my public confessional at Interface. The Puritan heritage of Massachusetts (not to speak of my own Baptist boyhood) comes to mind, and I picture pilgrims in public stocks, peeking out from a hole in the wood to a scornful public. I think of the Salem trials, and realize that, unlike the witch-hunters of America's past, I am my own accuser, publicly proclaiming the guilt for my sins — the quickie divorce and betrayal of vows by a man who writes and speaks as a Christian. If I've failed the hip new litmus test of walking the walk while I'm talking the talk, at least I'm admitting it.

There's a friendly-looking audience of twenty-five or so people, most of whom have signed up to take the workshop the next day. I look them in the eyes and tell them my story. I try not to cringe or flinch when I bring up the recent marriage and divorce, which feels like opening a fresh wound. I say how discouraging it is to mess up so badly just when I thought I was finally "on the path," and how this has led to a new darkness and a crisis of prayer.

I'm braced for censure, or at least disillusionment from the audience, but I notice some of them nodding and smiling, and I realize they know what I'm talking about; they've been there themselves. I realize that what I think is so unique to my own experience turns out to be — as usual — commonplace. The hubris of imagining we've "got it together," followed by a jolt of reality that plunges us back to earth, is probably one of the most familiar and often-traveled arcs of human experience. And yet we think each time, "This is different, this time I've really got it right."

They understand — more than I do — and share their own ups and downs of the spirit, in discussion that night and in the work of the exercises in drawing and writing the next day during the workshop. As people read their stories, the blessings and travails of their own journeys, they bring back episodes in my own life, and strike chords of memory with others in the room, as always happens. The realization comes over me, like a huge, undeniable wave, that we all have the same story. Oh, we all have our own variations on the themes of love and loss, of despair and hope; our dramas take place in different settings, with different casts of characters, but strip away the outer elements and you realize finally there is only one story, and we all are plugged into it; part of it, living it.

As people draw and talk and write and read aloud, often with stories more powerful than those I hear in conventional writing classes I teach, I see that one of the reasons this workshop works is that I'm not "teaching" anything. I'm not telling anyone what or how to write, but simply, like a stage manager, setting up the space for them to do it in, and trying to make the circumstances as comfortable as possible by not judging, grading, advising, or criticizing, but simply acknowledging, appreciating, honoring. "When people read their stories," one participant says, "It's sacred ground." As the day goes on, I see that I don't have to worry about how I'm doing in leading the workshop because I'm not "doing it" so much as it is coming through me.

I don't mean I think that I'm channelling Henry James or St. Theresa or Jesus himself — or any other great writer or spirit of the past — but that I'm facilitating a process, and my principal job is not to get in the way, just to be there, be empty and clear like a pipe through which water flows, an instrument through which music comes. At the end of the day I'm exhilarated. Instead of feeling tired from leading the activities of a workshop for seven hours, I feel refreshed, in body and mind, and most of all, spirit.

Rather than having to give up leading the workshops, I feel now they're my connection to Spirit. In this time when church seems foreign to me — or rather, I feel foreign or displaced inside it — the workshops give me an opportunity to be in touch with Spirit by providing ways for others to tell the stories of their spiritual journey, to see their experience through the lens of spirituality, whatever that deeper dimension means to each of them, rather than the lens of secular achievement, success, and "standing" in which we usually view (and are taught to view) our lives.

, , ,

I'm still going to services at King's Chapel, but not with the regularity much less the devotion I went with before. When I go, it is out of a sense of duty rather than passion, a faint hope of find-ing again the spark that I feel my own betrayal of marriage vows extinguished. It's uncomfortable for me to go, because I'm angry — at church, at God, at the minister. I'm ashamed of my anger but there it is, gnawing at me like a cur, a mangy, mongrel dog of the soul that snaps and growls and bites and clenches me with its sharp little teeth and won't let go. I'm angry as a child is angry, a bawling little brat who blames his pain and misfortune on others.

I'm angry at Carl, my minister and friend, for not advising me to stop the marriage, for conducting the damn service! I'm angry at my spiritual director, who told me maybe the ritual itself, the saying of the sacred vows, would make it all right. I'm angry at my friends who encouraged my marriage and sup-ported me in doing it, believing it would be a great and good thing, having only my own best interest at heart — but damn them, damn them not knowing better than I did that it was hopeless and doomed, misguided and wrong. How dare they not know what I couldn't figure out myself? How dare they all not save me?

Worst of all, and hardest to admit, I'm mad at God, too. How come she didn't save me? Just like Mama always did. And wasn't this doomed marriage an attempt to please her (as well as Her)? Don't I tell people before the marriage, when it still glows with the promise of fulfillment (social and theological even more than personal), that I know that my mother, who died nine years before, will be comforted and pleased at last to see me "settle down" with a nice girl from Indianapolis?

I try to please you and look what happens!

I want to keep those voices quiet, I want to purge myself of the anger, clean out the bile. I go on weekend yoga retreats at the Kripalu Center, in western Massachusetts, and at the Sivananda Yoga Ashram on Paradise Island in the Bahamas. The classes I'm taking with Carol Nelson in Brookline are fine, and bring more relief than anything else I'm doing, but they're only for an hour, and I want "longer-lasting relief" — like the ads for stomach medicine promise. At Kripalu there are classes and sessions in yoga and chanting all day long and at night as well, so there's opportunity for longer cessation of the inner gabble, a chance for a weekend marathon of blanking out the mind ("clearing" it is the more positive way of seeing the process) and stretching the body. I go for it.

I feel further purging and emptying through these more intensive retreats. Both of these facilities are Indian in their spiritual trappings — photos of white-haired gurus with fresh flowers beside them, sessions of chanting in Sanskrit — yet never do I feel my Christianity attacked or threatened, never do I feel intimidated or challenged in my own religious beliefs and practices. I don't mind the words now, especially because they aren't "my" words, the words I failed with. They are Sanskrit and sound like different tones in music. There is nothing disturbing.

At Kripalu, formerly a Jesuit retirement facility called Shadow-brook, its buildings and acreage sold to a yoga teacher and guru in the sixties, there is still in the main meeting room where yoga and chanting sessions are held a huge mosaic of St. Ignatius, with a halo, looking at the heavens while stars pour down on him in streams like gold threads. "We left it there because it felt so nice," says one of the staff.

At the Sivananda ashram on Paradise Island, yoga sessions are held on a platform on the beach with sea spray caressing your body, or, if the surf is too loud to hear the instructor, classes are conducted on a platform on the bay side of the property. Attendance is required at meditation and chanting sessions every morning, and at night there are sometimes readings from the *Bhagavad Gita* or bonfires on the beach in which guests are asked to lead songs and invited to sing hymns of their own faith. I come away refreshed and lighter from exercise and silence, the mind-stilling rest that comes from chants and meditations.

, , ,

I learn that hopelessness can open opportunity. When you feel you've messed everything up and so have nothing to lose, when you're not trying to protect your status quo, you're not afraid of taking on projects that might in happier times seem on the risky and frightening side and so less appealing. In the first flush of my fantasy with Sally, when I see myself as a newly minted member of the contented class, a person who has finally got it all together and is waiting to live out my life "the way it's s'posed to be" with a loving wife, a solid married man of substance and community roots, I turned down an invitation to lead my workshop in spiritual autobiography at Sing Sing prison. My first thought is "What if something bad happens? What if I'm held hostage? What if I'm caught in the midst of a prison riot like Attica?" It would just be my luck to have something prevent me from enjoying my long-awaited life of socially approved contentment. I make excuses. I say no.

Now I say yes. I look forward to going to Sing Sing. It's not that I hope to be killed in some prison melee and so be put out of my misery, but rather that I've lost the illusion that I have anything to protect. I think of Janis Joplin singing that freedom's just another word for nothin' left to lose. Hey. I'm free to go to Sing Sing. It feels good. Good to be free. Good not to be afraid. Fear paralyzes, dries us up. Fear kills. I think how often the message of an angel in the Bible is *"Fear not."*

I'm invited to Sing Sing by Reverend Bill Webber, one of the founders of the East Harlem Protestant Parish, whom I knew when I was living in that neighborhood and writing my first book. Now he directs a master's degree program for men in the New York state prison system who have earned their B.A. degrees while serving their sentences. Bill created the program while he was dean of the New York Theological Seminary. He is still on the faculty there, and the seminary sponsors this program.

Bill guides me in as we pass through huge locked doors that are opened by guards who clank them shut behind us as we move down long, cold hallways of steel. The class is held in a basement room with a coffee pot and a long table with sixteen men sitting around it. They are mostly black, with some Latino and a few white men, ranging in age from twenties to sixties, all in prison for a minimum of fifteen years, for crimes ranging from narcotics possession and/or sales to murder. I don't know who has committed what crime; I only know I am talking with a group of articulate, intelligent human beings of deep religious faith — most are Christians, some are Muslims — who are trying to keep their souls and bodies alive while shut up in cages like animals for years and years.

As the men do the exercises of drawing and writing about a spiritual experience of childhood, reading their stories and sharing their lives, I feel a genuine kinship with them. There is no pretense here, no "side," or affectation, no attempt to alter the truth in order to "look good," just a plain and direct expression of experience of spirit. In their imprisonment they are on some level oddly free as far as telling the truth of their lives, for they too have nothin' left to lose.

As I sit with these men at this table, the thought comes to me that there's something here I've been missing. In all the "New Age" programs I've tried, I've always avoided the "men's group" activities, feeling put off by the idea of beating drums and crying about my childhood in some room with a bunch of guys. There are no drums here and no one's crying, but there's a camaraderie, a sense of knowing and being known despite the vast difference in all our backgrounds, and the thought comes to me: "I've found my men's group."

I say I'll return and I do. Every time I go, I come away with a sense of uplift and exhilaration, from a sense of the hard faith that sustains these men, and the appreciation they have of any outsider who volunteers to come here. I think of a poster I have by Sister Corita that I've kept for twenty-five years, with a message by Albert Schweitzer that I sometimes forget and that always comes back to me when I live by its wisdom:

"I don't know what your destiny will be, but one thing I know, the only ones among you who will be really happy are those who have sought and found how to serve."

, , ,

I return to Glastonbury Abbey for a weekend. Brother Tom O'Conner, the very monk who spoke to our retreat on "How Do We Know When It's God," has been ordained and is now Father Tom. He gives the Sunday sermon on Jesus giving water to the Samaritan woman he meets at the well. Jesus knows she's been married five times, yet he doesn't disdain or despise her. As Father Tom points out, "He knows she has a past — but she also has a future."

A wave of relief comes over me.

So do I.

But I'm beginning to wonder where my future will be. My discomfort with sitting in a pew at King's Chapel seems to extend in a lesser way to other places of my life in Boston. From the pond in the Public Garden to the haunts on Charles Street, everything seems slightly tainted; the glow is gone. As I trudge up and down Mt. Vernon Street for the umpteenth time in the spring of 1990, a year after my disastrous marriage, I realize the way I feel now about this city I've thought of as home for so long — nearly thirty years — is simply "stale." Not that the city itself is stale, but that I feel stale in regard to it. I'm restless, and my old routines in Boston seem like rote. I'm not consciously thinking of leaving, but something is stirring, wanting to stretch. The answer is already there but I don't yet see it. The map is right on my desk but I don't recognize it.

One thing I do recognize is the power of going to the body as the path to prayer and meditation. I more and more see the wisdom of the body for discernment; its reactions and responses are more dependable than words. We are facile with words, and we can fool ourselves — and others — with them. The body isn't fooled. When it starts to protest, resisting our intentions and actions through headaches, trembling, nausea — any and all of the signs of anxiety and disturbance — we had better pay attention. Does it react this way whenever the new course is thought about or planned or advanced? Stop, look, and listen. Don't just listen to the words of others, listen to the message of your own physical being. Pay attention. The poet Mary Oliver says, "I don't know how to pray, but I know how to pay attention." That's the deepest kind of prayer.

Chapter 8

DOORS

———◆———

I'm not only stale on Boston, I'm stale on my work. In the dying autumn of '89 when Sally departs, the ideas I've had for my next writing projects all seem dead, burnt out, like so much else at this time, and I have no idea what to do next. I need a subject, something that stirs me, but my mind feels as blank as my soul.

Then one day I open a magazine and James Baldwin appears.

It's a photo of the great black writer whom I knew in the Village when I lived in New York in the fifties, and the picture accompanies a memoir I wrote about him as a literary friend and mentor of my youth. The article was commissioned by Art Cooper, the editor of GQ, over lunch one day in New York the year before, and in the crush of the recent events of my personal life I'd forgotten about it. Seeing your work in print is always a boost, and I feel good about paying tribute to Baldwin, whose clarity of prose is an inspiration to me, and whose friendship was one of the nurturing forces of my youth as a writer. Still, nice as it is, a magazine article doesn't solve my larger problems of finding a project for the coming year's money and work.

I open a letter from Seymour Lawrence, who published four of my five novels, congratulating me on the Baldwin piece in *GQ*. He thinks it's one of the best things I've written and says he's especially moved by the evocation of the period and place — New York in the fifties. He thinks I should write a book about it. He wants to publish it. Light fills my head, as the door opens.

Why didn't I think of that?

The subject seems a natural for me. I went to New York in 1952 to go to college at Columbia, graduated in '55, and lived in Greenwich Village until 1963, when a Nieman Fellowship in journalism took me to Harvard for a year and I stayed on to live in Boston. I knew the writers of the time, from Baldwin to Kerouac, listened to Miles Davis at Birdland and Charlie Mingus at the Five Spot, wrote my first book (*Island in the City*) about Spanish Harlem, covered elections, trials, and union politics for *The Nation,* did profiles of William F. Buckley and Adam Clayton Powell for *Esquire* under its great editor Harold Hayes . . . In short, I was there, on the scene and part of the scene in one of the great eras of our greatest city. Write a book about it? Yes! It was right under my nose and I didn't see it.

I learn again that writing, like spirituality, is not just an isolated enterprise, but requires community. I would never have written the essay on James Baldwin if Art Cooper hadn't got me thinking about him as a mentor and given me an assignment with a deadline; nor would I have written the book on New York in the fifties if Sam Lawrence hadn't pointed out the idea I hadn't noticed, and given me a contract and the money to live on while writing it. Look at the acknowledgment page of any book and you'll get a sense of the importance of community in the supposedly isolated work of the writer.

I'm writing in what was once the dining room of my apartment on Mt. Vernon Street, fitted out now as my study with bookshelves and filing cabinet, a long table to spread out papers on, a typing table that fits underneath or beside the table and holds my first computer, a Radio Shack special. Above me on the wall are framed covers of some of my books, photos of me and friends, and heroes whose faces inspire me — Miles Davis with his trumpet, Babe Ruth with his bat, a collage of Henry James and Edith Wharton done by my artist-writer friend Eve Babitz. A gift from April Smith — a hand-carved wooden angel from a church in Mexico — oversees and (hopefully) blesses my work from a perch on top of the filing cabinet. From where I sit, I see through the window of the door to the courtyard, a quiet scene with old trees bowing their branches into and over it. A perfect place to write.

At least it *was*.

I wrote *Returning* in this room, and other work I'm proud of, but now the room — like so many other places I love in Boston — seems stale, almost stifling. It reeks of my broken marriage. Though I've hidden the chewed-up apple core that Sally left on the mantel in the living room, I still see it in my mind's eye, symbol of our dried-up dream. I pace, drink coffee, sharpen pencils, shuffle papers, performing all the rites and tics that writers use to delay their work or prepare to do it. I have a subject I want to write about and a book contract to support me while I write it. But nothing happens. No words come.

Have words failed me not only in prayer, but in the work I know and love? The very thought is too scary to entertain. But something is happening — or not happening. I complain over coffee to Ivan Gold, my longtime writer friend from Columbia days who's lived here since coming up from New York to teach at the Boston University writing program in '74.

"Come to the Writers' Room," he suggests.

Ivan heads a group that has organized and drummed up financial support for office space to be used by professional writers who have a book contract; a similar setup flourishes in New York. The space is a series of cubicles with desks on the second floor of the Transportation Building downtown across from the Boston Common, rented out to writers for a nominal fee. Ivan is working on a novel there and says a cubicle is available right across from his own.

An anonymous office with no associations of the doomed marriage sounds like a godsend. I move in my computer and printer, a couple of reference books, a ream of paper, and I'm ready to go. There's no magic outpouring of prose, but at least I begin; words and sentences grow into paragraphs, and pages appear. I report to "my office" every morning like the other scurrying white-collar workers who crowd the streets and flow into the Transportation Building (except my collars aren't buttoned and I wear a sweater instead of a tie). There's a rhythm established, a welcome relief in the anonymity of the place, as well as the extra dividend of having Ivan in the cubicle across from me.

Talking isn't allowed in the room, but when I'm stuck I motion to Ivan, and unless he's in the midst of creating one of his elegant sentences, he follows me out and we go downstairs to Fuddrucker's for coffee. We were friends in New York in the Village in the fifties, and when I can't remember a name or place or date, the odds are Ivan knows the answer, and if not, by talking of the times, I come up with some other memory that serves just as well.

, , ,

On Monday nights I'm still going to Carol Nelson's yoga class in Brookline, which becomes even more valuable now while I'm writing a book. After sitting bent over a keyboard all day, I'm aching to stretch, and yoga not only relaxes the body, it clears the mind. But I don't return to the prayer group again, and it's still hard to join in the prayers and hymns of the Sunday service (I only mouth the words); I only show up about once a month now. I go to events at the parish house, though, to see my old friends of the King's Chapel community, and take part in courses and programs. No one asks why I'm not in church as often, nor do they pry or even mention my marriage and quick divorce. They are warm and welcoming, as always, supportive and friendly and kind, and I'm grateful for their grace and understanding.

Around this time, as the nineties begin, I meet a new woman who I think is my soul mate, sex mate, spiritual ally (she's active in her own church in the suburbs, even does yoga!), everything I always wanted, all in one person who seems perfect. She harbors the same illusions about me, and on one level it's all true; but maybe by the very fact that it's all true, we soon begin to set each other off like high explosives — screaming arguments, tearful make-ups, jealousies and scenes, vows never to see one another again, followed by passionate reunions. It's a wild roller-coaster ride, and it goes on and on, up and down and out and over and back, for the next two years. It's exhilarating, exhausting, fulfilling, draining, addictive, glorious, and hellish.

While all this is going on, I'm reporting to the office every day, my cubicle in the Writers' Room, and plowing ahead on the New York book. That's what the process seems like — *plowing*. I thought this one, whose subject I lived and know so well, would be more like . . . "sailing." But no. I hammer away, piling up pages, feeling like a weary farmer who is pushing a rusty blade behind a couple of stubborn, recalcitrant mules. I worry and wonder what I can do to make it come alive, to sing as I feel it should, and finally after a year an idea comes that might be a key, a clue I discover in the very words I've been writing.

I keep talking about the unusual sense of community of that time and place, a sense of camaraderie and cooperation among different groups and individuals in Manhattan, which seemed to me then like some fabulous small town hidden under the skyscrapers and lights, the turbulence and motion and glitz, if you lived there and loved it and knew how and where to look. There was a rare sense of mutual support among many of the writers, with older, established ones (like Baldwin) serving as mentors, younger ones cheering each other on — as Villager Seymour Krim did when he sent out postcards of praise to the author when he read a good article or story.

So if this was such a great community, why don't I talk to other people who were part of it, adding and blending the stories of my friends back then with my own? A few are already gone, like the marvelous Michael Harrington, a graduate of Dorothy Day's Catholic Worker, head (and heart) of the Young People's Socialist League, and author of *The Other America*, a book that helped shape Lyndon Johnson's antipoverty program. Gone too are Seymour Krim, whose skyrocket prose preceded Mailer's klieg-lit style, and the vibrant sociologist C. Wright Mills, all significant figures of the era. But most of the others are still there — many who never left, like Nat Hentoff, Gay Talese, Norman Podhoretz, and Marion Magid, while some who left have returned, like Joan Didion and John Gregory Dunne.

I decide to spend some time in New York and talk to them all, as many as I can find. In the early spring of '91, I rent the West Ninety-sixth Street studio of novelist Lynne Sharon Schwartz, who's gone for two months on a visiting-writer gig, and commute between New York and Boston to teach my once-a-week writing class at Emerson College.

When I go to New York to interview people, a funny thing happens. I feel at home. I've visited fairly often in the decades since I left, but I haven't lived there for twenty-eight years. I enjoy the renewal of old friendships, and it seems as if no time at all has intervened since when we last saw one another at the White Horse in 1957 or in Washington Square Park in the summer of '59. But there's something deeper than nostalgia that gives me this feeling of being at home.

One night I have dinner with a woman friend who went to Barnard when I was at Columbia and dated one of my best friends in college. As we talk of our lives then and now and in between I feel a great rapport, a comfort of being known and understood, and I realize that this woman, like all the other friends I've talked with, doesn't blink an eye when I confess my recent failed marriage, that she has true stories of her own life that are different but just as socially incorrect and off-beat as mine, and they seem perfectly understandable to me; I identify with them completely.

It dawns on me as I ride the rocking Seventh Avenue local back to my rented studio on Ninety-sixth Street that one of the reasons I originally went to New York and lived in the Village was to break away from the ordered life laid out for me in Indianapolis: marriage, children, a house with a yard, a job with security and a gold watch at retirement. I'm happy for friends who find fulfillment in those accepted patterns — I love and respect the friends from my high school days — but for me those patterns feel like a trap; the white picket fence of domestic bliss seems the barbed wire of a prison camp. Yet that's what I was trying to fit back into with marriage to Sally, the hometown girl, and all the old rebellion came bubbling back.

Most of us came to Manhattan in the fifties looking for freedom from convention, from middle-class expectation, from sexual, political, and cultural restriction, and found in the ultimate City — capital of anonymity — the privacy and challenge we sought. Seeing again old friends who stayed in New York and talking about what brought us here in the first place reminds me of the lines of John Reed's purple-poem ode to New York. We recited it on Village rooftops at dawn after all-night parties, spoke it with the requisite satirical tone to show we saw through its sentimentality, yet hearing it produced an eerie identification, an exciting sort of chill:

> "Who that has known thee but shall burn
> In exile till he come again
> To do thy bitter will, O stern
> Moon of the tides of men!"

For the first time I think about moving back myself. Tempting as it is, it still seems like a pipe dream; I have no real plan for returning to live in New York. But going there to do the interviews really gives new energy and life to the book. I finish eight months later, in the fall of '91, and publication is scheduled for the following May, when I'll also celebrate my sixtieth birthday.

I go down a few months beforehand to lead my workshop on "Creating from the Spirit" at the Auburn Theological Seminary, an outstanding venue for adult education on the campus of Union Theological Seminary, a few blocks north of Columbia University on upper Broadway. I stay on a few more days in New York to attend a literary party, where I run into Victor Navasky, whom I met when he came to Manhattan from Yale Law School in the early sixties and started a political humor magazine called *Monocle.* I had fun writing for it and going to the parties its issues provided an excuse to celebrate. Victor is now publisher of *The Nation,* where I got my start as a writer, and when I say I've been thinking of coming back to live in New York for a while, he says he'll give me a desk at *The Nation* in return for doing some reviews and articles.

"You started out there," he says, "so you might as well —" before saying "end up there" he smiles and says, "come back."

It feels right, like a welcome, an affirmation.

Am I taking this as a "sign"? A "sign from God"? From "the universe"? Or is it an example of what Jung calls "synchronicity"? However it's labeled, it feels good, it brings a sense of harmony and peace, and I'm now trusting that interior reaction. If the offer had stoked fear in me — the kind of trepidation that battered me before the marriage — I would have said "Thanks, but no thanks." I tell Victor to save me the desk.

When I go back to Boston, I talk to my friends about the move, and most of them understand.

"I know it seems crazy," I say to Ivan Gold over cappuccinos on Charles Street. "I'm about to be sixty years old, and here I am pulling up stakes to go back and live in Greenwich Village, like some sort of — some kind of young . . ."

I can't think of a suitable term, and Ivan strokes his beard and says wisely, "There ought to be a Yiddish word for it."

"*Meshuganuh?*" I ask. That means crazy.

"Not quite," Ivan muses, and after another thoughtful cappuccino comes up with . . . "*trumbanik*. Accent on the first syllable. It means something like 'gadabout.'"

"That's it," I say. "The *trumbanik* goes to New York."

Ivan confesses that he too would like to return to New York. "In my mind," he says, "I never left."

My old friend Shaun O'Connell comes up with a literary analysis of my move, relating it correctly to the writing of *New York in the Fifties*.

"You were seduced by your own book," he says.

My off-and-on girlfriend, whose match with me was made in Heaven/Hell, takes the news calmly, thinking perhaps, as I have done in the back of my mind, that maybe this is a blessing for both of us; maybe my leaving town is the only way we'll ever be able to break our cycle of love-hurt, attraction-repulsion, off and on, out and in. (A month or so after I move, she becomes engaged to another man.)

Theresa is surprised but thinks New York sounds exciting, at least for a while. I assure her my move is only temporary — "one year at a time" — which is how I envision it. Maybe that's why I don't feel torn about leaving the special people and the places I love — the pond in the Public Garden, Charles Street and Beacon Hill, the King's Chapel parish house — I'm only leaving for a little while, taking a break, but of course I'll return. Don't I always?

Just before the trip to New York that clinches my decision, I'm chosen as a member-at-large of the King's Chapel parish council. I've served on this lay body before, and then on the vestry, but being invited back at this time is especially sweet. It's an unspoken acknowledgment that in spite of my big mistake — what many could validly call my sin — of breaking the marriage vows said in this very church, I am still accepted and still regarded as part of the church family. Like Jesus giving water to the woman who's been married five times, my fellow church members give me this precious gift. The gesture embodies the spirit of what I mean by "Christian." I give thanks to God, and to my church family, but explain that I'm moving to New York — at least for a while. With accustomed grace, they wish me well.

, , ,

I'm in church. In New York. I notice I can't even fit the terms "church" and "New York" in the same sentence. I think of them as two conflicting concepts, like "Indiana" and "existentialism." This dichotomy that persists in my mind dates back to the time when I came to New York in the fifties. I didn't come to go to church, but if anything, to escape it. My church then was Columbia, and Hamilton Hall, where classes are held, my chapel; professors like Mark Van Doren and Lionel Trilling my priests. The White Horse Tavern in Greenwich Village becomes my baptismal font, my communion wine and wafers the chianti and bread at Louis' Tavern off Sheridan Square.

Finding the right church is like falling in love. I visit many churches in New York, all of them fine, attractive, welcoming — but none strikes that chord of deep response that I felt when I first walked into King's Chapel. I wonder if I'll ever find it again — maybe when it comes to churches I'll only fall in love once.

I enjoy in different ways All Souls Unitarian and Marble Collegiate, yet I don't feel personally drawn to them or to others I visit in my New York church-hopping. When I tape an interview in a series called "Faces on Faith" for the Video Department of Trinity Episcopal Church on Wall Street, I enjoy getting to know the producer, Linda Hanick, and over lunch I ask if I can go to church that Sunday with her and her family. She says I'm welcome to join them, but explains that although she works for Trinity, she and her husband and two daughters attend another Episcopal church, called All Angels, on Eightieth and Broadway. Linda lives in Brooklyn Heights, but she and her family don't mind taking the subway to the Upper West Side to go to All Angels, where they like "the spirit."

I know what she means when I hear the first hymn. There's an upbeat, dynamic feeling to it, and I learn that the hymns here are not all from the Episcopal hymn book, but some are of a category called "praise music" that is used in some Catholic churches as well as other Protestant congregations. "The whole congregation is the choir," one parishioner tells me, "singing in parts and harmony." The music is played by musicians who I learn work in pit bands for Broadway shows and sung by a congregation that stands and belts out the lyrics as if they really mean them. So much of church hymn-singing seems gray and perfunctory, as if parishioners are simply doing their duty, and the words they mouth might be in Urdu or Sanskrit for all the personal meaning they hold for the singers. But here people raise their voices as if they know what they are singing, and it comes from the heart as well as the throat. I notice three or four people in the congregation raise their right hand in the air as they sing, as if in affirmation of the message, a gesture of belief and triumph.

Maybe this harks back to the enlivened spirit of the Baptist church of my boyhood, where I was drawn to the vigorous hymns and the gestures that went with them, like extending your arm in an imaginary toss while singing, "Throw out the lifeline, someone is drifting away." I like that some parishioners here express the spirit by raising their arms in the air, and I wish I had the courage to do the same, to proclaim my faith in that unashamed, physical show of unabashed joy in Jesus Christ, but my layers of education (not knowledge, but education) and social conformity hold me back. At least I can enjoy being in a congregation with others less constrained.

People don't dress up to go to church at All Angels. There's a New York kind of casual look, as if they've just come from — or were on their way to — bagels with cream cheese and coffee and the Sunday *Times*. It doesn't seem at all disrespectful but rather gives the impression that church is a natural part of these people's lives — like the bagels and the *Times* — rather than some kind of once-a-week special performance that is alien to their daily concerns. The church building itself is informal — it might be mistaken for any brownstone on the West Side — except for the big banner emblazoned with its name that hangs in front.

Once every month at All Angels there's a practice of breaking up into groups of three or four and sharing the concerns of each person so the others can pray for them too. A young woman cellist from Kansas tells of her nervousness about an audition coming up the next week for playing in the orchestra of the Metropolitan Opera Company, while a middle-aged writer speaks of his problem with an article he's having trouble finishing, and a woman whose mother has cancer expresses her feeling of helplessness before the disease. I feel close to these people, in their cares, in their openness and faith, in finding a nourishment of spirit here. I ask for their prayers for my own concerns, and pray for theirs.

With words. I am praying with words, addressing Jesus Christ, addressing God, on behalf of these fellow believers and seekers who only ten minutes ago were strangers. When we pull our chairs from the small circles of prayer back into rows, and the service continues, I recite, with the congregation, the Psalm for the day, the Fortieth Psalm, which begins:

> I waited patiently for the LORD; and he
> inclined unto me, and heard my cry.
> He brought me up also out of an horrible pit,
> out of the miry clay, and set my feet upon a
> rock, and established my goings . . .

Yet again, I think; as he/she has done all my life, from child-hood on to this very moment. And I realize this Psalm is not just a rhythmic string of words, an expression of comforting senti-ments (there is nothing soft or sentimental about the "horrible pit" and the "miry clay"), but is rather speaking of my own life, and the lives of those all around me in the congregation, as well as those outside on the streets of New York and across the oceans and continents, wherever God's children (I mean all human beings) are born and strive and love and die, no matter what their faith or language.

The words are not empty but resonant with meaning. I'm no longer reciting by rote, mouthing and mumbling the lines of the liturgy just for the sake of courtesy and form, as I have since the words blanked out three years ago after my betrayal of the mar-riage vows, and I found my prayer in silence. Now I am praying the prayer, the Psalm; I am praying with words. I say a prayer of thanks to All Angels — the church — and the Holy Spirit.

I never join this church, nor become part of it as I did at King's Chapel, which I'll always think of as "my church." But going to services at All Angels when I live in New York in the nineties is a real refreshment of spirit, an opening to interior doors that were closed for the past three years.

, , ,

I'm grateful to find my way back to prayer with words, but it doesn't mean I no longer want to practice the silent prayer. I need to find a yoga class as well as a church. The prayer of the body I found in yoga has sustained me through the wordless time and has come to be part of my life, my rest and renewal. Of course one can practice yoga anytime, anyplace, without any props or teachers or companions, but doing yoga alone is not nearly as fulfilling and satisfying as doing it in a class with other people. I keep finding that community is a key ingredient of spirituality, and it holds as true for yoga practice as it does for the practice of faith in church, synagogue, or mosque. Solitary prayer, like solitary yoga, is enriching and meaningful, but from time to time it's important to practice with others, to gain the strength that comes from bodies and spirits joining together in a common enterprise, a mutual sharing in which the individual is strengthened and nourished by the group.

After several months of trying, I realize that finding the right yoga class can be just as hard as finding the right church or synagogue. Finally, on advice from Carol Nelson, my yoga teacher in Boston, I try a class in astanga yoga (also called "power yoga") taught by one of its leading practitioners, Beryl Bender.

I've been hearing about astanga for the last year or so, with opinions ranging from "It's the original, true yoga" to "It's not yoga at all, but a form of aerobics using yoga principles." Like religion, yoga has its own dogmas, divisions, loyalists, and fanatics. One of my former yoga teachers at the health spa Rancho La Puerta tells me how proud she is to be able to be doing astanga even though she's forty years old! I've just turned sixty, and my yoga skills — if you can even call them that — are still at the most basic beginner level, though I've been practicing now for five or six years.

"Do you think I can even do it?" I ask Carol, and she assures me that Beryl "takes you along slowly" and "helps you build up your strength." I sign up for the class.

Beryl Bender is a slim, well-toned blond woman in her late forties with a direct, no-nonsense but pleasant manner. There are a dozen or more regulars at her downtown class in a Soho loft, some of them professional dancers and athletes, almost all of them — mostly men and women in their thirties and forties — in the kind of toned condition of physical strength and discipline worthy of health magazine photos. I am out of place in this company, but Beryl and her husband and teaching partner, Thom Birch, make me feel at home. I enjoy not only the challenge but the result.

On the first night of the advanced class I notice that about halfway through the hour-and-forty-five-minute session a pool of water like a small pond has accumulated beneath me, and I wonder if there's a leak in the roof. It takes me a moment to realize that this is my own sweat. I have never sweated like this in my life, and it is cleansing and relieving. I know if it is possible to "sweat out" the toxins in my body, as the holistic health people proclaim, by God I have done it; my system must be as pure as a lake in the high Himalayas. I walk home the several miles from Soho to Horatio Street feeling light and buoyant and alive.

> , , ,

Living in New York again revives the scenes of my youth there, and I start a novel drawing on the same period as the memoir *New York in the Fifties* I just published. I haven't written a novel since the one that transmogrified my Hollywood experience into *Selling Out,* published in '85. In between giving workshops and writing occasional essay-reviews for *The Nation* and articles for *GQ,* I begin the new novel.

I roll the literary dice again, gambling I can make this my next major project in terms of time and also income. I want to finish the whole thing before trying to get a publisher, but as money starts to run low, I put together the hundred or so pages I have with a rough outline to see if it's ready to take to market. Two writer friends and one professional adviser say no. I read it again and see that what I have is flat, fragmented, far too incomplete to show for a contract. I wonder if I haven't used up the juice of that era in the memoir I've already written about it. I know I must put those pages aside and decide later, when I have the time and money, if I also have the desire to revive it.

This is a blow. I'd counted on devoting the next year or so to this novel. Now reality blows away those illusions. I hear the familiar sound of a door slamming shut. And each time it happens, it's hard to have faith that another one is going to open.

At least the blow is softened by a juicy magazine assignment for a trip to Ireland, my first visit to the land that's part of my own heritage. I have to remember, though, that this is not going to solve the problem of finding another book project. My agent suggests I "think of a short nonfiction book" to write, which is good advice but easier said than done. To put it bluntly, I tell a friend, "I need a miracle."

A few days later an editor I don't know from a publisher I've never worked with calls to say my name was suggested at one of their meetings as a good person to write a short nonfiction book they have in mind.

"What's it about?" I ask.

"Miracles," he says.

Sometimes God takes you literally.

， ， ，

I'm naked and shivering as two men in blue aprons dunk me into the cold water of a rectangular pool at Lourdes — the French village that is world famous as a place of miracles since a shepherd girl named Bernadette had a vision of the Virgin Mary here in 1848. The water from the spring she discovered is said to have healing powers, and people from all over the world come to take the baths, visit the grotto shrine, walk in torchlight processions, and pray. I've come here as part of my research on the book *Expect a Miracle,* and the dunking is like another baptism, reminding me of the one I received at the Broad Ripple Christian church at age eleven when the minister granted my wish to experience the ceremony of full immersion this church performs.

No lightning strikes or voice comes out of the sky when I'm dunked in the waters at Lourdes any more than when I was baptized in Indianapolis, yet this whole journey I'm taken on by writing the miracles book reaffirms my faith and my sense of wonder. I encounter every variety of miracle experience, meeting an Irishwoman whose doctor and medical records affirm her story of rising from a stretcher to walk after being paralyzed for three years when she hears a voice at an Irish shrine of the

Madonna called Knock. Most of the miracles I find are not of that classic definition of "an extraordinary event in the physical world that cannot be explained by the laws of science," but rather the more modest "a wonder, a marvel."

I witness again at Lourdes how service brings fulfillment to the servant as well as the served, for everyone who comes with a physical pain or illness or disability is assigned a volunteer to help them, to take them from place to place, to be sure all their needs are met. This service creates the sense of joy there, produces the healing of spirit that the place now emphasizes and that makes the infirmities of the flesh, even if not healed, easier to bear. That's why so many people return to Lourdes, making it the most popular pilgrimage site in the world.

My own miracle at Lourdes — in the sense of "a wonder, a marvel" — comes when a friend from my college days at Columbia acts as a kind of Virgil for the second time in my life. It's Sam Astrachan from the Bronx, who in my senior year in college and the year that followed introduced me to Dorothy Day and the Catholic Worker movement in the Bowery, to Jack Kerouac at Johnny Romero's Bar in the West Village, to the Fulton Fish Market and the Festival of San Gennaro in Little Italy — to New York in the fifties, which became my home and the subject and source of so much of my work throughout my life.

Now Sam lives in the south of France with his French sculptor wife, Claude, who went to Lourdes with her family as a child. They drive me clear across France — I hadn't realized they live seven hours from Lourdes by car — and translate for me, finding just the right people I need to interview, making my whole work there possible. It's also the renewal of a friendship that's held over all these years and cities. We've had reunions in New York, Detroit, and Boston, and now — who could have guessed? — at Lourdes.

My Jewish friend Sam and his wife walk with me in the evening procession when people from every race and culture join in singing the Ave Maria, and carry a candle that creates with all the others a moving sea of light. A young woman volunteer from Ireland says when everyone raises their candle, "It's like the raising of glasses at a feast." Yes, like a toast, and I make one now to Sam as I think of him beside me raising his candle at Lourdes, and I say, "*L'chaim,*" To life.

, , ,

The last exercise of the workshop I lead on spiritual autobiography is drawing a road map of your spiritual journey. On a large sheet of newsprint you sketch a line like a winding road or chart or graph to trace the ups and downs and ins and outs of your experience, illustrating with crayon drawings the peaks and pitfalls and turning points along the way, like bridges burned, bursts of sunlight, forks in the road, dangerous curves, spires of ambition or achievement, personal or professional battlegrounds, hearts broken, hearts in love — whatever symbols serve to signify meaningful events in your own life story. Then I ask people to pick one of the turning points and write about it. After leading these workshops for a couple of years, I begin to see a pattern, one that continues to be affirmed whenever I hear the results of this exercise: the turning points that seem at the time they occur to be the worst, most painful blows of fate are most likely to be the events that lead to the greatest fulfillment, though we can't see this outcome till later.

When I say we can only see the outcome later, I mean much later — like many years, or maybe half a lifetime. When the wound is still fresh, the scar still red and angry, it's impossible to see any "good" coming from a deep disappointment or setback or injury to body or pride or self-image, which all of us in some way or other sustain along the way. Suggesting such an outcome then sounds like the worst kind of cut-rate uplift, the sort of easy "positive thinking" I most abhorred when I heard it as a college student in the fifties, and still disdain when I see it repackaged now in New Age quickie, soul-soothing formulas.

"When one door closes another opens" is one of the most commonplace clichés and reminds me that sometimes thoughts or ideas become clichés because they are true. It sounds even more Pollyannaish to add that the doors that open next often lead to larger and more fulfilling life than lay on the other side of the doors that closed, but that's true in my own life.

My first major experience of this kind comes when I'm rejected by every one of the sophisticated fraternities during rush week at socially conscious Northwestern, and, feeling like a leper with my acne and inappropriate gangster-style neckties (they were splashy and loud instead of cool and rep), I flee back home to Indiana University, spend a semester in a rooming house with fellow outcasts, then join a friendly fraternity.

Now I secretly feel like a phony and turncoat, leaving behind my old "Independent" rooming house friends. I think I'm betraying them, which now is like betraying myself, for I see that I too am "them." All of us really are "them" to someone else, to some other group or faction or race or religion, all of us are simply bags of bone and skin when you strip away our medals and money and titles and pretensions, all the layers of clothes and jewels and accomplishments we hope will make us special, blessed, safe, loved, envied, elite, aloof; so we cherish the trinkets of status we hope will spare us from pain and keep us alive forever and make us forget we too will end up (at least in this bodily form) as dust and ashes, ashes and dust.

If anyone had told me at the time that my rejection at Northwestern would later lead to a far greater opportunity, one that would shape my whole life as a writer — would *give* me my life as a writer, my very identity — I'd have spit in his eye. Yet being turned away in Evanston, Illinois, leads me in my sophomore year from Indiana to New York City and Columbia. Here I find my education with literary lights like Mark Van Doren, Lionel Trilling, and C. Wright Mills, my early publication in *The Nation*, my life as a young writer in Greenwich Village — to put it more succinctly, my life.

It's not until thirty years later when I flee from Hollywood that I feel as naked and alone as I did coming home from Northwestern in 1950. In the spring of 1980 I'm broke, sick, split from the longest and best relationship I've ever known, and guzzling wine every day like water. My fuzzed-up brain, addled with booze and anxiety, can compute that this is a turning point, all right, but the idea that it's leading anywhere but down seems like a cruel joke. Yet this is the very turn that leads me to recovery of health and the clarity of body and mind that awakens spirit, brings me to church on Christmas Eve, and begins my own midlife journey back to faith at age forty-eight, creating the whole new life I am given for what I think of as the Second Half. I also think of it as the Best Half.

There are so many turns I think at the time are disastrous that lead to brighter, fuller kinds of experience, I can't enumerate them all. The most difficult challenge of the spiritual path is simply to trust. At each new crisis we fear if things don't work out according to our plan, we have failed, blown it, betrayed ourselves and been betrayed. The hardest thing to accept is that maybe our plan isn't the best; that maybe there is another plan, one we can't see at the time or are unable to understand the significance of if we can, yet it keeps happening, and we keep doubting.

I find the most healing response to those doubts in Henri Nouwen's *Reaching Out.* Rather than giving us pat answers or dogma, Father Nouwen poses a question:

> What if the events of our history are molding us as a sculptor molds his clay, and if it is only in a careful obedience to these molding hands that we can discover our real vocation and become mature people? What if all the unexpected interruptions are in fact invitations to give up old-fashioned and outmoded styles of living and are opening up new unexplored areas of experience? And finally: What

if our history does not prove to be a blind impersonal sequence of events over which we have no control, but rather reveals to us a guiding hand pointing to a personal encounter in which all our hopes and aspirations will reach their fulfillment?

Then our life would indeed be different, because then fate becomes opportunity, wounds a warning, and paralysis an invitation to search for deeper sources of vitality.

⁊ ⁊ ⁊

When I speak of my own turning points, of doors that open after others close, I feel fortunate, and grateful too, but I don't want to try to sell false expectations or formulas for easy uplift. The doors we go through (sometimes are pushed through kicking and screaming) don't always open to what we want.

What of those doors that lead to early death, or the nightmare of the Holocaust, or seemingly senseless suffering? I hear a response that helps me in Bill Moyers's discussions of Genesis with people of every faith. Talking about "The First Murder," the story of Cain and Abel, the Catholic novelist Mary Gordon says, ". . . faith requires that you get out of the story. Faith requires that you say 'There is a larger Story than this story, and it's not narrative. . . .' "

I want narrative because I was raised on that kind of story, that's what story means to me, *that's what makes sense.* Yet Gordon's comment opens up the possibility that there are other kinds of stories — quantum physics stories, perhaps — that I can't understand but that still have some meaning beyond our human understanding. "If you're going to have faith," Gordon says, "you have to say, 'Outside the boundary of the story, there is a meaning, a plan. There is a God I do not understand.' "

Trusting a God we do not understand is where faith comes in. And why it is so hard. I suspect we make it harder than it has to be, though. I know I do. As I look back I see that in the struggle to "know when it's God," the simplest rule of discernment is best, and is probably all we need. As William Barry writes in interpreting the Ignatian rules, "when we are out of tune with God's one action, we experience ourselves as alienated, unhappy, unfulfilled, even though we do not know the source of the malaise."

Whenever I feel shaken and shaking in times of crisis, when a decision I'm about to make or the struggle to make it brings mental and physical rumblings (thoughts in chaos, pulse rising) it is "wrong," or not the will of God. When I go forward anyway — fortified with the advice or reassurances of "experts" (psychiatric, spiritual, religious, lay, or medical) as justification, I bring on pain and suffering to myself and others. It seems so simple. Yet it's often so hard to trust our own instincts, which surely are good, and God, within us.

Once while leading a retreat in the Yucatan, I take my group on a tour of the ecosystem in which our guide brings us to a river that flows to the sea. The way to experience this river is to get in the water and simply lean back, as if you're floating, and let the current carry you. At first our group of a dozen people are giggling and thrashing and then after a while we fall silent, simply being carried along without effort, taking in the sky and the birds that fly past, and the soft lapping of the water is the only sound. As I float along, exerting no effort, I think: *this is what trust is like, this is what it would feel like to really live in faith.*

Chapter 9

GETTING ON

———◆———

FROM THE WINDOW OF MY HIGH-CEILINGED STUDIO on Horatio Street in the West Village I can see the Hudson River, and if I stick my head out and crane my neck to the right, I can even get a glimpse of the Statue of Liberty. There's a sense of rightness and completion to my being here in the neighborhood I lived in so long ago, not only because of writing about it in *New York in the Fifties*. I first came to the city with my parents for the New York World's Fair in 1940, and chose as a souvenir a Statue of Liberty night-light that I kept by my bed through childhood and into adolescence, a symbol of freedom and adventure. Now here I am with the real Miss Liberty outside my window, and it seems preordained, like a station on what the Navajos call "the gleaming way," the path of spirit and life.

Following my "one year at a time" plan, I renew my lease in the summer of '93 and expect to do the same the following year. I'm working on the "miracles" book as well as writing occasional reviews for *The Nation* and doing my workshops in spiritual autobiography around the country every month or so.

After a year I've settled in, not only finding a church and a yoga class I like, but also a Jungian therapist who has a deep understanding of spirituality and serves as a wise and trusted guide, illuminating dreams, desires, and actions from a spiritual as well as a psychological viewpoint. I have no plan to go anywhere else — but later it seems such a plan is already in place.

It begins with a phone call back in '92 when I've just moved to New York. A woman's voice tells me she went to her dentist that day, was leafing through a magazine in the waiting room, and read an article about my workshop on "Writing Your Spiritual Autobiography." She wants to know if I'll give the workshop for the church she belongs to — the First Unitarian Church of North Palm Beach. It's the first of a cluster of invitations that over the next year keep taking me to a place I never imagined going — Florida. I'm asked to speak at the Broward County Library's annual "Night of Literary Feasts" in Fort Lauderdale, then the Miami Book Fair, Books and Books in Coral Gables, and the Seaside Writers Conference, sponsored by Florida International University in Miami. Having dinner outdoors on a balmy winter night on Ocean Drive in South Beach, it occurs to me this would be a great place to be in the cold season. I ask the people I met from FIU at the writer's conference if I can come down and teach a course in their graduate writing program in the spring semester beginning in January '94, and they find a way to make it happen. I sublet my New York apartment, assuming I'll return when the semester's over in May, then pack my bathing suit and laptop computer and head for the beach.

Miami Beach is the last place I'd ever imagined living. Like many people of my generation, I associated it with death and aging, a sun-drenched haven for wrinkled elders laid out to die. South Beach had the old Jewish population, while aging WASPs went west to the Gulf Coast. Isaac Bashevis Singer and his characters are followed by "Rabbit Angstrom," whose author, John

Updike, sends him to Florida (where else?) to die, in *Rabbit at Rest*. From watching *Miami Vice* on television, I gather that if you don't die of old age down there, you're liable to be killed in cross fire from drug lords. It sounds like a good place to stay away from.

So here I am living in Miami Beach and loving it. I find it no longer conforms to its former image as the mecca of *alter cockers* (Yiddish for old guys). Here on South Beach, elders on fixed incomes have been replaced by models on fashion shoots, and Rollerblades rather than wheelchairs are the menace of the sidewalks. But the beach itself is quiet except on weekends, the sun is warm, and the sound of the surf at night is soothing. I enjoy the writing class I'm teaching at FIU's North Miami campus, and by the end of the semester I ask if I can come again next spring.

"How would you like to come in September?" I'm asked. "And stay the whole year?"

It clicks, and the lock is sealed when I learn from my tenant in New York that the rent on my Village studio is going up to $2,000 a month. I've enjoyed my brief return to New York, but now here's a chance to get out before I go broke. I store my winter clothes with old reliable Ted the Horse and find an apartment on the ocean in South Beach. When friends ask, "How do you write — much less meditate! — in the midst of all the action?" I explain I live south of Fifth Street, the most residential tip of Ocean Drive, which I hope will retain its reputation as "the quiet part" at least until I finish another few books. In the meantime, I walk every morning on a lovely, unspoiled strip of white sand beach, and listen to the sound of the surf from my window at night (which works much better for lulling you to sleep than one of those "nature" CDs that re-create the sound).

My path to here seems best explained by a scene from the Salinger story "Seymour: An Introduction." Buddy Glass is about to make a crucial shot in a marbles game on the sidewalk outside his brownstone in New York when his older, wiser brother Seymour stops to watch and gives him the best advice he ever got: "Don't aim."

I didn't aim for Miami Beach and wouldn't have known how to land here if I tried (and would surely be advised against it if I asked the opinions of worldly counselors). I simply follow a path that seems laid out for me. I often think back to that first Florida phone call from the woman who read about my workshop in a magazine in her dentist's office.

What if she'd gone to a different dentist?

, , ,

It bugs me when people think I've come to Miami Beach to "retire." I quote Irwin Shaw's startled response when a reporter asked him on his eightieth birthday when he planned to retire. "Writers don't retire!" he explained. Thank God. It's one of the beautiful fringe benefits of my perilous profession. Why in the world would you want to stop writing? It's like someone asking when you plan to stop looking at the world, and the people in it, and examining your own heart and soul and mind, or when you'll no longer want to express in language (that beautiful, mysterious instrument) what you see, learn, know, feel, hope, and dream.

Like everyone else, I never really believed I'd get old. Oh, of course I knew it in theory, but not in my guts. In my twenties I imagined I didn't even want to live so long. My heroes then were the drunk romantics like Dylan Thomas, who joined the Dead Poets Society at age thirty-nine, and F. Scott Fitzgerald, who drank himself into his grave at forty-four before he finished *The Last Tycoon*, which Edmund Wilson thought would have been his "most mature" novel — the one he wrote when he finally sobered up.

But as soon as I get close to those years in my own life, I discover that death no longer seems so noble and romantic. The normal signs and marks of age surprise and shock me with each insidious appearance, beginning in my late thirties. The first is a trip to the eye doctor to see if I've developed glaucoma — the only reason I can think of for not being able to easily read the print in a paperback novel I'm teaching at the Iowa Writers Workshop. The optometrist asks me how old I am, and when I say thirty-nine, he explains I've simply reached the age when I need reading glasses.

Damn. "Reached the age." That phrase once signaled opportunity, as you "reach" the age of puberty, of driving, drinking, "consent," and suffrage. Then at midlife, that "reaching" of age switches from opportunity to alarm, signals for repairs, as you "reach the age" of needing glasses, Grecian Formula (if you don't want to betray you're gray), Rogaine (if you want to keep what hair you have left), bifocals, mammograms and estrogen for women, cardiograms and now Viagra for men, mandatory retirement, retirement homes, wills, selection of disposal (burial or burning, what style and price casket or urn, and where and who to scatter your ashes).

The next year after my glaucoma scare turns out to be "only" aging, I'm preening with pride after picking up a woman at a mall until she asks me, "What color did your hair used to be?" It's the same as always, isn't it? Brown? Not in her eyes. For some bizarre reason she sees — gray. Maybe she's color blind. It certainly must be a light gray or I'd have noticed it. In another few years I can't help but notice it.

Landmarks — more like land mines — begin to multiply, signaling age. With single people, it often comes in reactions from the opposite sex. After losing my love of seven years, I return to the dating fray in 1980 and take an early thirty-something teacher for a drink. I'm forty-eight, and I mention I'm working on a novel called *Under the Apple Tree* about a boy growing up on the home front during World War II.

"Oh," she says, "Did you fight in that war?"

"No! I was a little kid in that war!"

I can see it's all the same to her. History. Ancient history. The Fall of Rome, World War II, whatever.

I'm taking the MBTA Red Line from Park Street in Boston to Harvard Square, and from where I stand hanging on to the overhead bar, my eye is caught by a pretty young woman student sitting down across the way. She sees me and smiles. I smile back. Wow. Real eye contact — I know she's too young, but the attention is flattering. My heart begins to thunk faster as she stands up and approaches me.

"Would you like to sit down?" she asks politely.

She's offering her seat to an old man.

I refuse the offer. I want to prove I can stand up all the way to the Harvard Square stop.

Whatever the effect, I know that innocent and well-meaning young woman was trying to be nice.

On the night of my fiftieth birthday I go to a Red Sox game with a bright, witty woman I've recently met and we're having a great time. I'm thinking, 'Hey, I'm fifty, and feeling no pain!" After the fifth inning I get up to take a pee.

A group of teenage thugs behind me at the urinal trough start complaining about how long I'm taking.

"Hey, this gray-haired guy in front of me can't get it going!"

Another one shouts, "I bet it just dribbles out!"

Now they are laughing and hooting.

"Wonder how long since he's got laid?"

I want to tell them, "This afternoon, you jerks," but I know if I open my mouth they'll beat the crap out of me.

Happy birthday.

, , ,

One of the most unusual and frustrating aspects of "ageism" is that unlike any other prejudice — against race, nationality, gender, sex, sexual preference, disabilities or "challenges," mental or physical — everyone alive is going to someday be old — that is, if they're lucky. If they don't die first. Maybe the knowledge that they are doomed to become like us — or rather, the popular image of us — old, gray, decrepit, doddering, foolish — explains the particular venom, sarcasm, fear, and condescension with which "ageists" react to those who are older or just plain old, in years.

Or maybe the emotion of it all simply goes to the fact that the older you get the closer you are to death, and death is THE great fear in life, especially in American life in this day and age (it's almost as bad as being old!). I'm not aware of how terrified I've been myself of the prospect of death (*my own*, I mean), until a friend I haven't seen for a while brings the reality home to me over lunch in Boston when I'm in my late fifties and he's in his early sixties. He uses a phrase that sends chills through my body and soul when he tells me, "I'm at the point in life where I'm trying to plan the End Game."

The End Game!

Holy God! This man has evidently accepted the fact that he doesn't have all the time in the world left to him, that in fact his time on earth is limited, and at sixty-something the limits are within viewing distance. And in a few years I'll be sixty myself!

I'm so freaked out by the idea of "the End Game," and the calm, accepting way my friend speaks of it, that I avoid seeing him for the next two years. It isn't a conscious avoidance, and when I realize why I haven't been in touch with him, I feel ashamed and write him a letter confessing my fear of "the End Game," and of anyone who is mature and courageous enough to think about it, and even speak of it! I tell him I'm now ready to face such music of reality myself, and I'd be grateful for any advice he can give me for dealing with it.

He recommends I read *The Tibetan Book of the Dead* — which now, in its new translation and title for American marketing, is called *The Tibetan Book of Living and Dying*. It's even divided into two parts, the first one on living, the second on dying, so you can ease your way into the tough stuff. I buy the book, read the first section, then put it under my bed and completely forget about it. A few years later I buy the audiotape of the book, which I figure will be easier to take, and I go directly to the "dying" part, which lulls me to sleep on an airplane by the time we're twenty minutes into the flight.

I realize I'm not really interested in the process or philosophy of dying, and in fact am not really afraid of it. The fear lifts one beautiful morning when I'm taking a short flight from L.A. to San Diego on my way to the health spa Rancho La Puerta. I'm feeling good and at peace as I look forward to the week of exercise and healthy eating and living in a beautiful spot where I go every year and always feel especially energized afterward. As I'm in this benign mood, the small plane gently banks into a cloud and we become part of it. The idea comes to me very deeply that *This is what it's like,* this is what happens when you die, and it's peaceful, and then whatever comes next will come next, the great mystery.

"And all shall be well and all shall be well, and all manner of thing shall be well," I remember from the great English spiritual writer and nun of the late Middle Ages, Juliana of Norwich.

I know it's not the act of death, the process of dying, I'm afraid or upset or angry about; it's the sacrifice of leaving this world, with all I yet want to do in it. The sadness of it was expressed most powerfully to me in one of John D. McDonald's mystery novels, when his hero Travis McGee realizes he's getting older, and in September, his favorite month, wonders "how many Septembers" he has left. In his late forties after a hard and often violent life, he speculates perhaps he has seventeen more Septembers.

How many more do I have now at age sixty-six?

Despite my denials of being in denial about death, it's obvious I'm obsessed by the subject of age and aging. Is it simply by chance that as soon as I move to Florida in the spring of '94, I'm asked to write about a conference on "conscious aging" at Clearwater, over on the Gulf Coast? Talk about synchronicity!

Here I am wanting to know as much as I can about aging and how to handle it, how to get the most out of it, how to live up to my best potential as the years and gray hairs accumulate, and the ideal opportunity drops in my lap. This is not some stuffy academic or medical conference, this is put on by the Omega Institute of Rhinebeck, New York, a kind of East Coast answer to Esalen, a cutting-edge citadel of New Age learning where I've given my own workshops in spiritual autobiography and creativity. Omega sponsors events throughout the country, and Florida seems the appropriate place to study "conscious aging."

Best of all, this weekend won't be led by a bunch of boring statistical nerds with dry-as-dust monographs, but by the hip guru of sixties psychedelics and meditation Baba Ram Dass, whose trademark message is "Be here now." I tell Rick Fields, editor of the *Yoga Journal,* he's picked the right man for this assignment; I'm "personally involved in the subject." Hey, it's my future. I pack some T-shirts, an old copy of Ram Dass's spiritual manifesto *Be Here Now,* and cross the highway known as Alligator Alley to hit the Gulf Coast.

, , ,

I'm not surprised to hear the Omega Institute is drawing a big response for their programs on "conscious aging." I learn that a hundred years ago there were 2.4 million Americans over sixty-five — less than 4 percent of the population, and now the figures have risen to 30 million and 12 percent. The Census Bureau predicts that 35 million citizens will be over sixty-five by the year 2000 — the year of my fiftieth high school reunion! Omega has not only the statistics, but better still, the understanding. Their catalog confirms my own feelings when it says that "America's stereotypic vision of aging" is formed by "a society obsessed with youth, in which old age is regarded as a clinical problem."

Right on! I can feel the spirit of sixties rebellion stirring again in my blood. *Tell it like it is!* And who better to do that than the consciousness guru himself, Baba Ram Dass. In his previous incarnation as Harvard professor Richard Alpert, Ram Dass teamed with Timothy Leary to turn on undergraduates with psilocybin and spread the word of illumination-through-hallucination to the flower children. Bounced out of Harvard, Alpert looked East to find enlightenment with a guru in India, shedding tweeds and loafers for a robe and sandals and trading in his birth name for a Sanskrit moniker meaning "servant of God." Though we've traveled far different paths, Ram Dass and I are the same age, and I know his outlook on growing old won't be burdened by conformity to prevailing "gerontology," defined by *Webster's* as "the study of the physiological and pathological phenomena associated with aging."

So according to *Webster's,* I'm not just old, I'm pathological!

More than two hundred of us over-sixties, mixed with younger people who make a living by studying, caring for, nursing, or selling housing to "elders," gather in the Tiffany Ballroom of the Belleview Mido Resort Hotel in Clearwater early on a Saturday morning to begin the two-day session. Ram Dass appears in a red-and-white shirt hanging loose over khaki pants and brown moccasins without socks. The top of his head is bald now, and red from the sun, with white hair flowing out from the sides like foam, and he sports a white mustache. Some of his fans who haven't seen him since they sat at his feet with hundreds of others to hear the wisdom he brought back from India in the 1970s are shocked at the signs of his own aging. "He's gray," says one, while another, more surprised, gasps, "He's fat!" Looking down at his stomach later that morning, Ram Dass himself stops in midlecture to remark, "Wow, look at that — I'm fat! But you should have seen my guru's belly — I'm in 'guru training'!"

After our morning meditation and breakfast, Ram Dass settles down on a wicker couch on a platform overlooking our rows of hotel chairs. Some zealous elder (probably an American Legion dropout) has stuck a red-and-white bumper sticker on the couch that says "Sexy Senior Citizen." Ram Dass plucks it off and says, "As an antidote to this, I'll tell you a story.

> "An older man is walking down the street one day when a frog jumps up on his arm and says, 'If you kiss me, I'll turn into a beautiful princess and do whatever you want.' The man sticks the frog in his pocket and walks on. After a few more blocks the frog croaks, 'Hey, don't you want to kiss me so I'll turn into your beautiful princess?' The man says, 'At this stage of life, I'd rather have a talking frog.'"

This gets a rousing laugh from the audience, which doesn't seem to bode well for overcoming the "mythology of aging."

Ram Dass pulls a few Perrier bottles from a black knapsack, sets them on a table with a photograph of his guru, and tells us he's come to this subject through a sudden awareness of his own aging. A year or so earlier on a train from Westport, Connecticut, to New York City, a conductor asked him what kind of ticket he wanted — "senior citizen" or "regular." "I was pleased to learn I could buy a 'senior' ticket at half the fare," Ram Dass remembers,

> "but I wondered how in the world the conductor knew I was a 'senior citizen.' He didn't even ask for my ID.
>
> "A few years ago in an Indian village I met a brother devotee of my guru and he said, 'You're looking much older.' I drew back, offended, then I saw he was saying it with respect, not diminishment, like it was an accomplishment. My reaction showed how I'd bought into my culture's attitude, and I realized I'd have to be mindful. I remembered that when you put frogs in hot water they jump

out, but if you put them in cold water and slowly heat it, they sit there and boil to death. I realized, 'Unless I am mindful, I'll boil to death' — I'll slide into the model of aging in my culture and lose power, social role, economic and political power. I was awed by the dysfunctional mythology about aging in our society."

So am I. Our culture's cliché of aging is epitomized by Milton Berle's performance on *Beverly Hills 90210* as a doddering, out-to-pasture actor who flubs his old magic tricks and can't remember the names of movies he starred in during his prime. The hapless old geezer is pityingly patronized by one of the young studs of the show, no doubt as an example of youthful sympathy for "seniors," portrayed as a gang of pathetic decrepits who are lucky to get their tapioca down without dripping.

I agree with Ram Dass that we need "a new mythology of aging."

"In gerontology," he says, "aging seems to be presented as a problem. . . . It's possible to bring inner practice to bear on aging, so it's not overwhelming and doesn't contract or define us."

As he speaks, Ram Dass fingers a string of beads.

"When you're young you rehearse the future, when you're old you rehearse the past, but you're never in the present moment!"

ィ　ィ　ィ

I begin to see that Ram Dass's approach to "conscious aging" seems the same as it is for any other stage of life, as expressed in his popular books and lectures like *Be Here Now, The Only Dance There Is,* and *Grist for the Mill.* He teaches people why and how to be "in the moment," through meditation, "witnessing" of the self, and trying to consciously separate from the ego that runs our lives.

"Aging is just the particular grist for my mill right now," he tells me.

Aside from joking about his "guru belly," the only time Ram Dass mentions physical exercise or discipline during the weekend seminar is in a put-down he plays for laughs: "Our role model of aging was people who proved they stayed young — older men climbing mountains, playing golf, and sisters doing yoga at one hundred."

When I ask Ram Dass how he feels about the role of the body in conscious aging, he says, "You should honor the temple, take care of the body. I've been lax in taking care of myself. I have gout and high blood pressure."

He recommends Rabbi Zalman Schachter's book *From Age-Ing to Sage-Ing: A Profound New Vision of Growing Older,* where I find five pages on "forgiveness" exercises, but only three pages on "exercise, physical." Though Rabbi Schachter advocates "respect and reverence for the body," its role in "sage-ing" seems on the level of the "gentle stretching exercises and massage to promote flexibility and relaxation" offered in his workshops.

How can the "conscious aging" movement neglect the physical aspects of aging?

, , ,

At the end of the conference I ask Ram Dass some more personal questions about aging. Though the conscious-aging movement aims to refute the "mythology" of old age, I often wonder why little if anything is said about the myth that sexual desire and capacity ends in the later years. It's not true in my own experience, or that of some of men and women friends who are older than I am. Schachter's book has a total of two paragraphs on the subject and warns that if in our "elder" years we are still searching for "the more" in sex and pleasure, we are "flowing against the current of Thanatos."

I remind Ram Dass of the story he told about the older man

who can kiss a frog and turn it into his own beautiful princess, but prefers "at this age" to have a talking frog. "Which would you choose at your age now?" I ask. "A beautiful princess or a talking frog?"

Ram Dass smiles and says, "I'm gay, so he'd be a prince."

"So would you rather have a handsome prince or a talking frog?" I ask.

He thinks for a moment, then answers, "At this age, neither."

"Sex isn't gone with me," he continues, "but it's not as interesting. It's changed its power over me. I'm not driven by it the way I was for thirty-five years. I'm very relieved to have the space and time that leaves. But I'm all for older people doing it — I delight in hearing about people doing it at ninety."

In *The Only Dance There Is,* Ram Dass says he's able to experience "almost all of the states I have experienced with LSD" through his practice of pranayama (control of breathing). I ask if he still practices pranayama.

"I don't do it now," he says. "To be able to do it, you have to watch your diet. You can't be living and eating in Ramada Inns; it's too emotionally unstable."

Does he meditate every day?

"No, I do it most of the time. I try to make my life into a meditative practice."

Later, what sticks in my mind is Ram Dass telling how he didn't know his guru's age until he died at eighty-four. "I hadn't experienced him as any age. It never dawned on me he was an older man, his mind field was so present when I entered it. I want to attempt in my own aging to reach a stage of consciousness when I too will have no age."

I feel the same. "No age" sounds better than old age.

⟩ ⟩ ⟩

Three years after this conference, Ram Dass is not only working on his book on conscious aging, he is also planning to start a national call-in talk show on AM radio. He writes to his friend

Sy Safranksy, editor of a small, unique, and idiosyncratically marvelous magazine called *The Sun,* that the talk-radio business is a "tough scene" to break into, but he's optimistic. Then one day a month after writing to Safransky, Ram Dass is at his home in San Anselmo, California, with his portable computer on his lap, rewriting a chapter of his book on conscious aging, when he suffers a major stroke. I read in Safransky's magazine that "the stroke had left Ram Dass virtually without speech and paralyzed along the right side of his body." A year later, Safransky reports in the *Sun* issue of May 1998 that "Ram Dass is still confined to a wheelchair, though he's learning to walk with a special cane. He can read or write only with great difficulty because his vision was so impaired by the stroke. His speech has improved dramatically, but the effects of the aphasia are still apparent."

The news of Ram Dass's stroke, along with the deaths of Allen Ginsberg and Timothy Leary, shocked Sy Safransky into realizing "the truth of impermanence was like a banner headline I ignored until someone picked up the newspaper and whacked me in the head: Wake up! Maybe I was dreaming I could protect myself against life's uncertainties by eating less, by exercising more. Beautiful dreams."

I feel the same way as I learn of the death of friends of my own generation like Michael Harrington, and the generation just ahead of me like Murray Kempton. I buy the *New York Times* every day and read first the obituaries, then — perhaps as an antidote — the sports.

Like most people I know who are my age and older, what I fear most is lying somewhere vegetable-like or existing without most of my mind and body functioning. The most depressing passage in the New Testament to me comes soon after my favorite story, the account of Jesus appearing to the disciples in John 21, telling them where to cast their nets that then come up full of fishes, and inviting them to "Come and dine" at the fire he has made of coals. After Jesus dines with the disciples on bread and fish, he gives his instructions to Peter to "Feed my sheep," and then, out of the blue it seems to me, or simply as a piece of advice or preparation, he says to Peter:

"Verily, verily, I say unto thee, When thou wast young, thou girdest thyself, and walkedst whither thou wouldest: but when thou shalt be old, thou shalt stretch forth thy hands, and another shall gird thee, and carry thee whither thou wouldest not."

Once, on a five-day religious retreat with the Episcopal order of monks known as the Cowley Fathers, officially the Society of St. John the Evangelist, my spiritual director asks me to meditate on that passage. This is a silent retreat, and my only speaking is during the daily one-hour session with the director. He tells me to meditate on John 21:18 that day and evening until we meet again the next morning. I don't realize what the passage is until I look it up back in my room and find it's the one about getting old. When I read it, I get angry.

What does this, have to do with me?

I am fifty-five years old at the time, and functioning well. I don't think about age unless someone else brings it up. My spiritual director is forty. I interpret his giving me this passage because he thinks I'm an old guy and he's not. I fume and stew until our meeting the next day, when I tell him I don't like this passage, I'm not going to think about it anymore, much less meditate on it. He is noncommittal.

Now, ten years later, I face up to the reality of age enough to make my own living will, with instructions to friends. I tell my old friend Ted the Horse he should tell the doctors to pull the plug when I can't remember the names I memorized at age twelve and have known all my life: the starting lineup of the Broad Ripple High School basketball team that was the first Indianapolis school to make it to the state finals.

, , ,

Just before my sixty-sixth birthday I make a big decision. I've been thinking about it for the last two years, since a woman friend my age whom I complimented on her healthy good looks tells me her secret. She's had a face-lift. I rub at my neck, feeling the sagging part that makes me think of a turkey whenever I look in the mirror. I say I'd like to get rid of it, and she encourages me to do it.

When I learn I'm going to be in a documentary film of my book *New York in the Fifties,* I decide it's now or never. I go to a cosmetic surgeon where I live in Miami who is recommended highly by a friend I trust. I tell him I just want a "neck-lift," because the term "face-lift" seems almost pejorative, carrying an aura of guilt and shame, a superficial act that only actors and vain, superficial rich people do. Well, I know I can't possibly fit all those categories — I'm definitely not rich. In fact, I kind of hope a "neck-lift" alone might be less expensive than an actual "face-lift." He tells me, though, "It's the same incisions for one as for the other. As long as you're doing it, you might as well do the whole thing."

The doctor puts his hands in front of my ears and lifts. I see from looking in the mirror that this pulls up the skin of my whole face, eliminating some of the depressions left by scars from the acne that raged through my skin during my teen years. I'm still sensitive about that; the very mention of it brings back the memory of the suicidal pain brought on by some of that ravaging that seemed to sear my soul as well as my skin. The idea of getting rid of those last reminders seems a tremendous relief, and the benefit greater than the "socially incorrect" or "spiritually incorrect" guilt I might feel or flack I might take for getting a face-lift.

Is doing this God's will? Is it wrong to alter or try to improve the face God gave you? Did God give me the scourge of the acne? I sometimes thought that at the time in the depths of my Job-like despair and the unanswered prayers to erase the blemishes, the red blight that ravaged my face. I think of George Orwell, one of my literary heroes, saying that by the age of fifty you get the face you've earned. Did I "earn" the scars of the acne? Would Orwell, the moral purist, approve? According to his code, I might be allowed to erase the acne scars but not the sagging neck, which I guess I have "earned" — but how? By genes, dissipation, failure to exercise in my middle years of drinking and drugging? I'd say to George, "Listen, Orwell, I'm not trying to look like a different person, just a nicer version of the same person." I doubt, still, I'd get his approval.

Never mind Orwell — what about God? Is it God's will for me to have a face-lift? I read that according to at least one Christian's position, what I'm doing is an "abuse." Diane Komp, a "Christian physician at Yale Medical School," is quoted in *Christianity Today* as saying, "Almost every branch of medicine abuses. For example, cosmetic surgery is important to treat sustained serious burns; but it is the same technique used for tummy tucks and face lifts."

I remember that Ram Dass, with evident approval from his audience, told the conscious-aging conference he might do something physical for his health but not to make himself look "young and beautiful."

I've never been beautiful and I won't be young again, so I don't feel guilty on that score. I pray about it, and I don't hear a voice from on high saying, "Do it," or "Stop!" but when I talk to the doctor and the moment comes to make the decision, I feel at peace. I experience none of the inner shaking and quaking that I know now accompanies those acts that I soon regret. I take the plunge.

I haven't had a moment's regret. No one has failed to recognize me, or mistaken me for Paul Newman. The only comments have been, "You're looking good," or from older friends in my condo, "What's the name of your doctor?" Looking better makes me feel better, and feeling better I work better. I did it and I'm glad.

That was "elective" surgery.

Six months later comes the other kind — the kind where you have no choice, if you want to stay alive.

, , ,

Every year since starting my exercise and diet program back in 1980, I go for an annual checkup and stress test on the treadmill, supervised by Dr. Howard Hartley, now head of Cardiac Rehab at Brigham and Women's Hospital in Boston. It was Dr. Hartley and nurse Jane Sherwood who started me on the road to recovering my health back then.

Every year I've had a clean bill of health until the fall of '94, when after my stress test I'm shocked to hear Dr. Hartley tell me that all is not well. For the first time, the test indicates there is blockage in one of the arteries to my heart. I'm shocked, and scared. I ask what I should do.

"Continue what you're already doing," the doctor says, knowing I exercise every day, do yoga, eat a low-fat diet, maintain a low cholesterol level, and don't drink or smoke.

"If I'm doing all the right things," I wonder, "why is this happening?"

"When it's genetic, it can happen anyway," he says.

I remember both my parents had their first heart attacks in their late fifties. Both of them died of heart failure in their mid-seventies.

Dr. Hartley says that if I can keep the blockage from increasing, I won't have to have any surgery.

When I get back home to Miami, I feel the need to do more than I'm already doing to improve my health, to take some further action. I buy Dr. Dean Ornish's book *Reversing Heart Disease* and decide to go on the "reversal diet" he recommends, which is all vegetarian. For more than a decade I haven't eaten any meat, but now I cut out chicken and fish as well. After two years of this I add fish again, feeling the need for that variety, and so far all is well — that is, for the next three years the stress test indicates the blockage hasn't got any worse, though I haven't been able to reverse it. I don't have chest pains, shortness of breath, or any other symptoms, so I figure I must be doing all right when I go for my checkup in Boston in September of '98.

I'm able to do more work, longer, on the treadmill than I did the year before, which shows my heart muscle is strong, so I assume everything is fine. But it's not. This time Dr. Hartley has me take an echocardiogram as well as the stress test.

After the tests I go into Dr. Hartley's office, and he tells me the stress test and echocardiogram show the blockage has become worse and has begun in two other arteries as well. I'm stunned. I feel fine. My cholesterol is good. My weight is good. My habits are good.

But I need surgery.

I go back home and have an angiogram at the Miami Heart Institute, which confirms Dr. Hartley's diagnosis. They say I must have open heart surgery — a triple bypass. I take a deep breath and ask how soon I can do it. Today is Friday. They can schedule me for Monday morning. The surgeon who will operate comes to meet me and says he's been doing this procedure for twenty-two years and has a 98 percent success rate.

That's nice. Not needing open heart surgery would be even nicer. I take my morning walk on the beach and, as I always do, I say the Twenty-third Psalm. It takes on new meaning now, especially the lines "I will fear no evil, for thou art with me; thy rod and thy staff they comfort me."

In fact I am not afraid — this is something I have to do to prolong my life, and I just want to do it and get it over with. I don't want to know the details of the operation, nor do I want to watch a video about it or read any pamphlets about it. I just want them to do what they have to do and be done with it. Sunday night I have dinner with friends and see a movie.

I report to the Miami Heart Institute Monday morning at nine. I sign releases, turn over my personal belongings, including my grandfather's gold signet ring (leaving me, I feel, stripped of personal identity, anonymous), take off the clothes I'm wearing, and put on a hospital gown. After I'm stashed behind a curtain on a bed in the limbo of the nurses' station, with nothing to read or listen to, I'm told the surgeon who will operate has had to do an emergency procedure before mine. So now I won't be going into surgery until about eleven. Two hours. Now I am really getting nervous.

I pray the Twenty-third Psalm again, and go through several poems of Yeats'. In my twenties I could recite dozens of them. Now mostly fragments remain, but a few I still remember entirely, like "An Irish Airman Foresees His Death." Oops — not a good choice. I try the "Crazy Jane" poems, with their vivid sense of life. I summon what I can from the ones about custom and ceremony, the ones in which life "overflows without ambitious pains."

Minutes pass like hours. I've already handed over the books and audiotapes I've brought, so there's nothing to read or listen to, except loudspeaker calls for doctors or nurses. I think of a radio soap I listened to as a child, in which a sing-song voice was always intoning, "Dr. Brent, call surgery . . ." I don't even remember which show it was. Maybe it was *The Romance of Helen Trent,* and the doctor was "Trent" instead of Brent. In my mind I run through the other radio soaps of my childhood: *Ma Perkins, Our Gal Sunday, One Man's Family;* and then the kids' adventure series: *Jack Armstrong, the All-American Boy, Hop Harrigan, America's Ace of the Airways, Terry and the Pirates, Don Winslow,* and best of all, just before supper, *The Lone Ranger.*

It's almost eleven now, and I feel like I'm jumping out of my skin. I spot a phone and use my credit card to call Sara Davidson in Los Angeles. I can't keep the hospital johnny tied in back, but I don't care. I need to hear a friendly voice. Sara's machine is on but she hears me and picks up. I speak in spurts, sounding spastic. I say I'm in the hospital, waiting to go to surgery, and Sara tells me to take some deep breaths with her. She guides me through a meditation, an affirmation. I'm still scared, but calmer now. A nurse comes in and calls my name. I say goodbye to Sara and climb into the wheelchair, ready to roll to my fate. I repeat the names of the starting lineup of the Broad Ripple High School basketball team that went to the state finals. I can't wait for the anesthetic.

It's night when I wake up — in pain and terror. There are tubes coming out of my body, out of my chest, my arms, and even my mouth. I can't speak. I make sounds and writhe around and the nurse tells me to keep still. It feels like a nightmare, in which I am being held against my will, bound and gagged, and I can't even speak an appeal. Tears come to my eyes. I wonder in desperation how I will ever get through this.

I remember a true story my friend Norm Eddy, the longtime minister in East Harlem, told me the past summer. The current minister of Norm's old church, the Church of the Resurrection, the Reverend LeRoy Ricksey, asked his congregation to say the Twenty-third Psalm. He told them as they recited it to think what single word in the Psalm seemed the most significant. They spoke the Psalm together:

> The Lord is my shepherd; I shall not want.
> He maketh me to lie down in green pastures: he leadeth me beside the still waters.
> He restoreth my soul: he leadeth me in the paths of righteousness for his name's sake.
> Yea, though I walk through the valley of the shadow of death, I will fear no evil: for thou art with me; thy rod and thy staff they comfort me.
> Thou preparest a table before me in the presence of mine enemies: thou anointest my head with oil; my cup runneth over.
> Surely goodness and mercy shall follow me all the days of my life; and I will dwell in the house of the Lord forever. Amen.

Without hesitation a black woman in the congregation raised her hand, and said what she felt was the most important word in the Psalm.

"*Through,*" she said.

Through?

"Yes," she explained, "when it says, 'Though I walk *through* the valley of the shadow of death.'"

"Through" means you don't die, you get through it. Getting *through* our pain and challenges is the key; getting through gets us out.

Now I know in my guts what the woman meant. What I have to do is get *through* this ordeal. I wonder if I will. I am angry. I hurt like hell. Now that it's over, I'm told this operation feels comparable to being hit by a truck. I curse, and say if I'd known how it was going to be, I'd rather just walk down the street and have a damn heart attack. The doctors assure me this is the worst part; I'll feel differently in a day or so.

After three days the pain really does subside, and I am moved from intensive care to a regular room on the floor below. The worst is over. I learn to walk again, first a few tentative steps, then down the hall. From my room I have a lovely view of Florida's Inland Waterway. I look down below to a kind of canal where boats pass into the larger expanse of water. The water laps gently here against the banks. I smile as familiar words resonate in my mind:

He leadeth me beside the still waters. He restoreth my soul.

Yes. And my body, too.

On Saturday I get to go home. At first I go for short walks of five minutes each, then increase them every day. A month later I am taking my usual forty-five-minute morning walk on the beach. The third week home I teach my writing class, and another three weeks after that I go to Indianapolis to give a talk I had to cancel the week of the surgery. In ten weeks I'm able to resume my life completely as it was before. My prayers are of gratitude.

I get phone calls and letters of support from friends of my generation who have had this operation. "Bypass buddies." We are still in the game. But we know now in our body as well as our mind that the game doesn't last forever. We are playing what my friend who shocked me with the term so frankly called "the End Game." Rather than feeling depressed about it now, I'm exhilarated. I want to play what time remains in the spirit of George Bernard Shaw, when he wrote: "I want to be used up when I die, for the harder I work the more I live, and I rejoice in life for its own sake."

I rejoice in being *given* life, and a faith that shows me time and again there is more to life than meets the eye, and more beyond it than we have the capacity to know.

Chapter 10

PLAIN CHRISTIAN

———◆———

"Do you now renounce your earlier work?"

For a moment I'm speechless. I've just given a talk about miracles at St. Bartholomew's Episcopal Church in New York, and a young woman at the back raises her hand and asks this question. No one has ever asked me that before — yet I know at once what she means.

Before *Returning* was published in 1988, I wrote five novels, all of them frank in their treatment of sexuality and their use of language. I've never used sex as a subject or language to shock or offend, but rather to portray real-life situations as I knew them to occur, and to put in the mouths of my characters the words that such people really speak.

Not only are sexual issues dealt with openly, religious beliefs are probed and questioned. Sonny Burns, the troubled protagonist of *Going All the Way,* is a young man rebelling against the conformity of middle America in the nineteen fifties, and striking out against home, family, church, and God — a God that he feels other people are trying to force down his throat. He curses that God, and declares to a proselytizing evangelist that he not only doesn't believe in God, "I don't even like the guy."

So now, the questioner at my church talk wonders, has the author of these spiritual books turned his back on the author who wrote the secular novels?

For a moment I imagine myself as a white-haired man in a white robe, wagging a finger at a younger, snarling version of me as a hard-drinking rebel cloaked in black. I smile at the incongruity of it. The audience waits a bit nervously for an answer, interpreting my reverie as hesitation, but I say with pride, "I *embrace* my earlier work."

True. But this question becomes more frequent, more persistent.

A publisher's escort driving me to bookstores in Phoenix says he's had a problem arranging my appearances. I ask why, and he explains, "I told the managers of the main bookstores you'd be in town, and they ought to have copies of two of your books that just came out in paperback — *Creating from the Spirit,* and *Going All the Way.* Well, several of the managers said 'That's not the same author.' They thought there was one Dan Wakefield who wrote the spiritual books, and another one who wrote the novels. I had to convince them you're the same guy."

Am I?

Who am I?

More to the point, which "I" am I?

Any human "one" contains more than one persona, even more than two. The answer of the demon in the exorcism story in Mark —"I am legion" — is not limited to unclean spirits, but stands for all the aspects of a human individual wrapped in one big sack of skin. Each of us is "legion." In one of his wisest observations, C. S. Lewis says, "The prayer behind all prayers is this: May it be the real Thou whom I speak to, May it be the real I that speaks."

The first part of that prayer depends on faith, the second part on knowing which is "the real I." After making a decision like the one to get married to Sally, I wonder who the "I" was who said, "*I do.*" Perhaps the key to becoming whole is finally to recognize and admit that our separate identity is composed of many personas.

I laugh in recognition when I read in Robert S. De Ropp's autobiography, *Warriors' Way*:

> I have made the voyage of life aboard a ship of fools with a motley crew, each member of which thought itself important. I have been a mystic and a scientist, an author, house builder, a boat builder, a gardener, a fisherman, father of four children, a Whole-Earther getting his food from the soil he cultivated. These various characters made up the crew of my vessel, and their often conflicting aims determined the course the vessel took. They argued, fought, stole from each other. Each tried for a time to become master of the ship. But now there is harmony aboard, and the various fools have made peace with each other. Their aims do not conflict, because none of them considers himself important. It's the effect of aging.

When De Ropp (author of such significant works as *The Master Game* and *Drugs and the Mind*) wrote those words, he was sixty-five. I'm now a year older, and still working on making peace among my own "fools" or "selves." Though I haven't yet achieved the "full harmony" described by De Ropp, I'm closer than I've ever come to that goal, which perhaps is the primary work of our life.

I'm glad that two of my own cast of characters — the writer of spiritual books and the secular novelist — were forced to meet and come to terms with each other. What brought them together — and helped me find a better way than marriage to make peace with my own roots, my own hometown — was a movie of one of my books. Nothing seemed more unlikely.

> , , ,

By the fall of 1994, I've long ago given up on a movie ever being made of my first novel, *Going All the Way*. When it came out in 1970, it seemed a good bet to make it to film — it hit the *Time* magazine bestseller list, was chosen as a main selection of the Literary Guild, and was nominated for a National Book Award a year later. But since then there have been four different movie options, and three scripts written — the last one back in '84, when I freaked out over the chance to go to Hollywood and collaborate with Don Devlin. I've always wanted to see this novel as a movie, but I gave up any such fantasies after that last debacle.

I'm flattered when two bright and talented young men (they are both thirty when we meet) look me up in 1994 and say they want to make my novel their first feature film. Mark Pellington has won the MTV award as Best Director for a music video, and directed documentaries for PBS. He is passionate as he talks about his vision for the story of the two unlikely friends who meet on a train as they return home to Indianapolis after the Korean war — the shy, introverted photographer Sonny Burns and the casually confident Gunner Casselman, a former high school football star. Mark leans across the table and says with intensity:

"You know those guys Sonny and Gunner? *I'm both those guys.*"

He even understands we have more than one persona!

I'm also pleased that he and his partner, Tom Gorai, want me to write the script, keep it set in the fifties, and shoot the movie where the novel takes place, in my hometown of Indianapolis. None of the previous filmmakers suggested this seemingly obvious way of doing it. Some of them tried to "update" the story, but it doesn't make sense when extracted from its period. Mark and Tom show they mean business when they get financing for me to write a screenplay.

, , ,

Now I'm facing a deeper question: what am I getting myself into?

Don't I know enough about the pitfalls and pratfalls of movies, the disappointments and disasters that are par for the course, the impossibility of the writer, who is always low man on the totem pole in movieland, having any control over the final product? My only previous novel that was made into a film, *Starting Over,* had nothing at all to do with the book, and I was shut out of anything to do with the movie.

Around this time I get a letter from Indiana University Press saying they hear *Going All the Way* is out of print and they want to bring it back as a classic. Isn't that enough? Isn't it better to leave it as a novel, rather than trying yet again to put it into another medium, one it's resisted all these years? And hasn't there been enough emotion and controversy in my life stirred up by the novel much less making it as a movie? Do I want to whip all that up again?

There are unhappy rumblings about the book out of Indianapolis when it's published in 1970. My friend and fellow Hoosier Kurt Vonnegut sums it up in a review in *Life* magazine: "Wakefield himself, having written this book, can never go home again. From now on, he will have to watch the 500-mile Speedway race on television."

Well, not quite, but almost. Some people — not my old friends, but ones I barely knew beyond their name and saying hello — think I have written about them, exposed their innermost secrets. Others think I have besmirched the place I was born and grew up in, that I'm making fun of Indianapolis. Some are shocked by the specific sexual descriptions and language. I try to explain I use such language not to provoke but to portray reality, the way people really talk and behave. Still, some at home are outraged, others feel hurt. I send my parents a copy of the book, and we never speak about it. They receive angry calls, letters, and threats toward me, and so do I.

For a decade or so I don't go home again in a public way, but just to visit my family and close friends. Not until 1984, when a librarian at the Indianapolis-Marion County Public Library invites me to speak about the novel, assuring me all is forgiven, do I return, writing in advance for the library bulletin, "Like the aging warrior, I come in peace." I've been going back ever since.

, , ,

There seems to be both a blessing and a curse on this novel. Are the latest efforts to make a movie of it jinxed? Will I be jinxed if I have another go at it? Why unleash these forces again? Or why avoid them? *How do we know when it's God?*

When I think of "discernment," the feeling of inner peace and balance and well-being is the key. And in any undertaking, your gut instinct about the people involved is crucial. Whenever I meet with Mark and Tom I have a great time. Although they're from another generation, we're on the same wave length, liking the same books, laughing at the same jokes.

At our first script meeting it's not Mark and Tom I must reconcile with, but Dan the secular novelist and his later incarnation as the spiritual writer, the professed Christian. Mark asks how I feel about some of the scenes in which Sonny, the troubled young protagonist, expresses his anger about the religious beliefs that he feels are being forced on him. He's read *Returning* and knows I've gone back to church and the Christian faith. He and Tom don't want to ask me to write anything that goes against my current beliefs.

I've been thinking and praying about those issues, and after rereading the novel again I feel strongly that Sonny's rebellion against religion is part of his own spiritual quest. His rebellion is true to his story and his character, and I want to represent it in the movie as honestly as I did in the book.

These issues come to a head in a scene in the novel that also seems crucial to the movie. Sonny's mother, who is fearful he is falling under the influence of a friend of whom she disapproves, brings home "Luke Matthews," the pseudonym of an ex-convict who is now an itinerant evangelist, in hopes he can get Sonny to change his ways. Sonny tells him he doesn't believe in God and angrily dismisses him.

There is also a scene in the novel in which Sonny, in his burning sexual frustration, comes home one night and gets out a stash of hidden girlie magazines. He begins to masturbate as he pores over the provocative pictures — only to be discovered by Luke Matthews, who has been invited to stay overnight by Sonny's mother and is ensconced in the upper bunk over Sonny's bed.

I keep both scenes in my screenplay. I send it for comments to a few writers, one of whom has connections with the Sundance Film Festival, where we hope to enter the movie in competition. This writer, whom I don't know well, but whose work I respect, expresses his shock and anger that I — a person who's returned to the Christian faith — would include such scenes in a movie script.

His criticism makes me think of the woman in the audience at St. Bartholomew's who asks if I now "renounce" my earlier work. I write back to this critic that "it would never occur to me to betray my own truth of that era of life by some kind of 'religious revisionism' imposed retroactively with the outlook that came thirty years later."

Around this time I come across an essay that addresses the responsibility of a Christian writer. It appears in a magazine I read and write for called *Image: A Journal of the Arts and Religion,* and was written by a novelist whose work I admire, Ron Hansen, author of two westerns as well as *Mariette in Ecstasy,* a novel about a nun who receives the stigmata. Hansen tells us

St. Thomas Aquinas believed that "art doesn't require rectitude of the appetite, that it is wholly concerned with the good of that which is made. He says that a work of art is good in itself, and this is a truth the modern world has largely forgotten . . . what is good in itself glorifies God because it reflects God. The artist has his hands full and does his duty if he attends to his art. He can safely leave evangelizing to the evangelists."

This has been my aim in my novels, as well as in the later spiritual books. In that crucial sense, I know I'm "the same guy." I also know that this guy is a Christian.

, , ,

We're waiting every day, every week, to get the green light for the film. Even beforehand, Ellen Chenowith, one of the top casting directors (*Diner,* among others), is assembling a terrific cast — Ben Affleck (who is not yet the star he is soon to become in *Good Will Hunting*), Jeremy Davies (whose career will also take off with *Saving Private Ryan*), and some wonderful and talented young women with good screen credits — Rachel Weisz, Rose McGowan, and Amy Locane. The problem is, we don't have any stars, and before the production company will make the deal, they say we have to have at least two well-known actors or actresses.

Most of the parts are for people in their twenties, so that only leaves the roles of the mothers of the two young men, and we get Leslie Ann Warren for the sexy "bachelor girl" mother, but are having a hard time casting a conservative, midwestern house-frau mom of the fifties.

If they can't get a name actress for the role, the whole project may sink, and I begin to fear that the old curse of this novel is haunting me again. I begin to think about my mother, who died in 1980. I wonder if she dislikes the idea of the movie as she did the book — or maybe it's the idea of who will play the protagonist's mother. The novel is autobiographical — in the way that most first novels are — but not as much as most people think, who believe I "am" Sonny and the mother is a portrayal of my own mother. I never intended it any more than I intended Sonny to be "me." Still, I have a feeling my mother is somehow "involved" in this. How could she be?

A year after my mother dies, I'm looking for condos in Boston, and one afternoon I grab the phone on impulse and make an offer on one that I have mixed feelings about. After I commit myself to this purchase and put down the phone, I hear my mother crying. I know my mother's voice, and I know very well the sound of her crying. This is not a memory. This is me standing in a room in Boston a year after my mother's death and hearing her cry.

Now around the time of the movie being cast, I "see" my mother in my mind's eye as I'm taking my morning walk on the beach, and I have a sense of her presence. These morning walks are meditative times, when I pray the Twenty-third Psalm and think of Jesus, and of scenes from the past or of loved ones who have died. When I "see" my mother, it's the way she looked the last few years of her life. This is not a memory of another time, but a present sense of her "looking down at me" as I walk along the beach. She isn't expressing any emotion, she is just there, in my mental screen, as a presence in my consciousness. I feel as if she is waiting to see who will play the mother.

I'm thrilled when I learn Jill Clayburgh is interested in the role. I'm even more delighted when Mark tells me Ms. Clayburgh at first felt the mother was too manipulative, but after reading it again she comes to feel that the character's only fault is that "she loves her son too much." That is something Clayburgh, as a mother herself, says she can identify with. She accepts the role.

The next morning as I'm taking my beach walk, I see my mother again, this time more clearly, as if she is nearer, and this time she is smiling. I feel now we have the go-ahead not only from the production company, but from my mother as well, and that both are crucial; in fact, maybe one depends on the other.

Mark and Tom keep me involved in the making of the movie even after the script is done, which is not only unusual, in Hollywood practice, it's miraculous. I get to invite old high school friends to work as extras, so the whole experience of filming is like a series of episodes from the old TV show *This Is Your Life*. There's a lovely symmetry to the fact that the novel that once kept me away from here is now, twenty-six years later, bringing me back.

I think of Eudora Welty's observation in her essay about the role of "Place in Fiction" when she writes:

> There may come to be new places in our lives that are second spiritual homes — closer to us in some ways, perhaps than our original homes. But the home tie is the blood tie. And had it meant nothing to us, any other place thereafter would have meant less, and we would carry no compass inside ourselves to find home, ever, anywhere at all. We would not even guess what we had missed.

, , ,

One afternoon while driving back to the housing complex where the cast and crew are staying, I'm playing the radio when I hear a new pop song that moves me deeply, "It's All Coming Back to Me Now," sung by Celine Dion. The lyrics are about a love affair, but the memories of the goodness of it, the power and glory of it, remind me of my love affair with Indianapolis, the place where I started my life, and how I'm back here again with my old friends and these new friends making the movie, making a work of art I am proud of, and when I hear this beautiful, sure voice singing, "It's all coming back to me now," it's like the "all" is the richness of my own life, the friendships and loves, the people and pleasures, the mutual work and accomplishments, like gold pouring down, not in money but love, like the passage in Luke in which joy and fullness is "pressed down and overflowing."

That night at the wrap party a young woman comes up to say that she worked in the art department during the production and what a great experience it's been. "Before this," she says, "I was going through some bad times, I felt like I was lost, in the dark. And working on this movie, with these people, it's like I've come into the light."

The movie is chosen for the Sundance Film Festival and bought for distribution by Gramercy, an independent company that a year before had a hit with *Fargo*. The movie stirs the outrage I expected as well as the appreciation. The trouble is where it comes; the most venomous dumping is in the *New York Times* in a "politically correct" attack. The most moving appreciation appears in the *Boston Globe,* whose reviewer Renee Graham praises "the sheer audacity and elegiac beauty" of the film and rates it one of the ten best movies of the year. Roger Ebert's comments on his TV show are a real affirmation to me that the movie does what we hoped it would do.

> I've never seen a film in my life that is closer to the experiences in mind and in body and in sexuality that I had when I was just getting out of high school and going to college, than this film. In other words, the friendships, the girls, everything reminded me specifically of things that I had either seen or I had gone through.

Siskel gives thumbs down, saying he likes *American Graffiti* better.

The movie is a commercial failure, but a personal success, a deep fulfillment.

At the Indianapolis premiere, not only my high school friends are there, but so is Miss Jean Grubb, my high school journalism teacher and faithful friend, who is now ninety years old. Much to my surprise, before the screening the attorney general of Indiana, representing the governor, gets up and asks me to come forward. He presents me with a plaque that makes me a "Sagamore of the Wabash," the Indiana version of being a "Kentucky Colonel."

If the attorney general of Indiana had called me up in front of an audience when the novel was published, I would have feared an indictment. Twenty-seven years later, when the movie premieres, I am honored with a plaque that says that "the greatness of the sons of Indiana derives, in part, from qualities possessed by the noble Chieftains of the Indian Tribes which once roamed its domain" (the "Sagamores of the Wabash" being among them), and "it has been the immemorial custom of the State of Indiana to attract to its support those who have exhibited such qualities"; it is those who are recognized with this award.

I think of my early Boy Scout lore, my days at Camp Chanktun-un-gi, when I earn the rank of "Firecrafter" and am initiated in a ceremony as sacred as any I know. I go on to earn the highest rank of "Minisino" which perhaps sounds like it might be related to "Sagamore." All this flows forward into this evening and fills me. What I most cherish about the citation of the Sagamore is that it says I have "endeared myself" to the citizens of Indiana.

At last.

, , ,

Faith is not static, nor is it in my experience a state or condition you arrive at and settle down in comfortably, having "found it," like a hidden Easter egg, or an answer to the meaning of life. Faith is dynamic, changing and challenging, taking on new shapes and forms, fading for a while and then manifesting in ways you least expect, sometimes subtly, sometimes shaking the very foundations of your being, affirming the wisdom of the Yiddish proverb "God is an earthquake, not an uncle."

Observance of faith, like my understanding of it, alters with the circumstances of my life. Living on the beach now, my morning walks by the ocean are a kind of communion. I don't mean communion in its literal Christian sense as the Eucharist, but as meditation — on God, on Christ, Spirit, and the spirits of friends and loved ones who have passed from this earthly realm to whatever dimension lies beyond death, beyond the limits of our mortal understanding. Around the time I started seeing my mother during these walks, as the movie of *Going All the Way* is being cast, I "see" (in the same sense of visualizations in my mind's eye and as spiritual presence) others I have been close to, some who "appear" in my consciousness unexpectedly.

During this time, in a similar way, I "see" in my mind's eye my old friend from the Boy Scouts Jack Hickman, and hear in memory his voice. Thoughts of his kindness come to me, beginning with our first meeting at Camp Chank-tun-un-gi when I am a frightened, anxious rookie who can't get my sleeping bag unrolled and he shows me how and then instead of putting me down for my ineptitude, says not to worry, "These sleeping bags are pretty tricky." I see my first literary agent, James Oliver Brown, whose faith in me as a writer was like nourishment for so many years, and I hear his courtly words and his laughter. I see Amy Franz, my first Sunday school teacher, whose lessons were love for one another, especially the needy, the outcasts, those who seem "different." I feel her presence often since finding again my Christian faith.

The companion whose presence is always with me on these walks is Jesus. He is not "carrying my cross" for me as the "post-Christians" charged, but simply, as in Merton's poem "He Is Risen," walking before me, sometimes beside me, sometimes inside me, not as a visual image but simply as presence. He is not there automatically, but I always ask for his presence, an invocation I owe in particular to one of my great Christian mentors, the late Father Henri Nouwen.

, , ,

Back in '83, a few years after my going back to church, Carl Scovel gives me a copy of Nouwen's book *Reaching Out*, which becomes an inspiring guide to my own journey. Shortly after that I meet Father Nouwen in person for the first time.

"I've read your book *Prayers from the Genesee*," I tell him, "and what bothers me is that if someone as advanced as you are has doubts and difficulties with prayer, what hope is there for someone like me who's just starting out?"

Nouwen looks at me sternly and says, "Mr. Wakefield, Christianity is not for 'getting your life together.'"

Wow. This is no self-help, "human potential" guru. At first I'm taken aback, abashed. Am I getting it all wrong?

Nouwen believes Christianity is not simply another system designed for the never-ending satisfaction of self, but rather, goes beyond the petty ego trip to the service of others, the giving up of self, offering a journey that is not just sweetness and light but also darkness and thundering doubt, thorns as well as roses, nails as well as doves. Later, on another level, Nouwen's stricture comes to feel like the greatest comfort to me — because, I think, when in spite of all my efforts I still haven't "gotten my life together," it doesn't necessarily mean I'm not a Christian!

When I go to a conference in Berkeley in 1990 sponsored by *Image: A Journal of Religion and the Arts* to give my workshop in spiritual autobiography, the extra pleasure of the trip is that Henri Nouwen is there to speak at the Sunday chapel service.

I sit next to Henri at a dinner that's being given by a local family who are among the sponsors of the event, and the conversation at the table is pleasant and unobtrusive. I can see that Henri is bored, not paying much attention, his mind somewhere else. Then a woman at the head of the table begins speaking sincerely about issues that are troubling her with the Church, fear that its stands on issues of politics and women's roles may prevent her from continuing to be a Catholic.

Henri suddenly comes to life, leaning over his plate to speak urgently to the woman.

"All that is distraction," he says. "I don't mean to denigrate or even dispute your complaints, but those are beside the point. The only thing that really matters is your relationship with Jesus — I mean a personal relationship with the mystical Jesus."

The woman looks both stunned and confused and, imagining what she might be thinking, I ask Henri, "How does someone have a relationship with 'the mystical Jesus?' That sounds like a pretty awesome undertaking."

"Just give me ten minutes a day," Henri says with passion. "No — five minutes! Just take five minutes a day, every day for two weeks, to sit quietly and ask to be with Jesus, ask for His presence. And then come and tell me what's important."

Henri pushes his plate aside so he can lean even closer to the woman, and says with electric intensity, "People complain about the Church, they say the Church isn't interested in their problems. I spoke to a young man with AIDS a few days ago and he told me, 'The Church doesn't care about me, where is the Church in my life now when I'm dying with AIDS?' And I said "Who do you think *I* am? Who do you think any priest is? I *am* the church! And I care about you. That's why I'm sitting here with you, now.'"

The power and depth of this brief conversational plea to the disillusioned woman is worth the trip to the conference. I feel as Henri speaks to her I am in the presence of Spirit; the presence of the Spirit of Jesus Christ.

Henri's seemingly simple prescription — spending just five minutes every day asking for Jesus' presence — does not mean that you can automatically invoke a mystical experience, but rather that simply turning your thoughts to Christ if you are a

Christian creates a respite, a different kind of consciousness, a removal from the tumult of material thinking to awareness of the transcendent, the Holy, the healing.

The simplicity of the act reminds me of my faith as a child, when without question or instruction, simply from the instinct of belief, I hummed or sang aloud or in my mind a hymn that spoke of Jesus' presence, like "He walks in the garden with me," or "I walked today where Jesus walked." I dwelt for a while then in that calm aura of mind and heart, out of the battles of ego and stress that even in childhood are tearing at us. And all these years later this world-renowned Catholic priest, this theologian from Holland, brings back to me that access to grace I knew from a Baptist Bible school in Indiana.

, , ,

I am sure there are those who wouldn't — or don't — consider me a Christian now. I don't go to church on a regular basis anymore, but enjoy attending services where I'm giving a workshop or talk; when I'm in Boston on the weekend I go to King's Chapel, and in New York to All Angels. I don't contemplate marriage again, though I've been in and hope to continue to be in loving relationships with women.

I gather that having a face-lift is "spiritually incorrect" if not considered un-Christian, and I'm sure I've violated another correctness taboo by taking Zoloft, one of the Prozac family of serotonin medications. When I'm hit by an unexpected depression that leaves me frightened and panicky, a therapist tells me that even though I had a bad reaction to Prozac a few years before, it's worth trying this newer medication called Zoloft, which has fewer side effects. It takes me out of the depths, and doesn't make me feel I'm in some artificial state that's not true to my own being. Like most people who have taken it with good results, it makes me feel "normal" or "the way I'm supposed to feel." All the aches and pains and joys of life are there, but without falling into the pits.

But is it "Christian"?

Whenever I visit Boston, I try to get together with Carl Scovel, whom I still (and will always) think of as "my minister" as well as friend, and put before him my continuing (obviously never-ending) questions about faith. I wonder what he thinks about the morality of Christians today who take Prozac and its derivatives. Does it indicate a lack of faith to use medication as well as prayer to heal depression? This question has obviously come up before, for Carl immediately quotes a passage he knows by heart and citation:

"Ecclesiasticus 38:3. 'For medicine comes from the hand of God and a wise man would not refuse them.'"

When I get home, he sends me as further elucidation a sermon he's kept a copy of since he heard it preached by the rector of Trinity Church in Boston, in 1953. In this sermon on what the church thinks about healing, the Reverend Theodore Ferris says, "Our faith is neither in pills nor in prayer. It is in God, who may use both pills *and* prayer as channels of his healing power."

I discover there's an ongoing debate in churches as well as in the rest of society about whether taking these new antidepressant medications is cricket for Christians. Theologians, therapists, ministers, and lay people take pro or anti positions, debating their points with the passion of medieval philosophers arguing the meaning of life.

The respected periodical *Christianity Today* runs an article called "The Gospel According to Prozac," in which Archibald Hart, dean of the School of Psychology at Fuller Theological Seminary, says the same thing as the therapist who prescribes the medication for me: if you're depressed, taking it "is no different than giving insulin to a diabetic." In the same article David Wolfe, a Christian philosopher who pastors a church in rural New England, comes to a similar conclusion, and adds, "God loves us and wants us to function optimally as persons so we will be better equipped to do his will."

There's a proviso in the Christian counselors' sanction of such medication that the depression must be "clinical" or "severe" — but I wonder who is to judge severity outside the patient-therapist relationship. As James Baldwin quotes a Harlem preacher in *Notes of a Native Son,* you can't judge a man "if thou knowest not his wrassling." Those who feel religion alone should heal all psychic distress should take this to heart before condemning or condescending to believers who use medication.

, , ,

By now it's obvious I'm not a pious Christian — any more than I'm a "post" Christian. I'd like to just proclaim myself a "plain" Christian — the kind who's forgiven for his sins by the Jesus who forgives the woman at the well (she was married twice more than me!), who believes in the crucifixion and the Resurrection, and knows the human versions of both experiences.

It's a good thing King's Chapel, the church I return to, is Unitarian, which seems most tolerant of all views, including under its umbrella humanists, Buddhists, pagans — and even Christians. I'm a member of the Unitarian-Universalist Christian Association and have served on its national board, without any complaints about my "plain Christianity."

In Boston for a visit in the spring of '97, I go to King's Chapel on Palm Sunday, and for the first time since the debacle of my brief marriage, I am able again to connect fully and deeply with the liturgy, music, tradition, and ambience of this church that is so unique and sacred in my own personal history, as well as American history. I walk out with one of the palm leaves that are given to everyone in church that day, and wish I could be here the following weekend, not just for Easter Sunday but also for the moving rituals that lead up to it: the services of Tenebrae on Friday night, when the candles that light the church that evening are snuffed out and the Bible slammed shut as the people leave in the darkness of Good Friday, and then the Easter Vigil on Saturday night, when the candles are lit again, and at midnight it is proclaimed, "He is risen, Christ is risen."

, , ,

In my quest to understand — and work out for myself — what it means to be a "plain Christian," I am blessed by being able to connect to my faith and enrich it in the course of my work, not only through the workshops I give on spiritual autobiography and creativity but also through the religious leaders, thinkers, and writers whom I meet, talk with, and write about, like Father Henri Nouwen, theologian and Baptist minister Harvey Cox, and Rabbi Harold Kushner. I regard them as mentors as well as colleagues, from whom I learn, whose work and teaching deepen and refresh my own faith.

The other main guide to my understanding of what I think of as "plain Christianity" is not a theologian, minister, priest, or rabbi, but a novelist. Even more surprising, I am speaking of a contemporary American novelist, honored and respected in the literary world of our time — a time and a world in which most of the leading inhabitants still believe God is not only dead, but long buried.

Although I've known and respected Reynolds Price's stature as a fiction writer for many years, it's not until my minister lends me Price's nonfiction book *A Palpable God* in 1983 that I become aware of his eloquent witness as a Christian. The stunning lead essay of that book, "The Bible as Narrative," tells of Price's midlife crisis of faith as both a Christian and a writer, and includes a group of Bible stories he translated from the Greek as a way of confronting and working through his doubts. Translating stories from the New Testament affirms his faith, and leads him to proclaim their truth so clearly and boldly that it focuses and clarifies my own belief:

> I, like millions, am convinced and have always
> been by the stories themselves — their narrative

perfection, the speed and economy with which they offer all the heart's last craving in shapes as credible as any friend's tale of a morning walk. They well understand that they give us one choice — if we call them untrue, we must call them insane. They are plainly not deceitful; and I plainly call them true, in some awareness of the range of objections.

When I read it I am grateful for this clear statement of what I feel myself, but have been too unsure and timid to articulate. Inspired by the depth of Price's passion and understanding — and his rare model as an American literary figure of my time who writes with conviction of being a Christian — I begin to reread his books and look forward to new ones.

I'm shocked when I learn from a newspaper article that in 1984 a large cancer was discovered on Price's spinal cord, and he was given no hope of recovery. "The tumor was pencil-thick and gray-colored, 10 inches long from my neck-hair down," he writes of it ten years later in his memoir *A Whole New Life: An Illness and a Healing*. Price recovers from the cancer, though it leaves him paraplegic. Radical surgeries, radiation, severe pain, and reliance on prescribed drugs leave him consigned to a wheelchair — yet those dire circumstances end neither his life nor his brilliant career.

As his new work continues to appear, I'm impressed not only by Price's courage to write in spite of the pain and the battle with cancer, but also by the vision he sustains. His fiction makes God and religion a natural part of his characters' lives, not in the sense of "religious novels" but novels in which religion is taken as a serious factor in people's existence.

This everyday sense of the sacred, of religion as a natural element of life, makes Price's work unique — and to me specially welcome — contrasted with the dark and often nasty ambience that pervades so much current fiction. Most of his characters are — as he writes of his own parents — "religious but not churchly." God is sometimes absent to them, but never declared dead. They make just as many mistakes and no doubt commit as many sins as their atheistic counterparts, but there is a dignity to them bestowed by their author that derives in part from their faith in something beyond the surface of their own skins.

Holden Caulfield observes in *The Catcher in the Rye* there are some books you read that make you want to call up the author, while other books, though they may be good, don't produce any such desire. Price is one of those authors I'd like to call up or, better still, to meet, and in 1989 I figure out a way to do it. I'm giving some workshops at the monastery in Cambridge, Massachusetts, of the Cowley Fathers, the Society of St. John the Evangelist, and I read in one of their brochures that they also have a house for retreats and study in Durham, North Carolina — where Reynolds Price lives and teaches at Duke. I arrange to give a workshop for the Cowley Fathers in Durham, and while I'm there, have dinner with Reynolds Price.

We meet at a Mexican restaurant Price chooses, and he arrives in his van that is specially equipped with a ramp for his wheelchair. He is a driven by a student assistant who lives at his house, drives the van, and accompanies him on trips. He still is traveling to give talks and readings, and in a few weeks, will go to Cleveland to oversee production of one of his plays that's opening there. He is gracious and cheerful and tells me he believes that being confined to the wheelchair gives him more opportunity to focus on his work, and he hopes as a result to be more productive.

In the same situation, I imagine myself cursing God and questioning my faith. Price, instead, finds his faith deepened, experiencing a healing vision of Jesus that gives him hope through the worst of the suffering. He finds relief from pain through the alternative medical practices of biofeedback and hypnosis after prescribed drugs brought only grogginess and despair. Mining art out of illness, he transforms early childhood memories that surface in hypnotic healing sessions into the autobiographical book *Clear Pictures* that he publishes later that year.

I avidly follow his steady, prolific output of novels, poetry, plays, and nonfiction, marveling at the creative force and consistent quality of the work. I learn in 1994 from reading *A Whole New Life: An Illness and a Healing* that "in 10 years since the tumor was found, I've completed 13 books — I'd published a first 12 in the previous 22 years," adding that "panic came elsewhere but never in my work."

When his new nonfiction, *Three Gospels,* is scheduled for publication in '96, I'm asked by the magazine *Common Boundary* to go to Durham and do an in-depth interview with Price. I see it as an opportunity for me not only as a journalist, but more important, in my quest as a Christian to better understand and nourish my faith. *Three Gospels* is a translation of the New Testament books of Mark and John, with Price's commentaries, as well as his own "gospel," or story of the life of Jesus.

We talk in the living room of the wood-and-brick home Price built near a pond surrounded by trees outside Durham, where he's lived for the past thirty years. The room is decorated with contemporary landscape and portrait paintings, many by friends, as well as a wall of icons of Jesus he acquired on trips to Israel. An array of angels of all shapes, sizes, and colors, sent by friends during his illness, floats from the kitchen ceiling.

Price comes into the room in his wheelchair, greets me with a warm smile and a handshake, and asks his assistant to bring me coffee. He says he'll be traveling throughout the country soon on a major book tour for *Three Gospels.* His voice is clear and resonant (it can be heard on commentaries he does for National Public Radio's "All Things Considered") and he speaks openly and freely as we talk for most of an afternoon and during the following morning.

I'm happy to see that in *Three Gospels* Price goes against current theological fashion by upholding the literal truth of the stories of the New Testament. I wonder how he feels about the Jesus Seminar — a group of scholars working to determine the historical facts of Jesus' life, by voting with colored tiles on what passages of the Gospels recounting the life and sayings of Jesus are true, not true, probably true, or doubtful. It seems to me these theologians are trying to "disprove" the miracles and healings of Jesus, as well as the authenticity of his words.

Price says,

> I have many reasons for feeling that the Jesus Seminar has been more flash than substance. I've read a lot of their publications, and some have been very interesting and useful. I don't think they're charlatans or people who have set out to overturn anything. But it really is sort of touching and amusing to see them trying to apply scientific method to human history — or take the hopeless stand that if you can't prove that Jesus said so-and-so, then he didn't say it. How are you going to prove what was said two thousand years ago?
>
> Just look at the sayings attributed to Jesus, printed in red in many New Testaments. There is this immensely eloquent, insightful voice that you don't find in the surrounding narrative. Beyond saying that something extremely exceptional occurred and is being reported in the narratives of the four Gospels, I just don't know how you get this tiny, semiliterate community of the eleven disciples who survived the crucifixion — and you take over the Roman Empire a little more than two hundred years after that.

I tell Price about my interview with John Dominic Crossan, a Catholic priest and theologian who is one of the scholars of the

Jesus Seminar. I asked Crossan if he read Price's essay on John 21, the story of Jesus appearing to the disciples after the crucifixion as they are fishing on the Sea of Galilee. Crossan hadn't read it, and I explained to him Price argues from the point of view of a writer why this story seems a literal account of an actual occurrence. I told Crossan I agreed with this view, and he said, "I think you've both been taken in by a good novelist."

Price says,

> I think it's the most wonderful story in the world, and it still is to me — I don't care what Crossan or anyone else thinks. It has a ring of reality that doesn't sound like fiction writing to me. If it is fiction writing, then whoever John was invented the techniques of the modern novel single-handedly, overnight, in the first century!
>
> If you are going to call John a great novelist, then you have to examine all the New Testament documents and especially the Gospels as lives of Jesus. If they are fiction, it would mean there was suddenly this outburst of great writers who invented forms that had not previously existed in known literature. If you look at the Gospel narratives and the words of Jesus, you are reading about a human being who, it seems to me, cannot be assumed to have been invented by four guys writing semiliterate Greek thirty-five to fifty years after his death. There is no other parallel phenomenon in the arts of the world in which four geniuses suddenly rise up out of the working class and make up a story. It's like saying Tolstoy, Dostoyevsky, Flaubert, and Dickens suddenly all turned up in this little clandestine group of threatened people and invented this stuff.
>
> So many people like Crossan think the Gospel writers just made up the story. Well, try it sometime,

Mr. Crossan. Try making up a story that is going to compel the fascination of a huge majority of the human race ever afterward. Sorry, it can't happen that way. Whatever happened, whatever the explanation is, it is very difficult to explain how you turn these terrified "quislings" around and have them going off into the mouths of lions and Roman emperors — and that turn occurred virtually overnight.

I tell Price that Crossan also believes Jesus was "healing the illness" of people in a psychosocial sense but not "curing the disease" in a biological sense. I ask if he thinks Jesus really did heal people of disease.

"Look at me," Price says without hesitation.

He was given no hope of recovery from cancer, but the cancer is gone and has not reappeared.

> , , ,

Price recounts in *A Whole New Life* that one of the crucial occurrences of his recovery from cancer was a remarkable kind of "vision." In plain, simple, convincing language, he writes of "an actual happening" that took place shortly after the onset of his cancer. In the daylight of a July morning, he is suddenly no longer in his brass bed but on a slope by the Sea of Galilee, the scene of Jesus' first teaching and healing. Jesus is there and beckons him to follow him into the water. Jesus pours handfuls of water over Price's head and says, "Your sins are forgiven," and Price asks him, "Am I also cured?" Jesus says, "That too," and then Price is back home again in his bed. I ask if he has had other such visionary experiences before or since, and how such happenings relate to his faith and he says,

> That single thing, which I continue to call a vision
> for lack of a more descriptive word, is the only

such experience I've ever had. I'm not somebody who looks out the window and sees an angel walk across the backyard. Only once in my life did I have that sense of being transported to a completely alternate place and time, and have this absolutely real action occur. I was moved by that experience all the more because it was unprecedented in my life.

I come away from the interview with Price as I do from his work, feeling reaffirmed and clarified in my own faith. I don't consider myself a mystic any more than Price does, yet I share his belief that "there is something else beyond us," and though I've never had an experience comparable to Price's "vision" or "happening" of being transported to another time and place, I believe in its authenticity.

I've had my own glimpses of what Yeats called "the trembling of the veil" of our earthly five senses. My childhood experience of being filled with light and the light being Christ was the first and still the most powerful. Like Price, I don't look out the kitchen window and see angels in the backyard, but in later years I've known brief openings or touchings of a sacred or spiritual nature.

One Sunday in winter after coming home from church at King's Chapel, I'm lying on my bed fully clothed and preparing to read the paper when I look out the window at the soft, silent snow and a feeling of extraordinary goodness and peace comes over me. It's more than a feeling, it's an almost tangible comforting, like being covered and enveloped in the deep sense that all is well. I try to describe the experience to a friend, who shrugs and says, "Well, why shouldn't you feel good?" and I realize how difficult it is to convey such moments, to try to transmit a feeling or sense of such grace, an unexpected blessing.

Once I'm simply walking down the street by myself when I feel or sense a hand holding my own right hand, not with a grip but the lightest yet surest of presences, a tender yet firm and affirming sign or signal. Without trying to analyze the sensation, a sure knowledge comes, without any words but a deep knowing of what this is, or rather, who: *Jesus.*

I go with a girlfriend to see *Thelma and Louise,* and though I'm enjoying the movie, it is hardly stirring any thoughts or feelings of a spiritual or religious nature. Then, toward the end of the film as the two women speed through the New Mexico desert in a convertible, with police in hot pursuit, they realize they've already broken too many laws to go back to the world they came from; knowing they can't return, one turns to the other and says, *"We're free."*

As the words are said, I suddenly feel a rush, a sensation of heightened awareness coursing through my whole body, and with this comes a series of scenes moving swiftly and colorfully through my mind. I am not only seeing, but in some distillation of past experience it's as if I'm reliving these events and occasions of happiness and fun and fulfillment, with people and places I love, from earliest childhood to the present. The whole beauty and wonder of my life is being unrolled before me. Tears of joy and gratitude stream from my eyes, and I can't even follow the rest of the picture. When it's over, and my friend and I leave the theater and go out into the night, I feel weak and drained, trembling a little, and startled, in awe of the experience.

"I have to lie down," I say.

We were going to a restaurant, but I know I can't do it until I regroup, gather my senses, and return to "normal." I feel I've received some incredible gift, one that is all the more appreciated and moving for being so completely unexpected and unasked for. It's a powerful affirmation of life, of my own life, and makes my complaints and disappointments of the moment seem silly, even shameful. I thank God for this gift, this glimpse of what's real and valuable and true, the gold we can't see because of the limits of our ordinary consciousness. I feel like

I'm just coming out of an "altered state," but it's not the result of drugs or hypnotism or any other psychological or chemical inducement.

I think such "varieties of religious experience" (what Price calls the sense of "something beyond") are more common than we think, but most people learn not to talk about them for fear of being misunderstood or thought to be kooky, or simply from the difficulty of conveying the ineffable. I don't for a second believe, though, that having such experiences makes you a better person, or a better Christian or Muslim or Jew, any more than I think the absence of such experience is an indication of a lack of spirituality or religious authenticity in anyone.

I don't believe I'll be a better or more "genuine" Christian because of such experiences, and certainly not by trying to induce them, but rather by attending to the more mundane duties and opportunities of my daily life to practice the Golden Rule and the principles of the Sermon on the Mount.

The real challenge of religion is trying to live by its principles in our work, which for me now not only means writing but also teaching. Reynolds Price, who has taught writing at Duke for more than thirty years now, says he believes that "teaching is very much a form of religious work, though I certainly don't set out specifically or secretly to proselytize my students in any direction." Though I've always thought of teaching as a kind of service, I haven't regarded it specifically as a form of religious work until I hear Price speak of it that way, and I realize it is, or can be that, in the broadest sense.

Being a "plain Christian" does not mean to me trying to make other people think or believe as I do. In teaching workshops or giving talks or in writing I never try to "convert" anyone to my own faith. I try instead to do as those Christians who inspired me by their actions but never tried to sell me their beliefs in my period of militant atheism. In workshops and talks I identify myself as a Christian but never try to convince anyone else to believe as I do. I feel privileged to be able to give my workshops to different denominations, in Unitarian churches that are Humanist rather than Christian, in Jewish synagogues, at Sing Sing prison, where the class usually includes Muslims as well as Christians, at adult education centers where Jews and Christians of all varieties join with agnostics and atheists in the search for meaning, the quest for spirit in the broadest sense of that concept, the one the dictionary defines as "the animating or vital principal in humans and animals, as opposed to the purely material elements; that which gives life, the breath of life."

I also teach in the graduate writing program of a state university, where religion is a subject only if it is the subject of someone's writing, and then the writing, rather than the belief, is studied, criticized, and commented on. Yet I feel Price is correct when he speaks of the possibility of teaching as a "form of religious work," in the sense of a reverence or honoring of the people I am teaching and the subject I am teaching them.

The only conscious aspect of any "religious" or "spiritual" approach I try to use in my teaching is something I learn from a young woman rabbi when I'm writing my book on miracles. Rabbi Nancy Flam, a cofounder of the Jewish Healing Center in San Francisco, conducts a service I attend that she holds for any who wish to come for healing, whether of a personal, emotional, or spiritual nature. She teaches from the Torah and includes music and ritual, but the heart of the service comes when she asks if anyone wishes to express the concern that brings them here. When a person speaks, Rabbi Flam listens — not as we usually listen, with only a portion of our attention, but with full attention, and her concentration is so complete I feel as if I can see a line going from her to the person who is telling her their problem. When I ask her about it later, she says she thinks of her work as "the ministry of presence," and she says "I never try to give any advice or tell anyone what to do about their concern, I just try to be fully present to them."

Being fully present to another human being is a gift, and I believe it as valuable in teaching as it is in healing. In conducting a class or having a conference with a student, my main goal is to be "fully present" to them and their work, which I believe is the basis for being able to be of service to them as a teacher and as a human being.

Rabbi Flam also tells me of the more specifically religious aspect of her ministry of presence, and its role in healing, which I think is profound.

> I've experienced God's presence in that connection. The person who's listening, who's being with the other one, the one who needs to be healed, is being a conduit for Divinity to express itself. In that way, our hands are really God's hands. That's why it's important to keep in good shape physically, to exercise and get enough sleep. We have to take care of our bodies because we are the vessels.

My own faith and understanding of faith have always been enhanced by Jewish thinkers and leaders and by Judaism as a religion, which of course is the source of Christianity. One of the books that most illuminates my understanding of my Christian roots is Rabbi Harold Kushner's inspiring *To Life: A Celebration of Jewish Being and Thinking.*

Rabbi Kushner's great bestseller *When Bad Things Happen to Good People* was often cited and quoted in my prayer group at King's Chapel by people who found solace, wisdom, and understanding in its message. Coming to know Rabbi Kushner himself — a man of wry humor and plainspoken insight — is a gift not only of friendship but also of spiritual inspiration and wisdom.

The Christian tradition cannot be imagined or understood — or have occurred — without Judaism, without Jesus the Jew, and the anti-Semitism that has grown from a distortion of Christianity and of Jesus' own teachings is a wound afflicting us all, one that must constantly be addressed and tended in an effort to heal.

Harvey Cox, a Baptist minister as well as a leading theologian at Harvard Divinity School, is married to Nina Tumarkin, a professor of Russian history at Wellesley and a religious Jew, and by mutual consent they are raising their son in the Jewish religion. Harvey says, "I told the rabbi who married us that I had no objection to our son being raised a Jew, as long as I could have a part in his Jewish education. When he is in his teens, I want to then be able to tell him about 'the Christian Addendum.'"

Christianity indeed may fairly be described as "the Christian addendum" to Judaism, and it seems to me recognition of that is as healthy as it is wise. After the sin of anti-Semitism, the greatest "distraction" or negative factor of being a Christian today is the identification in the media and in many people's minds of Christianity as an automatic adjunct of "the Religious Right." It's perfectly legitimate for there to be a "religious right" as well as a religious left and center and any points in between, but to identify this one element as definitive of Christianity is a gross distortion.

The political activism of the Christianity I believe in is found in the work and words and legacy of Martin Luther King; of Gustavo Gutierrez, a leading theologian of the liberation theology movement that creates "base communities" and hope for a better life among the poor of Latin America; the work of Henri Nouwen in behalf of that movement (expressed in his book *Gracias*) and his life of ministry in the L'Arche community; the daily-life ministries of the Reverend Norman Eddy and the late Reverend Margaret Eddy and all the other men and women of the East Harlem Protestant Parish who put their lives on the line in the neighborhood where they found the greatest need and their own calling; Dorothy Day and her Catholic Worker movement that began in the Bowery and spread to hospitality houses in cities throughout this country. These are the kind of Christians whose lives and faith inspire my own, the kind of Christians whom I think of as responding to Jesus' words when

. . . seeing the multitudes, he went up into a mountain: and when he was set, his disciples came unto him:

And he opened his mouth, and taught them, saying,

Blessed are the poor in spirit: for theirs is the kingdom of heaven.

Blessed are they that mourn: for they shall be comforted.

Blessed are the meek: for they shall inherit the earth.

Blessed are they which do hunger and thirst after righteousness: for they shall be filled.

Blessed are the merciful: for they shall obtain mercy.

Blessed are the pure in heart: for they shall see God.

Blessed are the peacemakers: for they shall be called the children of God.

Blessed are they which are persecuted for righteousness' sake: for theirs is the kingdom of heaven.

Blessed are ye, when men shall revile you, and persecute you, and shall say all manner of evil against you falsely, for my sake.

Rejoice, and be exceeding glad: for great is your reward in heaven: for so persecuted they the prophets which were before you.

, , ,

The discovery of the Dead Sea Scrolls in Naj' Hammādī brings us the Gospel of Thomas, which is not a narrative of Jesus' life like the other gospels, but a collection of sayings attributed to him. One of them comes to mind often when I take my walk on the beach in the morning, reminding me not to miss anything — not just on the beach but in the day and the days to come. His followers ask Jesus, "When will the kingdom come?" and he answers:

"It will not come by watching for it. It will not be said 'Look, here it is,' or 'Look, there it is.' Rather, the father's kingdom is spread out upon the earth, and people do not see it."

I stop and take a deep breath, and look, at the ocean's blue expanse, the pillowing clouds, and see as well the blessing of the life I have, the unexpected path that brings me here, and I say a prayer of thanks. When I look with full awareness, I do see the kingdom, but most of the time, like most of us, I'm too busy planning the future and reimagining the past (what I *should* have done and said). Most of the time I'm like the people I see on the beach with their heads down and ears plugged while they sweep the sand with metal detectors in search of buried coins and lost jewelry, while the real treasure lies all around them.

Glimpses of the kingdom shine through the smog of my own ego, through the noise of TV and CD and radio, the numbing assault on the senses that we sometimes relieve through prayer, meditation, and genuine attention to others, or simply a conscious awakening, awareness of the life we're given. We can find it in Scripture, the sacred texts of any faith, as well as in the living Scripture of the world, the bark of an oak tree, a stranger's smile.

We always forget the kingdom is here and lapse again back to somnambulism, but sometimes by grace we're jolted awake by a light so powerful it pierces our fog. It happens to me in a workshop I lead while I'm writing this book. Wendy M. Wright, a professor of theology at Creighton University in Omaha, Nebraska, reads aloud what she's written in a fifteen-minute exercise in spiritual autobiography, and it sounds like I'm hearing the essence of my own story. I learn again all of us who seek the spirit have the same story; it's the only story, retold through centuries in different tongues as I hear it now come as sure as Scripture from Wendy Wright:

> How dark the seeing. How fragmentary. Mostly it consists of learning to free fall. Learning to trust the constant somersaulting. Learning to live with spiritual vertigo. Learning to love the darkness. Learning to trust the brief glimpses. Learning that blindness is its own seeing. Learning that the falling is in itself beautiful. That at the bottom of the well of my heart, I free fall into You.

How to Meditate
A Guide to Self-Discovery
by Lawrence LeShan

The bestselling classic. LeShan's easy-to-follow and realistic approach allows readers to bring meditation effortlessly into their lives, no matter how great the demands on their time. *How to Meditate* is an unrivaled source of inspiration and practical instruction for anyone seeking inner peace, relief from stress, and increased self-knowledge.

"A practical guide to meditation. Drawing upon such disciplines as Zen, Sufism, yoga, Christian and Jewish mysticism, LeShan describes specific exercises and programs ranging from breath counting and simple mantras to group movement and sensory awareness." — Sam Love, *Washington Post Book World*

Available wherever books are sold